THE ESSENTIALS OF
INDIAN PHILOSOPHY

The Essentials of

# Indian Philosophy

M. HIRIYANNA



MOTILAL BANARSIDASS PUBLISHERS
PRIVATE LIMITED • DELHI

*4th Reprint: Delhi, 2015*
*First Indian Edition: Delhi, 1995*



ISBN: 978-81-208-1304-5 (Cloth)
ISBN: 978-81-208-1330-4 (Paper)

MOTILAL BANARSIDASS
41 U.A. Bungalow Road, Jawahar Nagar, Delhi 110 007
8 Mahalaxmi Chamber, 22 Bhulabhai Desai Road, Mumbai 400 026
203 Royapettah High Road, Mylapore, Chennai 600 004
236, 9th Main III Block, Jayanagar, Bengaluru 560 011
Sanas Plaza, 1302 Baji Rao Road, Pune 411 002
8 Camac Street, Kolkata 700 017
Ashok Rajpath, Patna 800 004
Chowk, Varanasi 221 001

*Printed in India*
by RP Jain at NAB Printing Unit,
A-44, Naraina Industrial Area, Phase I, New Delhi–110028
and published by JP Jain for Motilal Banarsidass Publishers (P) Ltd,
41 U.A. Bungalow Road, Jawahar Nagar, Delhi-110007

# Preface

*

IT is now some years since my *Outlines of Indian Philosophy* was published, with the intention chiefly of providing a handy text-book for students in our Universities. A simpler and shorter account of the subject is required for the general reader, and the present attempt is to meet that requirement. It is hoped that the book will be found suitable for the purpose, and that it will receive the same welcome as was generously accorded to its predecessor.

The subject-matter of the two books being identical, there is naturally a certain likeness between them; but it will be seen that no portion of the earlier volume has been verbally reproduced here. The present work, in accordance with the aim kept in view in writing it, leaves out many of the details included in the previous one. The difference between them, however, does not consist merely in these omissions: There is also variation in the treatment of some topics, as, for instance, in the first two chapters dealing with early Indian thought. At least in two cases, again, there are important additions. In the earlier book, Buddhism was dealt with in reference to two stages of its growth. There is a third phase, representing the doctrine as it was originally taught by Buddha; and a brief résumé of it, as it has been reconstructed by scholars in recent years, also finds a place here. Similarly, the account of the Vedānta has been amplified by the inclusion of the Dvaita system of it. In treating of such a subject as Indian Philosophy, it is difficult to avoid the use of Sanskrit terms; but their number appearing in the body of the work has been reduced as far as possible, and a Glossary is provided to help the reader in finding out their meanings readily.

I have utilized in the preparation of this book two of my articles contributed to the *Aryan Path*, and another to the *Heritage of Indian Culture* (published by the Ramakrishna Mission). I am grateful to the editors of these publications for their courtesy in permitting me to do so. Specific references to the articles are given at the appropriate places in the Notes appended at the end. I wish to record my feeling of indebtedness to the late Dr. J. E. Turner of the University of Liverpool for his kindness in reading the book in typescript and for his valuable suggestions. Finally, I desire to express my deep gratitude to Professor S. Radhakrishnan for the kindly interest which he has always taken in my work. It is no exaggeration to say that, but for his help and encouragement, neither this book nor the previous one would have been written.

*April* 1948. M. H.

# Contents

Chapter One

# VEDIC RELIGION AND PHILOSOPHY

*

THE earliest source of our information regarding Indian thought is the Veda, which signifies, as it has been stated, not a single work but a whole literature. This literature is usually regarded as consisting of two parts, viz. Mantras and Brāhmaṇas.[1] Several of the early Upanishads are included in the latter; but, on account of their great importance in the history of Indian thought, they deserve to be reckoned as a separate portion of the Veda. Broadly speaking, the three parts mark successive stages in the growth of Vedic literature, and also stand for teachings that are more or less distinct. The determination of the exact chronological limits of these stages is not possible. Even the duration of the Vedic period, as a whole, is not definitely known, though the question has exercised the minds of scholars for long. All that is certain is that the Veda proper, including the chief Upanishads, is older than Buddha, who is known to have died about 480 B.C. The later limit of the Vedic period may accordingly be taken as 500 B.C. As regards the earlier limit, the belief that was generally current till recently, and which has not yet been given up wholly, was 1200–1500 B.C. The view that is now replacing it is the one set forth by Dr. Winternitz in his *History of Indian Literature*, which fixes the beginning of the period somewhere between 2000 and 2500 B.C. instead of 1200–1500 B.C. It is not known what changes, if any, will be found necessary in this conclusion when the momentous discoveries made in recent years in the Indus valley near Mohenjo-Daro and Harappa are fully understood. These details, however, are not of very much importance for us here. We shall therefore proceed to consider the teaching of the Veda in its triple division.

## I

The word "mantra" may be regarded as equivalent to a "hymn" or "religious song." The hymns or religious songs contained in the Veda are of varying age, the oldest of them being separated from the latest by several centuries. They were at a later stage, that is, long after the period of their production, brought together and have been preserved in the form of separate collections (*saṁhitā*). Two of them, to which we shall occasionally refer in this work, are called the "Rigveda" and the "Atharva Veda." We do not know what proportion of the sacred songs existing at the time were included in these collections, but we may safely assume that the whole of the material is not found in them. "We have no right to suppose," says Max Muller, "that we have even a hundredth part of the religious and popular poetry that existed during the Vedic age."[2] We shall, in the present section, take into account only the earlier mantras, postponing the consideration of the later ones to the next section dealing with the Brāhmaṇas to which, in their teaching, they are more akin. We have, however, to remember that several of these early hymns are too obscure to admit of a satisfactory interpretation. This obscurity, together with the incompleteness of the hymn material we possess, makes it hard to reach anything like certainty regarding the character of the beliefs which prevailed in that age as a whole. We shall therefore content ourselves with citing here the view now commonly accepted by scholars, that these early mantras inculcate a form of nature worship, and that this religion of nature was, in its essence, transplanted from their original home when the ancestors of the future Aryans immigrated into India.

In this religion the various powers of nature like fire (*agni*), wind (*vāyu*) and the sun (*sūrya*), amidst which man lives and to whose influence he is constantly subject, are personified, the personification implying a belief that the order which is observable in the world, such as the regular succession of seasons or of day and night, is due to the agency of these powers. They are accordingly looked upon as higher beings or gods, whom it is man's duty to obey and to propitiate. Hence the hymns may generally be described as chants or prayers addressed to deified powers of nature, regarded as responsible for the governance of the world. The gods thus worshipped are very many. Some of them like Agni, the god of fire, who is represented as the carrier of gifts to the gods, belong to a period anterior to the occupation of India by the Aryans, while others, like Uṣas or "dawn", worshipped as a goddess and described as a blushing maiden pursued by her lover, the sun, are later creations by them in their new home.[3] Although the Vedic pantheon is thus quite large, some deities, as they appear in the hymns that have been preserved, are more important than others. But we may note, by the way, that Śiva and Viṣṇu, the two great gods of later Hinduism, although not unknown to the age, are not among the former. Of the relatively more imposing deities, it will suffice here to refer to two, viz. Varuṇa and Indra. In the words of one of the mantras, they are "the two monarchs that support all living beings." The distinctive feature of the one is his unswerving adherence to high principles; that of the other, his eagerness to protect his devotees by vanquishing their enemies in battle.

The latter, viz. Indra, is the leading deity of the hymn-collections taken as a whole. He represents mainly valour and force; but he combines with those traits certain others, which one would not like to associate with the idea of the divine. Thus he is vain and boastful, and is uncommonly fond of an intoxicating drink extracted from a creeper called *soma*. But he seems to have come to hold so exalted a position among the Vedic gods through some accidental circumstance. That circumstance might have been, as indicated by his description as the "protector of the Aryan colour" and as the "destroyer of the dark skin," the necessity that arose for seeking the aid of a martial and self-assertive deity by the immigrant Aryans in subjugating the hostile tribes who were prior residents of the land which they had invaded. Or it might have been the havoc frequently played by famine in their new home, as shown by the description of Indra as the "thunder-god" and as "the liberator of the waters by slaying the demon of drought." Prof. Radhakrishnan writes, "When the Aryans entered India they found that, as at present, their prosperity was a mere gamble in rain. The rain-god naturally became the national god of the Indo-Aryans."

Indra, however, was not the sole type of divinity known to the Vedic Aryans, for there are clear, though not so frequent, references in these hymns to another important deity, Varuṇa, who is essentially a god of righteousness and is the guardian of all that is worthy and good. He is omniscient, and is described as ever witnessing the truth and falsehood of men—as being "the third whenever two plot in secret." He is not only able to find out the inmost sin of man, but is also beneficent and will graciously forgive the sinner, if he be truly penitent. "Set us free from the sin we have committed" is, indeed, the burden of every hymn addressed to Varuṇa. The songs composed in his praise are some of the sublimest in the Veda. But to judge from their number in the collections as they have come down to us, he is quite unimportant; and he continued ever after to be so, as shown, for instance, from his position in the later Purāṇic pantheon where he is not the Highest but only a god of the sea—"an Indian Neptune" as he has been styled. He represents probably an earlier ideal, which under the stress of new and changed circumstances like those alluded to above, was superseded by Indra, as the latter also receded to the background in course of time and became but a glorified ruler of the celestial regions. But we should add that it was only the embodiment of the ideal specifically in Varuṇa that was lost and not the ideal itself, for we find it rising into great prominence in later Indian theism.

There is one aspect of the idea of divinity in this period to which we should call particular attention, viz. its intimate association with what is described as *ṛta*. *Ṛta*, which etymologically stands for "course," originally meant "cosmic order," the maintenance of which, as already stated, is the purpose of all the gods; and later it also came to mean "right," so that the gods were conceived as preserving the world not merely from physical disorder but also from moral chaos. The one idea is, in fact, implicit in the other; and there is order in the universe, because its control is in righteous hands. Of this principle of righteousness, Varuna is the chief support. He, it has been said, is "the real trustee of the *rta*." But the other gods also, not excluding Indra, show it in some degree or other. In fact, "guardians of *ṛta*" is in the Mantras a common epithet of the gods; and all of them are conceived as willing the right, and seeing to that will being carried out in practice. The word bears a third meaning also in the Veda to which we shall refer later. It has almost ceased to be used in Sanskrit; but we shall see that under the name of *dharma*, the same idea occupies a very important place in the later Indian views of life also.

According to these early mantras, the world is not only governed by the gods but also owes its existence to them, for it is they who have created it. It is represented as consisting of three parts—heaven, the world of mortals and the intermediate region—each of which has its own guiding divinities. The relation of man to the gods is depicted as one of complete dependence; but it is of quite an intimate kind, for we find Vedic Aryans addressing their gods as "father" and "brother." The expression of love for the gods, it has been remarked, "is almost a commonplace in Vedic phraseology, as conversely, the gods are represented as fond of the worshipper."[4] Since the gods are the powerful rulers of the universe, man must be devoted to them; and, since they are not merely powerful but are also righteous-minded, he must lead a morally pure life. There is no thought in these Mantras of the physical universe, or any aspect of it being unreal. On the other hand, the interest of the people in the everyday world appears then to have been quite keen, for the prayers addressed to the gods are mostly for worldly prosperity—for the grant of sons, cattle and wealth. Nor does there yet seem to have arisen any belief in transmigration. But the survival of man after death is recognized. That is to say, the soul is conceived as immortal; and the good and the pious, it is believed, go after death to heaven where they lead a life of perfect joy in the company of the gods. The fate of the souls of the wicked and the impious is not so clearly stated; but they also seem to have been conceived as surviving after death, because they are described, when mentioned at all, as consigned to "abysmal darkness" in contradistinction to the "white light" into which the virtuous pass after death.

## II

We have so far spoken of the earlier hymns, and shall now proceed to consider, within the limits set by our plan, the thought of the later hymns and the Brāhmaṇas. The word, which is derived from *brahman* meaning "prayer" or "devotion," signifies an authoritative utterance of a priest, relating particularly to sacrifice; and the Brāhmaṇas are so called because they are the repositories of such utterances. Speaking generally, the thought of the earlier hymns is seen in this period to develop on three lines: monotheism, monism and ritualism. The first two of these, however, are often found mixed up with each other. But the conceptions themselves, as will be explained soon, are quite distinct; and this is the reason for our dealing with them separately.

(1) *Monotheism:* The belief in many gods of the early hymns now becomes more or less definite monotheism. The tende to it appears already in those hymns in various ways. On the most important of them is the likeness of the gods to another, as they are described there. They all share certain features which suggest that their identity was already recognized, though but half-consciously. Thus all the gods are luminous, as shown by the common epithet of *deva* applied to them, which is derived from a root meaning "to shine;" and all, as noted before, maintain physical order and are friendly to the virtuous. This tendency now develops further; but it does not result in a fully crystallized conception of a supreme God, as required for monotheism in the ordinary acceptation of the term. It aims rather at the discovery, not of one god who is above other gods, but of the common power that works behind them all or, as we might otherwise put it, the principle immanent in all of them. "What is but one, wise people call by different names as Agni, Yama and mātariśvan." The conception of the supreme God in the later Vedic period may consequently be said to be more philosophic than religious. Omnipotence, for example, which is a characteristic of all the gods, becomes personified as the Highest under the name of the "all-doer" (*Viśva-karma*). He is the great architect of the universe, says one hymn, "who knows all, who

assigns to the gods their names and to whom all go for instruction." This attempt to derive a general, and virtually impersonal, conception of the supreme God from the common characteristics of deities is, with a remarkable freedom of speculation, made again, and again, so that we have, in the period, a number of such conceptions which succeed and replace one another.

The most prominent among the conceptions of the supreme God, so enthroned and dethroned afterwards, is that of Prajāpati or "Father-god", whose name implies that all created beings are his children. This title is found used first in its literal sense of "lord of creatures" as an attribute of various gods. But later it ceases to represent merely an aspect of divinity, and acquires an independent status. Thus in an oft-recited hymn of the Rigveda, to a question repeated nine times, "Who is the God to whom we are to offer sacrifice?" the answer is given that it is Prajāpati "who is the one lord of all created things." He is described elsewhere as born of *ṛta,* the principle of righteousness which rules the world; and the description shows that, though the deity is abstract, being the result of elevating a mere epithet to the rank of the Almighty, it does not lack the moral exaltation characterizing the earlier and more concrete gods. Indeed, he is often regarded as an ethical authority. Prajāpati represents the highest conception of unitary godhead in the later Mantras and Brāhmanas, taken as a whole. But even that is replaced, in course of time, by others; and still later, as for example in some of the Upanishads, the deity is reduced to a clearly secondary rank under the designation of Brahmā (*masc.*).[5]

(2) *Monism:* Another direction in which the thought of the earlier hymns develops is definitely philosophic, tracing the world not to a creator but to a single primordial cause which unfolds itself as the universe in all its diversity. As in the case of the previous conception, this causal principle or creative ground also is conceived of in diverse ways. Thus it appears as the Infinite (*aditi*) in one place, and as time (*kāla*) in another. In a remarkably profound hymn[6] which marks "the climax of speculative thought in the Rigveda," it is designated as "That One" (*Tat Ekam*)—a designation which, discarding all the earlier anthropomorphic mythology, un-

mistakably foreshadows the nameless Power of the Upanishads of which we shall soon have to speak. "In the beginning," the hymn says, "there was neither being nor non-being. That one breathed calmly, self-sustained." But it had within it, it adds, the latent power (*tapas*) out of which the whole universe, including the gods, developed afterwards. The point to be specially noted here is the conception of the ultimate entity as dynamic or self-evolving, and as therefore requiring no outside Power to guide and shape it.

This current of thought, as already stated, is often found blended with the other one of monotheism. The reason for it is that the supreme God, as conceived in the period, is not always identified with the other gods alone, but also with the whole universe of which he is the creator. "He is all and everything" is what, for example, is said in one place of Prajāpati. That is, the supreme God is regarded not merely as a creator, externally related to the world, but also as constituting its very substance, as the monistic principle does. It is now usual to represent the monism of the later mantras and the Brāhmaṇas as pantheistic; but it is not correct to do so, since the term as applicable to this teaching connotes the idea not merely of immanence but also of transcendence. Thus, for instance, what is known as the Hymn of Man[7] declares "Having covered the world on all sides, it extended beyond it the length of ten fingers." The primal principle, no doubt, is immanent in the world which emerges from it, but is certainly not exhausted by it.

(3) *Ritualism:* The purpose of invoking the several gods of nature was at first mostly to gain their favour for success in life here as well as hereafter. The prayers were then naturally accompanied by simple gifts like grain and ghee. But this simple form of worship became more and more complicated and gave rise, in course of time, to elaborate sacrifices as also to a special class of professional priests who alone, it was believed, could officiate at them. There are allusions in the later hymns to rites which lasted for very long periods, and at which several priests were employed by the sacrificer. The Brāhmaṇas, in which this elaborate ritualism is taught, altogether subordinate the earlier mantras to it. They do, indeed, utilize them, but often sundering them from their original

context, and sometimes even severing them from their original significance.[8]

More noteworthy than this elaboration was the change that came over the spirit with which offerings were made to the gods in this period. What prompted the performance of sacrifices was no longer the thought of prevailing upon the gods to bestow some favour or to ward off some danger; it was rather to compel or coerce them to do what the sacrificer wanted to be done. This change of spirit is explained by many among modern scholars as the importing of the magical element into Vedic religion, and is taken by them as a sign of the transfer of power from the gods to the priests. There is no doubt that belief in magic was widely current in the period, as is shown by the Atharva Veda, which is largely a book of sorcery and witchcraft. But, as indicated by the general tone of the rest of Vedic literature, it seems to have been confined to the lower strata of society. The altered spirit behind the offer of sacrifices more probably only means faith in the efficacy of Vedic prayers, as such, and not in the potency of priests. That would correspond with the unqualified reverence which, as we shall see, later came to be shown to the whole text of the Veda by the adherents of the various orthodox doctrines. The power of conferring good thus seems then to have been transferred from the gods not to the priests but directly to the Veda itself.

But whatever name we may give it and however we may understand its implication, it is certain that there was a profound change in the conception of sacrifice, and consequently in that of the relation between gods and men. All that came to be insisted upon was a scrupulous carrying out of every detail connected with the various rites; and the good result accruing from them, whether here or elsewhere, was believed to follow automatically from it. It is this sacrificial correctness that constitutes the third meaning of *ṛta*, to which we alluded above. Ritualistic punctilio thus comes to be placed on the same level as natural law and moral rectitude. To judge from extant works, ritualism in this extreme form appears to be the predominant teaching of the later Vedic period; but as the other two tendencies of monotheism and monism also undoubtedly prevailed then, the prominent place it occupies in those works is, in all probability, the result of the bias in that direction of the scholar-priests, who were responsible for the compilation of the Veda as it has come down to us.

## III

To take up now the consideration of the Upanishads. The word *upanishad* literally means "secret teaching" (*rahasya*) or the teaching which was jealously guarded from the unworthy and was imparted, in private, only to pupils of tried character. It has since come to be applied also to the treatises which embody such teaching. The number of these treatises, as commonly reckoned, is very large; but only about a dozen of them can be classed as genuine parts of Vedic literature. The rest, which belong to a later period, are relatively of inferior value. The classical Upanishads, as the former may be described, represent the flower of Vedic thought. They are written in rhythmic prose, where they are not metrical; and they possess, on the whole, a musical quality all their own. The reader, even when not familiar with their teaching, easily grasps their general import; and their power of transporting one out of oneself is remarkable.

Broadly speaking, the teaching of the Upanishads marks a reaction against that of the Brāhmaṇas which, as already pointed out, inculcate an elaborate system of ritual. In more than one place, they decry the value of sacrifices. To cite only a single instance, one Upanishad declares that it is not pleasing to the gods that man should know the ultimate truth, for that, by revealing to him their true place in the universe which is by no means supreme, will result in their losing the sacrificial offerings they would otherwise receive from him.[9] The gods, according to this view, are much like men; and their worship or sacrifices to them bring no lasting result, as devotion to philosophic truth does. But it has to be added that, within the Vedic period itself, this spirit of antagonism to ritual is modified and ceremonial life comes to be recognized as necessary, either directly or indirectly, for attaining the true and final goal of life.[10] The Upanishads thus came finally to represent the teaching of the Veda in its entirety, and not of its final portions only. Here we see illustrated a characteristic feature of all advance in Indian culture, viz. that when a new stage of progress is reached, the old is not discarded but is, sooner or later, incorporated in it.

There are great, almost insurmountable, difficulties in deciding what exactly is the teaching of the Upanishads in certain important respects. This accounts for the emergence in later times of diverse schools of Vedānta, all of which claim to propound the Upanishadic teaching. It is clear, however, that the prevailing view in them is monistic and absolutistic. That is to say, they teach that the ultimate reality is one and only one. Its unseen, but pervasive, presence is thus set forth in one of the Upanishads. "It is Brahman that is below and is above, that is to the west and to the east, that is to the south and to the north. Brahman, indeed, is this whole universe."[11] The teaching is also idealistic in the sense that this single reality is conceived of as spiritual in its nature, and that everything else is explained as existing in and through it. Referring to all things and to all living beings, another Upanishad says, "All this is based upon spirit; spirit is the foundation of the universe, spirit is Brahman."[12] This is not to say that either pluralism or the belief that the ultimate entities are many, and realism or the belief that matter is as real as spirit or mind, are unknown to the Upanishads, taken as a whole. It only means that, as already indicated, they are not conspicuous in them. They appear there like distant echoes of the teaching of the earlier portions of the Veda which, speaking in the main, is neither monistic nor idealistic. Such a bifurcation of the Veda is, no doubt, against Indian tradition, which has all along insisted on the unity of Vedic teaching. Its contention is that, because all portions of the Veda are alike revealed, there can be no disharmony in their teaching. But looking at the whole extent of Vedic literature and the vast stretch of time that separates the earliest from the latest portions of it, it would indeed be extraordinary if it did impart precisely the same teaching throughout.

What is the exact character of the doctrine of unity which is the predominant teaching of the Upanishads? It is necessary to call attention to certain details of the earlier Vedic teaching before attempting to answer this question. We have already indicated the presence of a monistic view in the later hymns. From the example cited in that connection and the name given in it to the unitary source, viz. "*That* One," it will be seen that the monism is the result of trying to account for the whole universe—nature, men and gods—regarded from the outside or objectively. There are other conceptions of the same kind in the older literature; and one of them, which gradually grows in importance, is Brahman. To the question raised in the Rigveda, "What was the wood, and what the tree from which they fashioned forth the earth and heaven?" the following answer is given later on in a Brāhmaṇa, "Brahman was the wood, Brahman was the tree out of which they carved heaven and earth." This conception is very prominent in the Upanishads. The origin of the term is not quite clear, and it will suffice to refer here to one of the several explanations now given of it. The word *brahman*, the reader will recall, signifies "prayer." Being derived from a root *bṛh* meaning "to grow or expand," it also stands for the power which of itself burst into utterance as prayer; and it is to this meaning that, according to some among present-day scholars, we should trace the philosophic significance of the term, viz. the power or primary principle which spontaneously manifests itself as the universe.

There is a second current of thought in the earlier literature which also we should take into account, if we are to understand clearly the monistic doctrine of the Upanishads. Its aim is the discovery, not of a cosmic principle—the source of the world as a whole, but of the psychic principle—the inner essence of man. Its origin should be ascribed to the belief that the proper study of mankind is man. Man's conception of himself, however, is notoriously vague; and anything from the gross body to the subtlest principle underlying individual existence may be signified by it. We have almost all the possible alternatives represented in Vedic literature, such as breath or life (*prāna*) and the senses (*indriya*). The culmination of this inquiry is represented by *ātman* or the self which is sometimes described negatively by denying that it is breath, the senses, etc., which are all the not-self (*anātman*), and sometimes as the true subject which knows but can never be known —"the unseen seer, the unheard hearer and the unthought thinker." The idea, in either case, is that it is unknowable in the ordinary sense of the term. One Upanishad brings out this uniqueness of the self by stating paradoxically that it is known only to those that do not *know* it, meaning that, though intuitively realizable, it cannot be made the *object* of thought.

Thus Brahman means the eternal principle as realized in the world as a whole; and ātman, the inmost essence of one's own self. These two conceptions—Brahman and ātman—are of great importance and occur not only independently in the literature of this period, but are sometimes correlated with each other; and their parallelism is pointed out by representing the self of the world as related to the physical universe in the same manner in which the individual self is related to its body. Thus in the Atharva Veda, the universal self or world-soul is stated to have "the earth for its feet, the atmospheric region for its belly, the sky for its head, the sun and moon for its eyes and the wind for its breath." The two conceptions are also sometimes identified; and it is this happy identification of them that constitutes the essential teaching of the Upanishads. It is represented by the well-known sayings "That thou art" (*Tat tvam asi*) and "I am Brahman" (*Aham Brahma asmi*). They mean that the principle underlying the world as a whole, and that which forms the essence of man, are ultimately the same. Here ended the long Indian quest for the pervasive cause of all things—the search, as the Upanishads express it, for "that by knowing which all will be known." Passages descriptive of Brahman alone or of ātman alone occur frequently in the Upanishads; but they are not peculiar to them, being also found in the earlier literature. Their explicit identification, on the other hand, is specifically Upanishadic.

It is necessary to point out the full significance of this identification. Brahman, as the ultimate cosmic principle or the source of the whole universe, is all-comprehensive. But such a principle need not be spiritual in its nature, and may well be a material or physical entity. Further, an objective conception like the above is little more than a *hypothesis* to account for the origin of the universe; and there is nothing compelling us to regard it as actually existing, there being no logical absurdity in denying it. Some thinkers already seem to have done so in the Upanishadic period and maintained that "in the beginning this world was just non-being."[13] The establishment of the spiritual character of this principle and the removal of the uncertainty about its existence are both accomplished by its identification with ātman or the self. For our own self is known to us to be spiritual and there is an intuitive obligation to recognize it, in some sense, as indubitable. If we start from the idea of the self, instead of that of Brahman, we meet with a similar difficulty, for, while the self points to what is spiritual and is an incontrovertible certainty, it is, as known to us, necessarily limited in its nature. Whatever view we may take of its nature, it is determined on one side by the world of nature, and on the other by the other selves. It is this deficiency of finiteness that is made good by its identification with Brahman or the all-comprehensive first cause of the universe. The outcome of the identification therefore is that the ultimate reality, which may indifferently be termed either Brahman or ātman, is spiritual and that it accounts for not only all the selves but also the whole of the physical universe. That is the meaning of monism or the doctrine of unity as taught in the Upanishads.

The spiritual and unitary character of this absolute reality is very well expressed by the classical phrase *saccidānanda.* As a single term defining its nature, it is met with only in the later Upanishads; but its three elements—*sat, cit* and *ānanda* —are used of Brahman, singly and in pairs, even in the earliest of them. *Sat,* which means "being," points to the positive character of Brahman distinguishing it from all non-being. But positive entities, to judge from our experience, may be spiritual or not. The next epithet *cit,* which means "sentience," shows that it is spiritual. The last epithet *ānanda,* which stands for "peace," indicates its unitary and all-embracing character, inasmuch as variety is the source of all trouble and restlessness. "Fear arises from the other," as a famous Upanishadic saying has it.[14] Thus the three epithets together signify that Brahman is the sole spiritual reality or the Absolute, which comprehends not only all being (*sat*) but also all thought (*cit*) so that whatever partakes of the character of either must eventually be traced to it. In other words, it is the source of the whole universe, while it itself is self-existent and self-revealing, there being no other entity from which it could be derived or by which it might be made known.

Another of the chief difficulties in understanding the Upanishads arises in determining the exact relation of this unitary principle to the world and to the individual selves. There are several passages which teach that the world is but an appearance, and that it has no actual place in the ultimate reality. There are other passages, not less numerous, which grant reality to the world though, at the same time, they maintain that it is never apart from Brahman or the Absolute. Śaṁkara examines both these positions in his several commentaries, and concludes that the former is the true teaching of the Upanishads. The latter view, according to him, is put forward in them only tentatively. That is, it marks only the first step in the teaching; and the Upanishads finally retract this view, affirming in its place the other, viz. that Brahman and nothing besides it is truly real. Thus the reality conceded to the world in such passages is not meant to be taken as ultimate. The concession is merely for adjusting the final teaching to common or empirical ways of thinking, which assume diversity to be quite real. It represents but the "lower" truth (*aparā vidyā*) which serves as a stepping stone to the comprehension of the "higher" (*parā vidyā*)—a distinction which is sometimes explicitly endorsed in the Upanishads.[15] As regards the individual self, Śaṁkara takes it to be Brahman itself appearing as finite because of its adjuncts like the body which, as parts of the physical universe, are not real in the true sense of the term.

There have, however, been other eminent exponents of the Upanishadic doctrine, some of them like Bhartṛprapañca[16] being anterior to Śaṁkara, who maintained that the self and the physical universe, though they may be finite and imperfect, are real, but that they are not altogether different from Brahman. That is to say, they are both identical with and different from it, the three together constituting a unity in diversity. *As* Brahman, the ultimate reality is one; but, *as* souls and the world, it is many. The whole universe, on this view, actually emerges from Brahman and therefore necessarily partakes of its character of reality. The richness of its content indicates that Brahman, its source, is complex; only the complexity is sometimes manifest, and at other times latent. The former is the period of creation (*sṛṣṭi*); and the latter is that of dissolution (*pralaya*) which, according to immemorial Indian belief, succeed each other endlessly. At the end of each cycle, the variety returns to Brahman, but re-emerges from it at the beginning of the next cycle. The distinction made here between a latent and a manifest stage of the universe implies the dynamic character of ultimate reality, and the view is accordingly described as "the doctrine of self-evolving Brahman" (*Brahma-pariṇāma-vāda*). This view also, like the previous one, is monistic since it admits no reality outside Brahman. It may also be described as idealistic for, though it may not explain the world as an appearance, it denies ultimate meaning or value to it, except when viewed as an element in Brahman, the absolute spirit.

In whichever of these two ways we conceive of Brahman, it is the source from which the universe, in all its organic and inorganic aspects, comes into being. In the first place, it gives rise to the five "elements" (*bhūta*), as they are called, space (*ākāśa*), air (*vāyu*), fire (*agni*), water (*ap*) and earth (*pṛthivi*). Each of these elements has its own distinctive quality: Space is characterized by sound (*śabda*), air by touch (*sparśa*), fire by colour (*rūpa*), water by taste (*rasa*) and earth by odour (*gandha*). This classification, which has been accepted by nearly all the later Indian philosophers, it is obvious, corresponds to the fivefold scheme of the organs of sense—those of hearing, touch, sight, taste and smell, and should have been suggested by it. From these elements are derived, on the one hand, the whole of the inorganic world consisting of things like hills and rivers and, on the other, the organic bodies of plants, animals and men, all of which house souls which are ultimately Brahman itself or, in any case, not quite different from it.

What is the bearing of such a view of ultimate reality on our everyday life? The most striking feature of the latter is the conviction which it involves, viz. that diversity is real and ultimate. The presupposition of most, if not all, of the activities of life is that one man is different from another. The very efforts made through social and political organizations to unify men imply that they regard themselves as distinct. If man is distinct from man, his distinction from his physical environment is even clearer. It is not merely man that is distinct from matter; matter itself, whether it serves as an adjunct of the self like the physical body and the organs of sense or as its environment, seems to be diverse in its character, each object having its own individuality or, as the Upanishads express it, its own name (*nāma*) and its own form (*rūpa*). It is obvious that, if monism is the truth, no part of this diversity can be ultimate. That is the significance of the teaching of the Upanishads, so far as our common beliefs are concerned.

The diversity given in everyday experience may only be an appearance of Brahman and therefore false, as one school of interpreters of the Upanishads holds; but, even according to the other school, it is not the whole of truth, for unity also is equally real. And yet it appears to be the sole truth, owing to an inveterate habit of our mind which should be traced to our ignorance (*avidyā*) of the ultimate reality. This is what is meant by Māyā—the power or the principle that conceals from us the true character of reality. The ignorance may be regarded as negative, that is, as merely a lack of knowledge of the unity underlying the diversity given in common experience; or it may be looked upon as positive in the sense that it gives rise to a misapprehension, making us see the manifold world where there is Brahman and only Brahman. In the former case, our common knowledge would be correct so far as it went, although it did not go far enough to comprehend the unity also; in the latter case, it would be almost completely erroneous. The goal of life as conceived in the Upanishads is, in either case, to overcome this congenital ignorance, by attaining full enlightenment or *jñāna*. The enlightened state is called release or *mokṣa*. It is attaining one's true selfhood in Brahman.

This enlightenment, however, does not mean only an intellectual apprehension of the view that all is one, but also an actual realization of that unity in our own experience. In other words, the aim of studying philosophy is not merely to gratify theoretical curiosity, however disinterested that curiosity may be; it is also to live the right kind of life, consciously adjusting one's conduct to one's intellectual convictions. It is in this sense of devotion to worthier living and not in the sense of dogma or superstition, that religion is blended with philosophy in India. Acquiring such enlightenment means a long course of training. In the first place, the truth, as taught in the Upanishads, needs to be learnt from a proper preceptor (*guru*). This stage of the training is called *śravaṇa* or "formal study." But merely to accept the teaching, although it may be quite true, would constitute blind faith; and it does not become philosophy until its rational support is sought out. The beliefs of others are, no doubt, often of immense use to us, for we cannot know everything for ourselves. Man's advance is mostly due to his capacity for receiving and profiting by the thought and experience of others. But the matter is altogether different in the case of a subject like philosophy, whose relation to life is so peculiarly intimate. Others may teach us here the truths which they have reached as well as the method by which they did so; but, unless we successfully repeat that process and rediscover those truths for ourselves, we cannot get that depth of conviction which alone can be called "philosophy" in the complete sense of the term. If there are facts which are beyond the reach of reason and cannot therefore be absolutely demonstrated, philosophy should at least point to the *likelihood* of their being true. This is recognized in the Upanishads, for they prescribe what is called *manana* or "reflection" in addition to study (*śravaṇa*) in the sense of learning the truth from a preceptor. It means that philosophy, though it may begin as faith, does not end there.

The training prescribed in the Upanishads does not stop here. It includes also what is called *dhyāna* or "meditation," which means constant dwelling upon the truth of which one has become intellectually convinced. This meditation is otherwise known as *yoga*, of which more will be said in the sequel. A number of sections in the Upanishads are taken up with describing modes of exercise, or *upāsanas* as they are called, which prepare the disciple for contemplating the ultimate truth, by accustoming him to draw away his mind from all disturbing thoughts and fix it on one object only. The aim of the final contemplation is to enable him to grasp the unity of existence directly—as directly as he has grasped its diversity. Thus, if reflection (*manana*) is for getting intellectual conviction, meditation (*dhyāna*) is for gaining direct experience. Without the acquisition of such immediate or intuitive experience, philosophy, even if it represents a logical certainty, will be of purely academic interest. Such theoretical knowledge may be a mental accomplishment; but, being mediate, it cannot dispel the immediate conviction in the ultimacy of diversity and will not therefore become a permanent influence on life. The Upanishads base this part of their teaching on a fact of experience, viz. that a mediate knowledge of truth cannot overcome an immediate illusion—that seeing alone is believing.

But to be effective or even possible, the meditation requires not merely an intellectual conviction concerning the ultimate truth, but also detachment from selfish interests. This was the idea underlying the practice, referred to earlier, of keeping the Upanishadic teaching as a secret and imparting it only to true and tried pupils. "Give it to none that is not tranquil," says one Upanishad, for it was feared that an indiscriminate broadcasting of the truth that all is one might lead to its distortion and bring it into discredit. The ethical training, which detachment signifies, is generally taken for granted in the Upanishads, and is consequently not dwelt upon much in them. But where they refer to it, they definitely bring out its importance, as, for example, in the beginning of the Kaṭha Upanishad, where a youth who seeks to know from the god of Death whether the soul survives the body or not is tempted in several ways by the offer of wealth and power before the truth is made known to him. But it is not merely a spirit of self-abnegation that is presupposed by Upanishadic teaching; equal emphasis is laid in it on what is described as social morality. Thus in another Upanishad, Prajāpati, who is an ethical authority, as we know, enjoins the practice not only of self-denial but also of generosity and compassion.[17] The Upanishads describe Brahman itself as without evil—a description whose implication is that he who desires to attain Brahma-hood should strive to free himself from all forms of evil. As Max Muller says, goodness and virtue are "a *sine qua non* for the attainment of the highest knowledge which brings the soul back to its source and to its home and restores it to its true nature." The culmination of this ethical training is symbolized in formal renunciation or *saṁnyāsa*, which finds a prominent place in the Upanishads. It is the ascetic (*nirṛtti*), as distinguished from the activistic (*pravṛtti*) way of life taught in the Brāhmaṇas—a distinction to which we shall refer at some length in the next chapter.

To restate briefly the entire course of discipline: The necessary pre-condition for starting on the course of Vedāntic life is detachment. In other words, no one that has not undergone a course of ethical training calculated to kill all egoistic impulses is qualified for a serious study of the Upanishads. When this preliminary qualification is acquired, there is a three-fold training which is mainly intellectual: (1) learning the ultimate truth with the assistance of a teacher (*śravaṇa*), (2) reflection upon what has been so learnt with a view to convince oneself of the certainty or, at least, the probability of it (*manana*) and (3) meditation which aims at deepening and intensifying that conviction until it effectively uproots all beliefs that are inconsistent with it (*dhyāna*).

The goal of life, as already indicated, is the attainment of **release** (*mokṣa*) from the empirical state of *saṁsāra* or the recurrent round of birth and death. It is becoming Brahman or, what comes to the same thing, the realization of one's own true nature. In accordance with the double view of the ultimate reality found in the Upanishads, this is conceived in two ways. It is a condition, according to some like Śaṁkara, in which the self remains by itself—partless and peaceful; and, according to others like Bhartṛprapañca, it is a condition in which only the sense of diversity as ultimate disappears and an all-comprehensive reality is experienced as identical with oneself. In either case, it is a state of moral and intellectual perfection, transcending the distinctions we commonly make between the self and the not-self, and between good and evil. That this goal is achievable in the present life seems to be the teaching of the Upanishads, taken as a whole. It is known as *jīvanmukti* or "liberation while still alive." "When all desires lodged in the heart disappear," says the Kaṭha Upanishad, "then man becomes immortal and (even) here attains Brahman." Here, for instance, is a distinct mention of it. In the condition of *jīvanmukti*, the diversity of the world—even according to those who believe it to be false—does not cease to appear; but the belief in its ultimacy is once for all destroyed. This conception of release marks a great advance on the earlier Vedic belief that the final ideal of man can be attained only hereafter. Socrates is stated to have brought philosophy down from heaven to earth; the seers of the Upanishads, we may say, discovered that heaven itself is on the earth, could one but realize it. When in the end a person that has reached this stage is dissociated from his physical accompaniments, he becomes Brahman itself. That is final release (*videha-mukti*).

We have so far restricted our attention to persons who succeed in killing every passion and acquire complete enlightenment in this life. But their number must necessarily be very small. Of the others, who form the large majority, the Upanishads may be said to make two broad divisions—those that pursue the right path of life, though they are not able to acquire full enlightenment in this life, and those that yield to natural impulses, because they lack self-control. The former, the second best, progress from one state of existence to a higher without returning to the world of mortals, until at last they find release from the cycle of births and deaths. This progressive realization (*krama-mukti*) of the ideal of life is what some Vedāntins consider to be the *sole* form of release taught in the Upanishads. It corresponds to the eschatological view of the goal of man, as it was understood in the earlier stages of the Vedic period. Only the result is conceived here as absolute liberation from the conditions of worldly existence, and not as a sublimated life of joy in the world of gods. The latter class of people, on the other hand, viz. the self-indulgent who fail to bridle their desires, are born again and again, their condition in any particular life being determined by "the nature of their deeds and the nature of their thoughts"[18] in the past. The belief in the karma doctrine implied here forms a characteristic feature of Upanishadic teaching. But it will be convenient to defer its consideration to the next chapter. It is enough for the present to refer to the clear enunciation in the Upanishads of the moral law underlying the belief, viz. that "good deeds lead to good; and evil deeds, to evil."[19]

There is one other point to which a brief reference is necessary, before we close this section, viz. the place of theism in the Upanishads. We have already sketched its growth to the close of the Brāhmaṇa period. In tracing the subsequent history of it in the next chapter, we shall mention the place which monotheism, strictly so termed, finds in the Upanishads. But there is also another form of it in them, about which a few words should now be added. It has not been developed, like the conception of Prajāpati for instance, from the polytheism of the mantras; it is directly derived from the Brahman-ātman conception and, in consonance with it, the supreme God is here taken to be immanent in all that constitutes the universe, including gods and men. This fact is indicated by the name generally given to it in the Upanishads, viz. Īśa or Īśvara ("Lord") who lives as the "inner guide" (*antaryāmin*) in all objects in the universe.[20] Īśvara, in this sense, is only the personified form of Brahman. The term does not accordingly signify a creator other than the created, as God is conceived in monotheism, but a principle which is eventually one with it. To express the same in the terminology of later Vedānta, God as conceived here is the material as well as the efficient cause of the universe. This personified conception of Brahman, as may be expected, often passes insensibly into that of the Absolute in the teaching of the Upanishads.

## Chapter Two

# TRANSITION TO THE SYSTEMS

*

WE have very briefly treated of Vedic religion and philosophy and have now to deal, in somewhat greater detail, with the several systems of Indian thought. But these systems do not appear immediately after the close of the Vedic period; they do so considerably later, although the exact duration of the interval cannot be determined. It used to be thought, till some years ago, that none of the systems was much older than the Christian era. The present tendency is to assign them an earlier date;[1] but, even thus, there is a couple of centuries separating the Vedic period from what may be described as the period of the systems. Indian thought made rapid strides in this interval which, we may observe in passing, was one of great intellectual stir not only in this country but also elsewhere as, for example, in Greece. In this period, it was not merely the different currents of Vedic thought, mentioned in the previous chapter, that flourished; new and very important schools of religion and philosophy also definitely emerged then. Naturally the systems which we are to consider presuppose all these developments, and it is therefore necessary to indicate their general character before proceeding further.

## I

We shall begin by tracing the further history of the different currents of Vedic thought; but we shall not separate monism from monotheism in doing so, for, as already observed (p. 16), they are mixed up with each other so much that it is often rather hard to differentiate between them. It will suffice to remark that, so far as monism is concerned, both the views of the Absolute noted before (p. 22) are found in early post-Vedic literature. In the Gītā, for example, which belongs to this period, the ultimate reality is described in some places as pervading all things that exist; but in others, it is stated to stand aloof, unattached really to any of them. The chief sources of information for us here are (1) the Kalpa Sūtras, a class of treatises consisting generally of short aphorisms, in which is systematized the teaching of the Veda on its ritualistic side, (2) the well-known epic of the Mahābhārata which is a veritable storehouse of human wisdom, and (3) some of the "later" or "minor" Upanishads, as they are now called in contrast to those that form genuine parts of the Veda. In utilizing the last two of these sources, we should be much on our guard, because large portions of them belong to an age later than the one with which we are now concerned. They contain new material along with the old, and there is a good deal of difficulty in distinguishing between them. Consequently our statements in matters of detail, so far as they are based on these two sources, must be more or less in the nature of conjectures. But the general trend of thought in them is fairly certain.

(1) *Monotheism:* The impersonal form of theism, to which we alluded in the previous chapter (p. 15), continues in the Post-Vedic period also. We have seen that Prajāpati, the chief god of the Brāhmaṇas, came in later times to be regarded as a secondary deity under the designation of Brahmā (masc.) The intrinsic identity between the two conceptions explains the fact that Brahmā also is sometimes represented as the supreme God in early literature. That is the case, for example, in the Mahābhārata. But such representations of him occur, significantly enough, mostly in those portions of the epic which are the earliest among its theistic sections, implying that his supremacy, once recognized, waned gradually. His place is, in course of time, taken by two other deities, viz. Śiva and Viśṇu; and in the epic, on the whole, it is they that are prominent.

These gods are older than Prajāpati; but, to speak generally, they occupied in the beginning no very important position (p. 11). Their conception, however, is personal;[2] and this personal character becomes more and more pronounced as they gain in prominence, so that they finally come to represent a conception of the supreme godhead similar to that of Varuna

(p. 12) in the early mantras. The history of this personal theism, subsequent to the decline of Varuṇa worship, is lost; but we may conclude from the fact of its continuance later that it could not have wholly disappeared then. It should have remained mostly a belief of the common people, as theism in general still continues to be; and it was probably under the influence of that belief that these two deities came to be completely personified. In their fully developed form, both Śiva and Viṣṇu are described as gods among the gods (*deva-deva*), or gods above the gods (*devādhideva*); and each has a personality so clearly outlined that it is impossible for either to be identified with the other. This distinctness explains, at least in part, the generally sectarian character of theism in the present period.[3]

*Śaivism:* This is the creed in which Śiva is conceived as the supreme God. The beginnings of the conception can be traced back to the early hymns, where we find Rudra as the personification of the destructive powers of nature as exemplified, for instance, in storms and lightning. Indeed, the name Rudra literally means "howler." The hymns devoted to him in the Rigveda are only a very few; but some of the features, predominantly associated with Śiva in later times, are already found mentioned in them, such as his dwelling in the mountains, his having braided hair and his wearing a hide. In later stages, he comes to be represented as the patron as well as the pattern of ascetics. On account of his generally terrific character, he was invoked in those early times in order that he might become auspicious or *śiva*. This name of "*Śiva*" becomes his distinctive designation in the later portions of the Veda. He also comes there to be described as the great God (*mahādeva*). In the Śvetāśvatara Upanishad (in which the conception blends now and then with that of the Absolute), he holds the same conspicuous position and is declared to be knowable through loving devotion (*bhakti*). The Upanishad also states that divine grace (*prasāda*) is needed for salvation. It thus explicitly introduces a characteristic tenet of all personal theism, viz. the grace of God and its necessary counterpart, viz. man's devotion to him.

These features of the creed appear more prominently in later literature as, for example, in the sections of the Mahābhārata glorifying Śiva. Images of this God and of the emblems of his divinity are found among the relics of Mohenjo-Daro (p. 9), but the precise relation between the creed to which it points and the Vedic faith in Rudra-Śiva is not yet known. Here is one point on which the unravelling of the true nature of the Indus valley civilization, as it is now styled, is likely to throw fresh light. It is, however, clear that there is a certain blending of antithetical features in this conception; and it may in part be alien in its nature, the alien features being later assimilated to the Aryan conception. There are various indications pointing to its mixed character. The story, narrated in more than one old work, of Dakṣa's sacrifice whereto Śiva was not invited as being a "low god" is one of them. Another indication is that Śiva worship is largely based upon Āgamas (literally "tradition") which are not, according to some thinkers like Śaṁkara, entirely in agreement with the teaching of revelation or the Vedas.[4]

*Vaiṣṇavism:* This is the creed in which Viṣṇu is worshipped as the supreme God. As already stated, Viṣṇu also is a Vedic deity. He is represented in the mantras as one of the solar deities and, as such, is associated with light and life. His essential feature, as depicted in the hymns, is his taking three strides (*tri-vikrama*) which in all probability refer to the rising, culmination, and setting of the sun. It was this worship of the sun, "the swift-moving luminary," that gradually transformed itself into the worship of Viṣṇu ("the pervading") as the supreme God. He had already attained supremacy in the time of the Brāhmaṇas; and in one of the older Upanishads, the goal of human life is represented as reaching the supreme abode of Viṣṇu.[5] There was also an allied conception, that of Nārāyaṇa, whose origin may be traced in the Rigveda, and which appears in a well-developed form in the Brāhmaṇas. The name signifies "the abode or resting place of men" or, more generally, "the goal of all beings." One of the Brāhmaṇas states that Nārāyaṇa placed himself in all the world and in all the gods, and that they were all placed in him. In a relatively later Upanishad, the Mahānārāyaṇa, in which this God occupies the position which Śiva does in the Śvetāśvatara Upanishad, his cosmic character is thus described: "Whatever in this universe is seen or heard, pervading all that—both inside and outside—Nārāyana stands."[6] He is called in the epic "the son of *dharma*," implying that the conception is not cosmic alone, but also pre-eminently ethical in its character.

There is a third element also which goes to form Vaiṣṇavism, as prevalent in this period; but, unlike the other two, it is derived from a non-Vedic, though not a non-Aryan, source. Some time before Buddha and Mahāvīra, the last prophet of Jainism, there seems to have arisen in the North-West of India a religious reformer Śrī Krishna, son of Vāsudeva, who preached a theistic faith. The supreme God as conceived in it, who was termed "Bhagavān" ("the worshipful"), was of the Varuṇa type—a God equally exalted morally and otherwise also equally worthy of worship. It soon assumed a sectarian complexion in the form of Bhāgavata religion; and one stage of it is found taught in the famous Bhagavadgītā, so far as it is theistic —a work to which we have already alluded, and to the importance of whose practical teaching we shall refer later. It was largely prevalent when Megasthenes visited India, so that the religion must have originated some considerable time before. This monotheistic creed came, in course of time, to be combined with the Vedic cult of Viṣṇu-Nārāyaṇa; and it was this combination that chiefly contributed to make the God of Vaiṣṇavism even more personal than that of Śaivism. Somewhat later Śrī Krishna, the prophet of the Bhāgavata religion, was deified and identified with Viṣṇu-Narayaṇa as an incarnation of him.

Thus altogether three streams of thought mingle to form Vaiṣṇavism. Like Śaivism, it also contains elements drawn from sources other than the Veda; and the form of worshipping the supreme, which it commends, is for the most part based on Āgamas. There are certain special features characterizing this creed: To begin with, it is, as just pointed out, more rigorously monotheistic than Śaivism, which sometimes shows an impersonal phase. A second feature is that Viṣṇu assumes different forms or incarnations called *avatārs*. The word *avatāra* means "descent," and signifies that God brings himself down in order to present to us a higher ideal of life, and thereby to exalt us to him. According to Hinduism generally, progress in the world is not continuous. Things grow worse and worse at times, when God "intervenes catastrophically to inaugurate a reign of justice and happiness."[7] This theory of *avatārs* helps what has all along been a noteworthy feature of Hinduism, viz. its absorption of other creeds into itself by explaining the gods worshipped in them as but manifestations of the one supreme Being. "Those that worship other gods," says Śrī Krishna in the Gītā, "they also worship me, though but imperfectly."[8] It does not thus extirpate those creeds, but re-interprets them and utilizes whatever elements of truth they may contain. It was through such re-interpretation, for example, that the worship of Śrī Krishna himself was assimilated to the Vaiṣṇava creed, and that still later a place was found for Buddha among the ten principal incarnations of Viṣṇu. Yet another characteristic of Vaiṣṇavism is the great emphasis it lays on loving devotion (*bhakti*) as a means to redemption—a feature which we have already noticed in the case of Śaivism. The religion also discarded animal sacrifices, evincing thereby its antagonism to what was, at the time, a conspicuous feature of Vedic religion. A section of the Mahābhārata, speaking of the glory of Vaiṣṇavism, refers to the performance of a "horse-sacrifice" in which no animal was killed.

A special mark of monotheistic belief, whether Śaivism or Vaiṣṇavism, is the distinction it makes between God, the individual soul, and the world of which he is the author. The soul is usually conceived as eternal, but as entirely dependent upon God; and it therefore becomes the first duty of man to make himself a conscious and willing instrument in the fulfilment of his purpose. What the conception of the goal of life according to early Indian theism is cannot be definitely stated, for it is presented in diverse forms. Generally speaking, it may be taken as reaching the presence of God or becoming godlike.[9] The predominant means of achieving this end is, besides good conduct (*caryā*), loving devotion (*bhakti*) to God, such as will win his grace (*prasāda*)—a means whose potency, as the reader will recall (p. 13), is recognized even in the oldest portions of the Veda.

(2) *Ritualism:* The ritualistic spirit, which is so prominent a feature of later Vedic thought, is further developed in the post-Vedic period as shown by the Kalpa Sūtras whose aim, as already observed, is the systematisation of ceremonial. There are three classes of them. One of them, consisting of very

voluminous works, is taken up with the description of the elaborate rites which mark the chief subject-matter of the Brāhmaṇas. Another is concerned with the many simpler domestic rites connected with events like marriage and birth of children. We have little to do with either of these varieties of works here, since their chief interest is in ceremonial; and we shall not therefore dwell on them further. It is the remaining class of these Sūtras that are of importance to us, though even they are so only indirectly. Their aim is to regulate the conduct of the individual by requiring him to perform certain duties and thus fit him for the ritualistic life which, in accordance with a principle recognised from very early times but now become more articulate, will be fruitful only in the case of those that are morally pure. "The Vedas do not cleanse the ethically unworthy,"[10] says one of these Sūtras; and the Mahābhārata repeats the same idea when it declares that they "do not save him who is a hypocrite." They are called Dharma Sūtras, because their aim is to lay down the standard of *dharma*, whose meaning we may now proceed to consider.

The word *dharma* is of great importance in the history of Indian thought, but unfortunately it is not easy to define its meaning. Literally it means "what holds together."[11] and signifies that it is the basis of all order, whether social or moral. It is thus allied, in its ethical aspect, to *ṛta*. In fact, this conception, as stated before (p. 13), virtually replaces the other in the present period. It is sometimes used as a purely moral concept, and stands for right or virtuous conduct which leads to some form of good as its result. But its more usual meaning is religious merit which, operating in some unseen (*adṛṣṭa*) way as it is supposed, secures good to a person in the future, either here or elsewhere. Thus the performance of certain sacrifices is believed to lead the agent to heaven after the present life, and of certain others to secure for him wealth, children and the like in this very life. Even when the conception of *dharma* is thus predominantly ritualistic it does not cease to have an ethical significance in conformity with the principle just referred to; and it is that significance or the ideal of moral purity which these treatises formulate that chiefly counts for us here, although that ideal may not have been laid down in them as ultimate but only as a means to success in ritualistic life.

It is not possible to enter here into the details of the obligatory duties prescribed in the Dharma Sūtras. We may only note in general that they conduce to the cultivation of what are known as self-regarding virtues as well as to the fulfilment of social obligations. This will be clear, if we refer to two of the main classes of *dharma* taught in these treatises:[12]

(i) The first of them are described as "common" or "general" (*sādhārana-dharma*). They comprise virtues like self-control, kindness and truth-speaking which are equally obligatory on all.[13] They are further conceived, where they are altruistic or have a bearing on others, not as stopping short at mankind, but as including within their scope sub-human beings which are regarded as having rights though no duties.

(ii) In order to understand the nature of the other set of *dharmas*, we have to remember that the Aryan society was divided, as it still continues to be, into four classes (*varṇas*) which are well known, and that the life of the individual belonging to the higher three among them was similarly divided into four stages (*āśramas*). The four stages or orders of life are those of the religious student (*brahmacārin*) who learns the Veda leading a severely austere life, the householder (*gṛhastha*) who offers sacrifices to the gods and performs other duties like alms-giving, the anchorite (*vānaprastha*) who retires to the forest and there lives the life of the hermit, and the wandering mendicant (*saṁnyāsin*) who, abandoning all worldly or selfish concerns, devotes himself to meditation on the ultimate reality. Each class and each stage has its own specific duties to perform, so that it is wrong to think that those who don the mendicant's garb have no obligations to discharge. Their entry into that order signifies only the giving up of ritualistic life, associated with the householder in particular. It does not mean that they grow indifferent to the welfare of others. These duties, which are appropriate to the several classes of society and the stages of life, are described as "specific" (*varṇāśrama-dharmas*). Though, unlike the deeds of the first type, they are relative in their conception, they resemble them in that they are equally obligatory; only while the former are binding on *all*, irrespective of age or rank, the latter are so on particular classes or groups only. Many of them are of a religious character, but even they conduce to the cultivation of private virtues like self-restraint and the advancement of the common good, including in the long run the well-being of the agent also. It will suffice to cite, in illustration of this, what are called the five "great sacrifices" (*mahāyajña*) which every householder is expected to perform daily. They are studying the Veda, sacrificing to the gods, honouring guests, presenting oblations to ancestors, and offering food to birds, etc.

The usual view set forth in these Sūtras is that the discipline of the four stages is to be gone through in order. That is, they combine the training of active social life (*pravṛtti*) with that of renunciation (*nivṛtti*). It is the same as the course of life generally commended in the Upanishads, for there also *saṁnyāsa* (p. 27), because it marks the culmination of ethical discipline, presupposes the training of the other stages of life, particularly that of the householder. We know, for example, that the great Upanishadic teacher, Yājñavalkya, had been a householder for long before he renounced the world.[14] But in the Dharma Sūtras there are also references to a view which denounces *saṁnyāsa*.[15] That accords better with the spirit of ritualism and represents, in all probability, the original Vedic view which held out the attainment of heavenly happiness as the final goal of life (p. 13). But, taken as a whole, these Sūtras seem to represent a synthesis of ritualism with the Upanishadic view of liberation, such as we mentioned in the previous chapter (p. 18). Thus we find one of them holding up self-realization (*ātma-lābha*) as the goal of man, and another putting forward the view that the development of one's spiritual nature, if it became a question of choice, should be preferred to ceremonial sanctification.[16] The ultimate goal to be reached by this training is described as the "world of Brahma" (*Brahma-loka*)—a goal which is much like the progressive realization of the ideal (*krama-mukti*) as set forth in the Upanishads (p. 29).

## II

We have hitherto occupied ourselves entirely with the teaching of the Veda or of works ancillary to it. But there was in the period another type of teaching also which, in its origin as well as in its general spirit, was quite different. It appears in more than one form; but in all, it exhibits a striking feature of antagonism to the Veda. There is, of course, an element of opposition within the Vedic teaching itself as pointed out already (p.18), viz. that between the Brāhmaṇas and the Upanishads; but it was somehow overcome in the course of time. The opposition to which we are now referring is of a more radical kind. It is such as was never composed in the long history of Indian thought, and has persisted in some form even to this day. This teaching does not take its rise in the post-Vedic period but is older, for we find distinct, though but occasional, allusions to it in all the important stages of Vedic literature. We referred to one such instance (p.22) in explaining the Upanishadic conception of reality—a nihilistic view, maintaining that there is no positive source to which the world of experience can be traced. But this teaching appears there only indirectly, that is, as one which Vedic thinkers felt it necessary to repudiate. There is no direct record of it, which has come down to us in any of its forms from that early period; and we cannot therefore say what degree of development the teaching had reached then or what the precise extent of its influence was.

As regards its origin, it may in some manner have to be connected with the thoughts and beliefs that prevailed in the country when the Aryans first occupied it; or it may only be the result of a deeper split among the thinking sections of the Aryans themselves, which did not lend itself to be reconciled easily. To judge from the fact that the followers of this heterodox teaching also were generally Aryans, the latter explanation seems more probable, although the earlier thought of the land might also have considerably influenced it. But whatever its origin, it begins to play an important part from about the beginning of the post-Vedic period. It has greatly helped the progress of Indian thought as a whole, opposition instilling strength into the exponents of both sets of doctrines. While Vedic thought points to the North and the West as its home, this non-Vedic thought indicates the East as its main stronghold. We may note, by the way, that the centre of political interest in this period, as shown by history, also shifts in the same direction.

This current of thought also shows three chief varieties in

the present period. The first of them we may describe as naturalism (*svabhāva-vāda*); and the other two are represented by the well-known creeds of Jainism and Buddhism, of which one has all along remained confined to India and the other has become a world religion. Each of the latter has its own literature, though neither goes back to the period when its first great exponents spoke in human voice. The earliest part of this literature is some centuries later; but we may be sure that much of the tradition which they enshrine reaches back to that age. A peculiarity of these literatures is that they are not in Sanskrit but in Prakrit, the language commonly spoken at the time, showing that the movements in question were popular rather than priestly in their character. As for naturalism, there is no such literature; only stray references to it are found in the writings of both orthodox and heterodox schools. The best source of our information here is the Mahābhārata, which often, though but incidentally, refers to it. As, however, the information we can gather about the details of this doctrine is extremely meagre, we shall postpone what we have to say about it to the next chapter. The other two doctrines had developed considerably by the time the systems arose. But for convenience of treatment, we shall postpone the consideration of their early teaching also to the same chapter, where we have to deal with them in their systematized form.

## III

Even from the brief account of Indian thought which we have given, it is clear that a great mass of philosophical material had accumulated by about the third or fourth century B.C. It was the inherent heterogeneity of this material that led to its systematization; but the details relating to its early stages are lost, probably beyond all recovery. The primary sources of information for us as regards the resulting systems of thought are what have come down to us generally under the name of "Sūtras." Each of the orthodox systems has its own Sūtra, excepting only one, viz. the Sāṅkhya. Even that system is now found explained in a Sūtra, but there is convincing evidence to show that it is quite late. The heterodox or non-Vedic systems also have primary authorities of more or less the same character. The object of these treatises, whether they be of the one class or of the other, is twofold—to consolidate the teaching of the particular school to which they belong, and to criticize others where they diverge from it. Hence they contain cross references to one another, and therefore seem to be all contemporaneous. But it is most improbable that they were so, and we have to explain the mutual internal references as often due to later interpolations. The works consist of aphorisms (*sūtra*), which are so laconic that they are hardly intelligible without the aid of commentaries. We have such commentaries on every Sūtra; and the commentaries themselves have, in their turn, been commented upon. The literature of a system consists of its own Sūtra with commentaries and super-commentaries upon it, as also of certain independent treatises (*prakaraṇa*) which expound the doctrine as a whole with a view to aid beginners, or discuss one or more aspects of it from the standpoint of the advanced student.

The chief sign of the systematization of earlier thought about this time is seen in the attention that comes to be consciously paid to the nature and function of knowledge or to the problems of what and how we know. To express the same in Indian terminology, a common feature of all the systems is that they involve, if they do not actually start with, an investigation of *pramāṇas*, that is, the proximate means, as they are defined, to valid knowledge or *pramā*. They are usually regarded as a help not only in acquiring new knowledge, but also in verifying what is already known, so that logic, as conceived in India, is a science both of proof and of discovery. A *pramāṇa*, like perception, may reveal the existence and nature of things not hitherto known. It may also be the means of verification, as when an object apprehended by the organ of sight is tested by means of touch, or when a doubt arising in respect of something inferred is cleared by actual observation. There is much divergence of opinion among Indian thinkers concerning details relating to the scope and nature of *pramānas*, and we shall refer to some of them in dealing with the several systems. The number of *pramāṇas* also is a topic on which wide differences of view exist among the schools. In fact, one of the commonest, though somewhat mechanical, classifications of the schools is according to the number of *pramāṇas* they accept, ranging from one to as many as six or even more. Most Indian logicians, however, agree in accepting three of them—perception (*pratyakṣa*), inference (*anumāna*) and verbal testimony (*śabda*). We shall say a few words here about the last of them, whose inclusion among the *pramāṇas* is a striking feature of Indian logic.

We must first distinguish here between two aspects of *śabda* which may confound the beginner. When a sentence is uttered, there is, to begin with, a certain impression produced on our mind through the auditory channel. This is a case of perception, and the objects apprehended are *sounds* occurring in a certain order. Verbal testimony, as a *pramāṇa*, does not of course mean this. There is another, the interpretative or semantic aspect of sentences; and it is that with which *śabda*, as we are now dealing with it, is concerned. The utility of this means of knowledge in life cannot be exaggerated. Of the numerous facts which a man needs to know, it is only a small fraction that he can learn for himself; and for the rest he has to depend entirely upon the testimony of others which comes to him through their words—whether spoken or written, it does not matter. The value of testimony as a means of communicating information to others or of enriching our own experience may therefore be admitted readily. But it may be questioned whether so much is sufficient to constitute it into an independent *pramāṇa*. The dispute is thus solely about the logical status of verbal testimony, and not about its usefulness.

Some Indian logicians believe in the legitimacy of only perception and inference, and repudiate testimony as a *separate* means of proof or channel of new knowledge. The latter, according to them, will be valid only when it is based directly or indirectly on those two *pramāṇas* or on experience as commonly understood. Their view may thus be described as empiricism. This type of Indian thought is best represented by naturalism (*svabhāva-vāda*) to which we have made a passing reference, and whose general epistemological view we shall explain in the next chapter. This position is accepted by the other schools also, in so far as statements of ordinary men are concerned (*pauruṣeya*). But to suppose, as empiricists do, that the senses and reason are the *only* sources of knowledge is, according to those schools, to restrict the realm of reality too much. Though the human mind may not be definitely aware of what is beyond perception and reasoning, they say, it is not altogether unconscious of it. The very statement that common experience exhausts reality implies, by placing a limit on it, that the mind has travelled beyond that limit. Our reach exceeds our grasp. But it would obviously be futile to postulate such a transcendental realm as merely an unknowable something. There is also need for an appropriate *pramāṇa* whereby we may know it or, at least, those aspects of it which are of significance to us. It is on such a consideration that verbal testimony has been accepted as a separate *pramāṇa* in Indian philosophy. Jaimini, for instance, points out that the Veda is the source of our knowledge just where perception and inference fail to be of assistance to us.[17] Without entering into details, we may state that the chief function of verbal testimony in this sense is explained as the communication to us of a knowledge of the two higher ideals of *dharma* and *mokṣa* and of the proper means to their realisation.[18]

This *pramāṇa* goes back, according to some, to the intuitive vision of a saint (*yogin*), and the channel through which the knowledge intuited by him flows to us is spoken of as *smṛti* or "(mere) tradition."[19] We may take as a good example of it Jainism, which traces its truths to the insight of great prophets like Mahāvīra. For a knowledge of the world which transcends common experience, we depend according to this view entirely upon the authority of individual insight. In this appeal to the experience of an individual, others see a risk for, in their view, nobody's private insight can carry with it the guarantee of its own validity. As *Kumārila*, a well-known leader of orthodox thought, has remarked in discussing a related topic, a "vision" that has unfolded itself to but one single person may after all be an illusion.[20] This is not to impugn the good faith of the saint; it only means that the excellence of the character of a teacher is no guarantee of the truth of his teaching. To avoid this possible defect of subjectivity orthodox thinkers postulate in the place of testimony, based upon the intuition of a single sage, another, viz. *śruti* or "revelation"—otherwise known as the Veda which, it is claimed, will not mislead us since it has emanated from God or is supernatural in some other sense. As commonly explained, the *śruti* is tradition which is looked upon as immemorial (*sanātana*) in its character because its origin cannot be traced to any mortal being. There is the implication here, as contrasted with the previous view, that the realm of transcendental being is not directly accessible to the mind of man, however gifted morally and intellectually he may be.

But, theological considerations apart, it should be admitted that the truths for which the Veda stands, whether or not it is now possible to ascribe them to specific thinkers, should eventually be traced to some human source; and the fact seems to be implied in the description of those truths as having been *seen* by inspired sages (*ṛṣis*) of old. If it be so, the Veda also must be reckoned as communicating to us the results intuited by ancient sages. But there is a very important difference, as may be gathered from a condition which is sometimes laid down as essential to all "revealed" teaching, viz. that it should have proved acceptable to the best minds (*mahājana*) of the community. This may appear to be only a begging of the question at issue, for non-Vedic tradition also claims to have been accepted by the best minds of the community. What, however, is meant by this new condition seems to be that, if a doubt arises as to the validity of the views handed down from the past, adherents of the present school appeal, as those of the other do not, to a community of minds which they have satisfied. Thus the standard here becomes eventually a society of men, and not an individual; and, by virtue of the objective status which it thus acquires, its deliverances are taken to possess an authority which cannot belong to those of anybody's private intuition. Herein may be said to lie the superiority of *śruti* to mere *smṛti*, in the sense given to it above. The Mīmāṁsā and the Vedānta are the systems that accept "revelation," in this sense, as the means to a knowledge of supersensuous truth.

Indian schools of thought are thus broadly divisible, from this standpoint, first into two groups—one, which assumes that reality is confined to what is given in common experience and may therefore be described as positivistic or empirical;

and the other, which regards the realm of being as by no means exhausted by such experience and acknowledges a unique *pramāṇa* for knowing what lies beyond. The latter group is again divisible into two classes—one, which believes that individual insight is ultimately adequate for a knowledge of the transcendental realm; and the other, which seeks the aid of revelation for it. These may together be described as intuitionalistic, if we bear in mind the interpretation given of revelation above. Both alike mean that ultimate philosophic truths are neither deduced solely from postulates or premises taken for granted, nor logically constructed on the basis of mere common experience, but are directly seen.

The systems as ordinarily reckoned are six, viz. Nyāya, Vaiśeṣika, Sāṅkhya, Yoga, Pūrva-mīmāṁsā, and Uttaramīmāṁsā or Vedānta. These are often grouped by twos, taken in order, since they are allied to each other; and we shall follow this grouping in our treatment of them. The systems forming the last pair, however, are not so closely akin in their theoretical aspects, at least, according to some; and we shall therefore treat of them separately. They are the systems which are directly based on the Veda. The remaining four doctrines also, in their present form, declare allegiance to the Veda, although they put their own interpretation upon it; but it is doubtful whether they were Vedic from the beginning of their history. Having in view this, their later feature, they also are described as orthodox. To these we have to add three more, viz. Materialism (a later phase of naturalism), Jainism and Buddhism which, as systems, explicitly reject the authority of the Vedas and are heterodox. We shall first consider them briefly under the head of "non-Vedic schools." But before taking them up, it will be useful to refer to two features which are common to all of them, Vedic and non-Vedic, excepting only Materialism.

(1) *Belief in the Karma Doctrine:* This belief has, for long, had a profound influence on the life of the Indian people. There are two aspects of it which should be clearly distinguished. In the first place, the doctrine extends the principles of causation to the sphere of human conduct and teaches that, as every event in the physical world is determined by its antecedents, so everything that happens in the moral realm is preordained. If all that man does is thus preordained, it

may be asked whether the doctrine does not become fatalistic and therefore leave no room to him for the exercise of freedom. To answer this question, it is necessary to explain what exactly is meant by "freedom." To be controlled by extraneous factors in what one does is not to be a free agent; but freedom does not therefore mean the total absence of determination or mere caprice. To act with arbitrarily shifting motives would be to act from impulse, as many lower animals do. Hence freedom should be regarded as consisting not in unrestricted license, but in being determined by oneself. When therefore we ask whether belief in karma does not result in fatalism, all that we mean is whether it does or does not preclude self-determination. That it does not is evident, because the doctrine traces the causes which determine an action to the very individual that acts. Since, however, those causes cannot all be found within the narrow limits of a single life, it postulates the theory of *saṁsāra* or the continued existence of the self (*jīva*) in a succession of lives.[21] Thus the theory of transmigration is a necessary corollary to the doctrine of karma. The fact of moral consciousness, as students of Western philosophy know, is, according to Kant, the guarantee of personal immortality. In a similar way, the law of karma is here our assurance of the truth of transmigration. If we now look at life in this new perspective, the present conduct of a person and the good or evil that follows from it are due to his own actions done in one state of existence, if not in another. Destiny, as an old authority observes,[22] thus becomes only another name for deeds done in previous births. There being therefore no external Fate constraining man to act as he does, he is free in the sense referred to above; and the doctrine does not therefore lead to fatalism.

Here, no doubt, a question will be asked as to when the responsibility for what one does was *first* incurred. But such a question is really inadmissible, for it takes for granted that there was a time when the self was without any disposition whatsoever. Such a view of the self is an abstraction as meaningless as that of mere disposition which characterises no one. The self, as ordinarily known to us, always means a self with a certain stock of dispositions; and this fact is indicated in Indian expositions by describing karma as beginningless (*anādi*). It means that no matter how far back we trace the history of an individual, we shall never arrive at a stage when he was devoid of all character. Thus at all stages, it is self-determination; and the karma doctrine does in no sense imply the imposition of any constraint from outside. So deep is the conviction of some of the adequacy of karma to account for the vicissitudes of life and the diversity of human conditions that they see no need, as we shall point out later, to acknowledge the existence of even God, conceived as the creator of the world and as its controlling judge.

Granting that we alone are in the long run accountable for whatever happens to us now, it may still be said that we are not able to help ourselves in any manner, because we cannot alter the course of our past karma which leads to those happenings. It may be that the constraint is not external; but constraint it is, and there can therefore be no freedom of action. In meeting this objection, it is necessary to draw attention to a point to which we have already made a passing reference, viz. the idea of moral retribution underlying the karma doctrine (p. 29). Whatever we knowingly do, will, sooner or later, bring us the result we merit; and there is no way of escape from it. What we sow, we must reap. That is, the karma doctrine signifies not merely that the events of our life are determined by their antecedent causes, but also that there is absolute justice in the rewards and punishments that fall to our lot in life. This is the second aspect of the doctrine to which we alluded earlier. The law of karma accordingly is not a blind mechanical law, but is essentially ethical. It is this conviction that there are in reality no iniquities in life which explains the absence of any feeling of bitterness—so apt to follow in the wake of pain and sorrow—which is noticeable even among common people in India when any misfortune befalls them. They blame neither God nor their neighbour, but only themselves for it. In fact, this frame of mind, which belief in the karma doctrine produces, is one of the most wholesome among its consequences. Deussen refers thus to the case of a blind person whom he met once during his Indian tour: "Not knowing that he had been blind from birth, I sympathized with him and asked by what unfortunate accident the loss of sight had come upon him. Immediately and without showing any sign of bitterness, the answer was ready to his lips, 'By some crime committed in a former birth'."[23]

The implication of this idea of retribution is that the karma doctrine is grounded in a moral view of the universe, and that it therefore commits man to the obligations of a truly moral life. It points to the truth that there is an ideal of life which it is the first duty of man, as a thinking and self-conscious being, to sedulously pursue. In other words, the doctrine presupposes the possibility of moral growth; and the rewards and punishments, which it signifies, are not therefore ends in themselves but only the means to bring about such growth. They are thus really more than retributive; they also constitute a discipline of natural consequences to educate man morally. If so, the conclusion to be drawn from it is that freedom to choose between alternative ways of acting is not merely compatible with, but is actually demanded by, the law of karma. If man were only a creature of his congenital impulses—altogether powerless to rise above them, it would be poor comfort for him to know that he was not the victim of any alien Fate.

This does not, however, mean that he can avoid the consequences of his past karma. His life, in that respect, is characterized by the strictest necessity; and he has to accept all the unpleasant experiences of life as willingly as he does the pleasant. They are predestined results from which he can never free himself. The Mahābhārata says that the consequences of what a man does will seek him out later "as surely as a calf does its mother in a herd of cows." So far, karma does imply necessity. But, as stated above, it implies freedom also, viz. in the matter of *ethical* advance. There is no contradiction in thus pointing to both freedom and necessity as the implications of the doctrine, for they refer to different aspects of karma. Every deed that we do leads to a double result. It not only produces what may be termed its direct result (*phala*)—the pain or pleasure following from it according to the nature of the deed done; it also establishes in us a tendency (*saṁskāra*) to repeat the same deed in the future. The necessity involved in the karma doctrine is only in so far as the former of these results, viz. the pain or the pleasure, is concerned. As regards the latter, viz. the tendencies, they are entirely under our control; and our moral progress depends wholly upon the success with which we direct and regulate them, as they tend to express themselves in action. Nor does this double significance of karma lead to any bifurcation of life's interests or conflict in its purposes, for the ethical advance is what is intended to be made the sole aim of *all* activities. That, for example, is the explicit teaching of the Gītā as we shall soon see. By thus adopting the betterment of one's moral nature as the goal of all endeavour, one may grow indifferent to what happens in the present as the inevitable result of past karma.

(2) *Ideal of Mokṣa:* The other important point of agreement among the various schools is the recognition of liberation or release (*mokṣa*) from the cycle of rebirths as the highest of human ends or values. The Indians generally speak of four values—*artha*, *kāma*, *dharma* and *mokṣa*. Of these, the first two, which respectively mean "wealth" and "pleasure", are secular or purely worldly values. The other two, whose general meaning has already been indicated, may, in contrast, be described as spiritual. Philosophy is concerned only with the latter, but this does not mean that it discards the other two. It does acknowledge them also, but only in so far as they help, or are instrumental to, *dharma* or *mokṣa*. Owing to this judgment of preference which it implies, philosophy, as conceived in India, may be described as essentially a criticism of values. Indeed, its final aim is to determine what the *ultimate* value is, and to point out how it can be realized. In earlier times, the first of the two spiritual values, viz. *dharma*, alone seems to have been recognized. That, for instance, is the conclusion to be drawn from the original ritualistic teaching of the Brāhmaṇas; and there are still to be found some passages in old works which indicate that belief in the ideal of *mokṣa* was not accepted by all.[24] But this view has for long been superseded; and *mokṣa* has come to be acknowledged as the highest of human values by all the doctrines, so that all of them are now doctrines of salvation. The prominence which *mokṣa* attained gradually does not mean that the ideal of *dharma* is abandoned. It only becomes subordinated, in that the ethical discipline which it involves is made, as in Upanishadic teaching (p. 13), a necessary aid to the pursuit of *mokṣa*.

The nature of *mokṣa* differs widely, as conceived in the various systems. It may generally be represented as achieving self-perfection, and it will suffice for the present to draw attention to but one point about it. We have already mentioned (p. 28) that, while some Indian thinkers maintained that liberation is achievable only hereafter, others held that it could be achieved in this very life (*jīvanmukti*). This distinction persists in the age of the systems also. But whether here or elsewhere, the ideal of *mokṣa* is assumed in all the systems to be actually attainable. It may, of course, be held that a goal like self-perfection is never actually reached, but is significant only in so far as its deliberate choosing and its persistent pursuit are concerned. A modern thinker writes, "The ultimate values are not of the realm of fact, but are merely ideals which should regulate our conduct." The view of Indian philosophers, however, is that it can undoubtedly be realized—that "ought" means "can." All of them, including the heterodox, believe that the evil of *saṁsāra* carries with it the seeds of its destruction, and that it is sooner or later bound to be superseded by the good. In other words, none of the Indian systems is finally pessimistic; and the common view that they are mostly "gospels of woe" is entirely wrong. We have more than one interesting indication in the Sanskrit language of this faith of the Indians in the ultimate goodness and rationality of the world. The Sanskrit word *sat*, as noticed long ago by Max Muller, means not only "real" but also "good." Similarly the word *bhavya*, we may add, means not only "what will happen in the future" but also "what is auspicious," implying that the best is yet to be. Corresponding to this belief on the practical side, there is the belief on the theoretical side that ignorance or error will also be superseded in the end by truth for which, as one old Buddhistic verse puts it, "the human mind has a natural partiality."[25] If either evil or error were final, the world would be irrational.

Before we leave the topic of *mokṣa* and the ethical discipline which is an essential preliminary to its pursuit, it is necessary to refer to the two ways of life, already mentioned—one of action (*pravṛtti*) and the other of renunciation (*nivṛtti*). Each of them was, in all probability, adopted at first to the exclusion of the other. But before the Vedic period closed, as we have seen (p. 27), it had become permissible to change from the one to the other, after reaching a certain stage in self-discipline.

More or less the same practice obtained in the non-Vedic schools also, and it continues to prevail among them even in this period.

But so far as the orthodox schools are concerned, a profound transformation has since taken place in the view of the relation between these two ways. The positive way of life has been transformed by the incorporation in it of the essence of the negative one. It is true that even in its earlier sense, the path of action involved numerous checks on natural impulses and therefore implied the need for a great deal of self-restraint. But the restraint in it was only partial, because a person who followed that path was allowed to seek his own private happiness, provided he did so without resorting to wrong action. What particularly marks the later conception of it is the *total* exclusion of self-interest from it. It does not aim at merely subordinating the interests of the individual to those of the community, or of any other greater whole to which he may regard himself as belonging, but at their entire abnegation. The path of action accordingly comes to lay the same emphasis on self-renunciation as the path of *saṁnyāsa* does, and one acquiesces as little as the other in what is sometimes described as "reasonable self-love" or "enlightened self-interest." But it does so without reducing, in the least, the stress on the need for engaging oneself in social activity. Consequently, the abandonment of active social life is at no stage permitted. It must throughout be pursued, but in a spirit of absolute detachment. By thus combining asceticism and activity, the new form of discipline elevates them both. Asceticism thereby becomes much more than self-denial, and activity is freed from all egoistic motives. This remarkable change we owe chiefly to the teaching of the Gītā. Even if the Gītā did not initiate it, it has given wide and permanent currency to the new idea by presenting it in a splendidly devised setting. We shall now set forth, at some length, the way in which this is accomplished in the work.

The importance of the Bhagavadgītā, to give the work its full name, in the religious and philosophical literature of India is second only to that of the Upanishads. This poem of 18 cantos appears as an inset in the Mahābhārata, where it describes the two rival armies of the Pāṇḍavas and the Kauravas as ranged against each other on the battle-field. Arjuna who, taken all in all, is the most notable of the five Pāṇḍava brothers, is suddenly overtaken by despair; and he refuses to fight. The thought uppermost in his mind at the moment is that he should not kill his kith and kin but should withdraw from the contest, *whatever* the consequences of such withdrawal may be. He is far from sure that he and his brothers will win the battle; and, even if they do, the kingdom which they will gain, he feels, will be one that has been denuded of almost everything that they care for. In this despondency, he prefers to turn an anchorite. Then Śrī Krishna, who has undertaken to guide his chariot, advises him to begin the fight which it is his duty as a prince to do; and it is that advice which is believed to be embodied in the poem.

The teaching, when taken in its details, is full of perplexity because the work shares the heterogeneous character, previously mentioned, of the epic to which it belongs. We have already referred by the way to one aspect of it, viz. that while it is based in some places on the Upanishads, it presupposes in others a theistic view of the type designated as Bhāgavata religion. But whatever these perplexities may be, there is absolutely no doubt as regards the central point of its practical teaching. We have to note particularly two aspects of Arjuna's mood at the time, in order to understand the exact bearing of the teaching. The first is that he forgets that he is a warrior prince whose duty is to fight when occasion demands it. His desire to flee from the world is more in accordance with the ideal of *saṁnyāsa*. Renunciation, as we have seen, is normally meant for those that have succeeded in attaining a certain stage of spiritual progress; but Arjuna, as he is figured in the epic, is not one of them. The second aspect is that he feels that the fighting is in the main, if not entirely, for the good of himself and of those that are near and dear to him. In other words, his standpoint is really one of selfishness, although in desiring to renounce the world he may appear to be quite unselfish. Śrī Krishna points out these misconceptions, and succeeds in convincing him of the need for carrying out the resolve with which he has entered the battle-field. As a result, Arjuna decides once again to fight the enemy with the consequence that his cause, which is the cause of righteousness, wins.

It is clear from the context that the Gītā emphasizes the importance of social duties, whose significance we have already explained. But in emphasizing it, Śrī Krishna makes an innovation which invests the teaching with the whole of its significance. As pointed out before, these social duties were originally conceived as advancing the common good or the interests not only of society as a whole but also those of the individual agent. The Gītā, on the other hand, insists that such duties should be done with no thought whatsoever of the good that may follow from them. That is to say, the notion of duty becomes entirely separated from that of its consequences as they are generally understood. This innovation is not without a psychological justification. The correlation of social with individual good, as contemplated in the old codes, viz. the Dharma Sūtras, is, strictly speaking, impossible. It may not be very difficult to adopt this principle, so long as the same line of conduct serves to promote the interests of both; and it may therefore appear quite feasible to bring them both into harmony with each other. But on occasions when the two interests happen to collide, it becomes impossible to adjust their rival claims. It is to avoid this conflict that the Gītā commends the performance of duty in a totally disinterested way (*niṣkāma-karma*).[26] The conflict could, no doubt, be avoided by abandoning all selfish interest and pursuing only the good of the society of which the agent is a member. But such conscious assumption by any one of the role of a social benefactor is likely to result in a sense of self-importance which is ruinous to all spiritual growth. Hence the teaching that both the aims are to be discarded.

If the idea of duty is thus separated from that of its consequences, it may appear that there will be no means of determining its content in any particular context in life, and that therefore the Gītā teaching, while it may tell us *how* to act, fails altogether to guide us as to *what* deeds we should do. But really there is no such lack of guidance in the teaching for, according to it, the duties which a person has to undertake are determined by the place he occupies in society. This is another important principle enunciated in the Gītā, viz. that one's own duty (*sva-dharma*), be it never so low, is superior to another's[27]—a principle whose knowledge has filtered down even to the lowest ranks of our society as indicated, for instance, by the words which Kālidāsa puts into the mouth of the fisherman in the Śākuntalam. The significance of this principle is to elevate the moral quality of actions above their content. What really matters is the motive inspiring their doing—how actions are done and not what they are. "God cares," some one has stated, "more for the adverb than for the verb." Thus the work in which Arjuna engages himself as a result of Śrī Krishna's teaching is stupendous in its magnitude, being nothing less than setting right the world which is running off the rails. The actions, which ordinary people like ourselves have to perform, bear no comparison to it. While the one, for instance, would in a historical estimate count for a great deal, the other would be nowhere. Yet in point of their moral worth, the two do not differ in the least. Such a detached carrying out of one's duties, whatever they may be, is called *karma-yoga*.

It is, however, necessary to add that all consequences as such are not excluded according to this teaching. Both sets of them, viz. those that accrue to society and those that bear upon the agent, are retained; but they are transmuted in that the one becomes implicit and the other, spiritualized. The fact that the Gītā insists on the performance of one's own duty or the duty of one's station in life, clearly shows that the maintenance of social order is not lost sight of. Only it ceases to be the motive for which the action is done, and becomes only a consequence necessarily involved in it. Similarly in the case of the agent also, there is an end. It is his spiritual betterment.[28] Disinterested activity, in the literal sense of the expression, is a psychological impossibility; and to insist upon it in the name of morality is, as Śaṁkara observes, to reduce life to a form of meaningless drudgery.[29] So even deeds performed in the spirit of the Gītā teaching have an end, viz. "the cleansing of the heart" (*sattva-śuddhi*) or, if we like to put it so, the building up of character. What is meant by the Gītā counsel that all thought of fruits should be dismissed from one's mind in the doing of duty is, not that it should be emptied of all motive, but that the *diverse* purposes of the deeds that fall to one's lot in life should be replaced by *one and the same* end, viz. the moral improvement of the agent.

There is thus an end here as much as there is in all volitional activity according to the older teaching; only it is of a higher type, because it shuts out altogether the desire for inferior or utilitarian values, and aims solely at subjective purification. This subjective purification, it should not be forgotten, is only the proximate end of duty, for, as we know (p. 27) it is meant to subserve, through *jñāna*, the higher and final aim of liberation. In other words *karma-yoga* qualifies directly for *jñāna-yoga* or the acquisition of right knowledge and not for *mokṣa*.

So far we have alluded to only one of the two ways in which duty, as taught in this gospel, is to be done. It is based upon the absolutistic view. There is another which explains it from the standpoint of theism which forms as important an aspect of the Gītā teaching as absolutism. According to it, one should perform one's duties for the fulfilment of God's purpose or, to state the same in other words, for the forwarding of universal life. As in the previous view, here also the duties that a person has to perform are those of his station in life; but he should do them, subordinating his will completely and wholeheartedly to the divine will. This is dedicating all work to the Lord (*Īśvarārtha*),[30] and is known as *bhakti-yoga* or "the way of devotion." By thus working for the Lord, he renounces the fruits commonly associated with duties. He thereby purifies his heart; but, as distinguished from the previous view, salvation is achieved here through the grace of God rather than *jñāna*. Really therefore the distinction between the two teachings is not much; only while the former teaching may suit the few whose minds are well cultivated, the latter has decidedly a stronger appeal to common people with their simple trust in a personal God.

## Chapter Three

# NON-VEDIC SCHOOLS

*

OUR plan does not include the treatment, at any considerable length, of the three doctrines reckoned as non-Vedic. We shall refer to them here but briefly, for a general knowledge of them is necessary to properly appreciate, and sometimes even to follow, the account which will be given of the orthodox doctrines in the chapters to come.

### A. MATERIALISM

As already observed (p. 41), the information we can gather about the details of this school of thought, in its earlier stage, is extremely meagre. All that we know for certain is that, as shown by its general designation in that stage (*svabhāvā-vāda*), it traced whatever character an object might manifest to that very object and not to any extraneous agent. It accordingly rejected the idea that nature reveals any divine or transcendental power working behind it. "Fire is hot; water, cold; and the air is temperate to the touch. Who could have brought such distinctions into being, if they were not of the very essence (*svabhāva*) of those objects?"[1] That is, things are what they are; and their nature, by itself, explains all the variety of the universe and the order that is noticeable in it. The later materialism or Cārvāka system, to which we are now to refer, is a lineal descendant of that doctrine. To it is also applied the title of "Lokāyata," which literally means "restricted to the world of common experience" and points to its positivistic character. The chief tenets, ordinarily associated with this school now, are the following:

(1) It is stated that the Cārvāka admits the validity of only one *pramāna*, viz. perception, and rejects not only verbal testimony but also inference. This can only mean that the Indian materialist was aware of the lack of *finality* in reasoned

conclusions, because all of them rest implicitly, if not explicitly, on some inductive truth which, though it may be highly probable, is never demonstrably certain. It is this high probability that explains the successful prediction which is often possible of future events, as in the case of the rising of the sun tomorrow (say) after it sets today. There is nothing strange about such a view of inferential knowledge. In fact, the Indian materialist is here only upholding a position that is quite familiar to the student of modern logic. To deny inference in any other sense would be absurd, since the denial itself would be a generalized conclusion like those to which he objects on the score of uncertainty.

(2) We know that the Upanishads speak of five elements (p. 24). The materialist admits only four of them—all physical and given in perception—earth, water, fire and air, and discards the fifth, viz. space. He takes them to be the ultimate facts of the whole universe, and explains mind as a function of these elements, which enter into a unique combination in the living body. Thus the physical body as characterized by sentience is to the materialist the only self (*ātman*), and there is no "soul" apart from it. Strictly speaking, therefore, it is wrong to speak of the body *of* a man. But not all the materialists denied the soul altogether; and some among them were willing to acknowledge "a knowing self," unitary in its character, provided it was regarded as lasting only as long as the bodily organism did, and not as surviving it.[2]

(3) The Cārvāka, it is further stated, does not believe in any spiritual values (p. 50), and is content with the worldly ones of sensual pleasure (*kāma*) and wealth (*artha*). He is therefore represented as discarding morality, and preaching what is reproachfully described as the principle of "good digestion and no conscience." But no serious thinker could conceivably have inculcated such a teaching. The only thing the materialist could have meant is that there are no higher values, in the sense accepted by the generality of Indian philosophers—as underlying the constitution of the universe and as bound to triumph over the other values ultimately. He repudiates the authority of the Veda which, according to the orthodox, is the source of belief in such values (p. 44), saying that different parts of it are irreconcilably at variance

with one another, and that it is therefore impossible to make out what it really teaches. He admits the presence of suffering and pain, along with pleasure, in life; but it does not mean to him that either unmixed happiness can be had or should be sought. The part of wisdom, he thinks, is in trying to secure the greatest surplus of pleasure which is within one's reach; and the doctrine, on its ethical side, may therefore be described as crudely hedonistic.

As we have interpreted the doctrine, it is not without its own philosophic importance, and has many parallels in the history of human thought. Hindu as well as Jaina and Buddhistic thinkers, however, have all along represented it as upholding *literally* the tenets as stated above. It only means that for long the doctrine has become debased, and has lost its individuality altogether. But even at its best the materialistic theory carries no conviction with it, since it tries to account for the higher principle of mind by the lower one of matter. Starting with the existence of matter, it explains mind as only a function of it. But in thus starting, the theory has already taken for granted that there is no mind, although it is as much an implication of experience as matter. In fact, we have no conception at all of matter, except as it appears to an observing mind. Believing in the existence of the one thus amounts to believing in the existence of the other. The truth that may underlie the theory is that all the things of the world can finally be brought under a single head, but it is wrong to conclude from this that that unitary source is necessarily physical.

### B. JAINISM

This is a very old form of non-Vedic religion. Like Vaiṣṇavism, it also seems to represent a reform of Brahmanism, but only on far less conservative lines. For instance, it repudiates animal sacrifices (p. 36); but it does not believe in a supreme God. In all probability, it arose in the later Vedic period and was only revived by Vardhamāna, styled "the great hero" (*mahāvīra*), in the sixth century B.C. Jaina tradition itself makes this clear, as it represents him not as its founder but as its resuscitator. He is, in fact, believed to have been the 24th in the line of prophet-guides or "path-finders" (*tīrthaṁkaras*). The doctrine which he preached was at one time mistaken by oriental scholars for a sect of Buddhism; but it is really very different, and is also older.

Vardhamāna was born in a princely family at Kundagrāma in North Behar about 540 B.C. and he lived to the ripe old age of 72 years. He led a householder's life till he was 30 years old, but then, renouncing all, he wandered about leading a life of severe abstinence and meditation. In the thirteenth year thereafter, he attained illumination which secured for him freedom from all ills. He then became a *jina* or "spiritual conqueror"—a word from which the term "Jainism," meaning "the religion of the followers of Jina," is derived. It also shows why he came to be styled "the great hero." For many years after attaining perfection, he assiduously preached his doctrine and he died in 468 B.C. Although Jainism has since then spread widely, its influence, unlike that of Buddhism, is limited to India. But, as distinguished from the latter, it has continued to retain its individuality to this day, owing chiefly to its conservatism—"its scrupulous care for the preservation of ancient customs, institutions and doctrines." There are two principal sects of Jainism known as Śvetāmbaras and Digambaras. As these names signify, the saints of the former sect are clad but in pure white, while those of the latter go about naked, their belief being that nobody who owns anything—even a piece of loin cloth—is altogether fitted to attain salvation. There are a few other distinctions between the two sects, but they are not of any really philosophical significance.

## I

The distinguishing feature of Jainism, on the theoretical side, is its belief in the eternal and independent existence of spirit and matter or, more correctly, the animate and the inanimate, respectively called *jīva* and *ajīva*. But by spirit here we have to understand only the individual self, and not the supreme soul as in the Upanishads. For though acknowledging, as we shall see, that even material entities have their own souls, Jainism does not believe in any universal spirit or God in the common acceptation of that term. We shall now briefly deal with the conception of these two entities:

(1) *Jīva:* It is conceived as an eternal substance (*dravya*) of limited, but variable, magnitude. It is thus capable of adjusting its size to the dimensions of the physical body in which it happens to be housed for the time being. In this latter respect, Jainism is strikingly at variance with the other schools of Indian thought, which conceive of the soul as either atomic or omnipresent, and therefore as never changing its size. Knowledge or sentience is its very essence; and empirical knowledge, in its diverse forms, is a manifestation of it under limitations caused by the *ajīva* or inanimate nature—a sort of blinker put upon it during its mundane existence. The eyes, for example, are viewed here not as an aid to seeing, but as a check put upon the absolute sight of the soul. The ultimate aim of life is conceived as casting off these limitations completely, so that the soul may regain and reveal its true nature of omniscience. Its perceptions then extend to all objects. Or rather there is no perception at all then, in its ordinary sense, but only a mystic or direct intuition of all things. This full and comprehensive knowledge is termed *kevala-jñana*.

Spirit is intrinsically manifold; and, like Hinduism, Jainism also believes in the theory of transmigration. But there are two important distinctions. The Hindus, generally speaking, believe that it is God who allots rewards and punishments to all beings according to their karma. The Jains, on the other hand, who do not believe in a supreme God, declare that karma operates by itself. Here is an example of belief in the all-sufficient character of karma, to which reference was made in the previous chapter (p. 48). In this belief, as we shall see, it strangely bears a likeness to the Vedic doctrine of Mīmāṁsā. Again, while the Hindus take karma to be immaterial, the Jains believe it to be but subtle particles of matter, which is one of the *ajīvas*, finding their way into the soul and soiling its nature. The implication of this view is that the soul consists of parts for, otherwise, such an ingression of karma particles would be impossible. The souls, in their empirical condition, are divided into higher and lower classes, according to the number of sense organs they are believed to possess. An example of the lowest of them, possessing only one organ of sense, viz. that of touch, are plants. The highest are men who, in addition to the five senses, are endowed with "mind" (*manas*) and are rational.

(2) *Ajīva:* The *ajīva*, as its name indicates, is devoid of consciousness of life. It is regarded as fivefold; but it will do to mention here only three of them, viz. matter (*pudgala*), time and space.[3] Of these, matter is manifold, the ultimate stage of it being atomic. But it is only as aggregates of atoms that it becomes the object of common experience. It has the qualities of colour, taste, odour and touch. Sound also is an attribute of matter, or, more correctly, a modification of it, but only in its composite and not in its atomic form. There is accordingly no distinction in atoms as such; but qualitative distinctions between one material object and another, as known to us, emerge as a result of the different ways in which the atoms combine to make them. It is therefore the combinations that are classifiable as earth, water, fire and air. All these atoms or aggregates of them are supposed to harbour souls, so that the whole universe may be said to be throbbing with life.[4] Time is infinite and all-pervasive. All things are in time, and all change takes place in it. The universe, as a whole, is conceived as having had no origin and as not going to have any end, although it is constantly undergoing change. Space is viewed as extending beyond our world; and it is, like time, infinite and all-pervasive.

So much we may regard as forming the original basis of Jainism, on its theoretical side. Like the other doctrines, this also exhibits a good deal of growth in the period of the systems. We shall refer only to some of its broad features under the two heads of knowledge and reality:

(1) *Knowledge: Jñāna* is conceived here as self-luminous, so that it shows to the soul or self not only objects but also itself. It pertains to the self, but not in the sense of an external possession. It is but a mode (*paryāya*) of the self, and it is in this sense that we speak of the latter as possessing it. The self, we know, is not conceived here as an unalterable entity, but as capable of modifying its magnitude. It can also undergo changes of form, retaining its magnitude; and *jñāna* or knowledge, which leads to the revelation of objects, is one of them

The point to be particularly noticed is that the object known is regarded as existing outside and independently of knowledge. As surely as there is a subject that knows, Jainism says, so surely is there an object that is known. Experience without something that is experienced is meaningless. For this reason, the doctrine is described as realistic. It is also pluralistic, since it believes in the manifoldness of both spirit and matter.

The Jains divide knowledge into mediate (*parokṣa*) and immediate (*pratyakṣa*); but experience or knowledge, being only a state of the self, is in both cases regarded as necessarily immediate. The bipartite classification of knowledge has therefore exclusive reference to the way in which *objects* are made known by it. The fire, for example, that is inferred from observing smoke is known in a manner which is different from that in which a table that is perceived is known. The former knowledge is mediate, and the latter immediate; but knowledge itself, whether classed as inference or perception, is immediate.

(i) *Immediate knowledge:* The most important fact here is that this is not identical with perceptual knowledge, as it is commonly understood. It is much wider in its scope, and sensory knowledge is only one of its varieties. It is accordingly defined, not as what arises from contact of senses with their respective objects as in many other systems, but merely as vivid (*viśada*) knowledge, by which is meant a detailed or "particularized" apprehension of the object in question revealing its colour, the disposition of its parts, etc. It may involve the functioning of senses; but it need not do so, and may be extra-sensory. The fact is that as the self, according to Jainism, can by its very nature know all things directly, it needs no outside help. For example, *kevala-jñāna* is knowledge direct and immediate, but it does not depend upon the co-operation of any sense. "All that it presupposes," it is stated, "is the self." It is knowledge in its pristine form, and is termed primary perception (*mukhyapratyakṣa*). It may be described as intuition, comprehending, as it does, all things and all phases of them.[5] The possessor of such knowledge is an *arhan* ("the worthy one") or the perfected (*siddha*)—a conception which very much resembles that of the *jīvanmukta* in orthodox thought (p. 28). The other variety of immediate knowledge is common perception (*sāṁvyavahārika-pratyakṣa*). It is twofold according as it is got through the aid of the external senses or of the mind. That is, it may be sensory knowledge as when we see a table which is before us, or Inner perception: as when we realize that we are happy.[6]

(ii) *Mediate knowledge:* This includes various modes of knowing such as inference and verbal testimony. We shall refer to only one of them, viz. recognition (*pratyabhijñā*), whose conception here is rather unique. The common explanation of this mode of knowledge found in the Indian systems is that it is perception aided or supplemented by memory. Thus recognizing a person means that he is there before us now, and that his presence, when noticed, calls back to us our having seen him before. To the Jains, on the other hand, it is a new type of knowledge which, though based upon perception and memory, is not itself perceptual. The specific fact revealed in it is, as in the other systems, the identity (*ekatva*) of a thing in the two moments—one past and the other present. Such an explanation presupposes a belief in objects which, though changing, endure for a longer or shorter period. It is maintained here that neither perception nor memory, by itself, is competent to reveal this identity, because it involves a reference to *both* past and present. Hence the need, it is stated, for postulating a new kind of knowledge.

So far we have assumed the Jaina idea of this variety of knowledge to be the same as recognition in its usual sense, through which a thing experienced in the past is expressly identified with what is being experienced in the present. Other systems of Indian thought restrict its scope to this; but Jainism extends it farther so that it may embrace all cases where perception and recollection are involved and the resulting knowledge is unitary. Thus the knowledge that A is like B is reckoned as an instance of it, although it points to resemblance and not to identity between A and B. Similarly, "A is different from B," and "A is greater than B," "The mango is a fruit," etc., are all cases of "recognition" in this sense. In every one of them, what is perceived is different from what is recalled; but the two are similar in some respect or other. The similarity is explicit in the first of the examples, viz. A is like B; but it is implicit in the rest, for they involve comparison or classification which cannot refer to absolutely distinct things. This similarity (*sādṛśya*) is a second type of fact revealed through "recognition" as explained here. It will be seen that Buddhism takes similarity alone as the true object of recognition and regards identity, which common sense associates with it, as false or illusory.

(2) *Reality:* The Upanishadic conception of reality, according to our explanation, is of two kinds—one which takes change as actual and the other as unreal (p. 23). Of these, the Jaina view resembles the former; only it regards reality as multiple in its character. It is what changes almost perpetually or is dynamic, and yet keeps its identity throughout. There is one feature of this view in the present doctrine, to which attention needs to be specially drawn. Everything, it teaches, may be regarded as having a general (*sāmānya*) as well as a particular (*viśeṣa*) aspect. Thus a cow is characterized by cowness, which it has in common with other cows. It has also certain characteristics which are special to it, such as its particular colour or size by which we are able to distinguish it from other cows. Some thinkers view these particulars and universals, as they are called, as being separately real. The Jains, on the other hand, take the two as *together* constituting reality, so that things, whether spiritual or material, are necessarily complex according to them.[7] The particular or the general taken by itself is a pure abstraction. They are distinguishable in thought, but are not separable in fact. The relation between these two aspects of an object is one of identity in difference (*bhedābheda*). That is, the particular and the general as such are different; but as phases of the same substance (*dravya*), they are also one. In the case of a cow, for instance, these two, viz. cowness and the specific colour or size as such are distinct; but they are not absolutely so, for they belong to or characterize one and the same object and have no being apart from it. To the objection that the contradictory features of identity and difference cannot, like heat and cold, be predicated of the same object the Jains reply that our sole warrant for speaking about reality is experience and that, when experience vouches for such a character, it must be admitted to be so. The so-called contradictions may themselves be the ultimate truth about reality. Thought must follow the nature of reality in grasping it, and should not attempt to determine it.

The general or universal features may be of two kinds, described as "crosswise" (*tiryak-sāmānya*) and "lengthwise" (*ūrdhvatā-sāmānya*), which may respectively be taken as equivalent to what are known as the abstract and the concrete universals in Western philosophy. An example of the former we have in "cowness" which is presented simultaneously (*tiryak*, literally meaning "extending horizontally") in several cows; the latter is what underlies manifestations appearing successively in time (*ūrdhva*, literally meaning "extending vertically"), for example, cotton as the material of single yarns, thread and cloth. It will be seen that these notions are respectively based upon those of similarity and identity, which are alike known through "recognition" (*pratyabhijñā*). Two or more cows which exhibit the same cowness are similar; the cotton which appears in the yarn and the cloth is identical. When we say that A is a cow and that B also is a cow, it is the predicative element of cowness that is common to both; but when we say that X was a boy and that he is a youth now, it is the subject element that is so. Both sets of features, whether they be constant like cowness or changing like boyhood or youth, are described here as "modes" or "forms" (*paryāya*) of the substance to which they belong. Of these, it is clear that the latter are impermanent. The other set of modes like cowness also are so, according to Jainism. They are only special dispositions or configurations of the substance in which they appear and, as such, are to be regarded as different in different particulars. For example, the cowness of one cow is not numerically the same as the cowness of another.

We shall now understand the exact significance of the definition of reality given in the system, that it is characterized by origination and destruction, as well as by permanence.[8] The origination and destruction relate to the modes (*paryāya*) of reality; and permanence, to their substratum. It is reality, in this sense, that is divided into *jīva* and *ajīva* with its fivefold variety as mentioned above. All these six kinds of reality are termed substances (*dravya*)—a term which connotes that it has qualities (*guṇa*) and modes (*paryāya*).[9] The distinction between qualities and modes, however, is not very clear; and the recognition of the former is probably due, as has been suggested, to the influence of other doctrines. Of these six substances, all but time, besides being real, are extended (*asti-kāya*). Time is real, but has no spatial extension. It is an entity of only one dimension.

It remains now to add a few words about what is known as the *sapta-bhaṅgī* or "the sevenfold predicable." The thought underlying it is inherent in the doctrine, although its clear enunciation seems to belong to the present period. We have already pointed out that, according to Jainism, reality does not exclude contradictory features, which amounts to saying that it is indeterminate in its nature (*anekānta*). This does not, however, mean that it is altogether indefinite but only that it cannot be defined absolutely. It is this idea that is conveyed by the sevenfold statement as a whole; and it expresses the nature of reality in several steps, because no single mode of doing so is adequate to it. Broadly speaking, there were three separate ways in which reality was conceived at the time when this theory was formulated. Some said, "It always is" (*asti*); others, "It never is" (*nāsti*); and still others thought that reality was inscrutable, and that it did not therefore admit of being expressed in either of these two ways (*avaktavya*).[10] Jainism holds that none of these views is wholly correct. Each refers to but a single aspect of reality and is right only if we take it in relation to that aspect and not absolutely, as its supporters contend. It is this relative character of our knowledge of reality that is made known through the *sapta-bhaṅgī*; and it consists of seven steps since there are seven, and only seven, ways of combining the three predicates, taking them singly, in twos and all together.

To state the first four steps of the scheme: (1) maybe, a thing is; (2) maybe, it is not; (3) maybe, it is and is not; (4) maybe, it is inexpressible. In the case of a golden ornament, for example, we may say that (1) it exists, i.e. as gold, but that (2) it does not exist, i.e. as silver (say).[11] As a consequence of this double predication, we may go farther and postulate that (3) it both is and is not. From what has been stated thus far, it is clear that when we say the ornament is, we do not mean that it only is as something, but also that it is not as something else. The latter idea, however, is implicit, and not explicit like the former. The reverse holds true when we say that it is not. The third step is merely a combination of these two statements; and the emphasis is to be understood as being laid on the two elements in the predicate *successively*. Now it may be asked whether these two elements can be predicated of the ornament *simultaneously*, laying equal emphasis on both. The answer to this question, one expects, would be in the negative; but the Jains, with their comprehensive view of reality, refuse to regard any predicate as inadmissible in respect of it, and give an affirmative reply. They, however, add that the predicate cannot then be expressed by any word in the language, the implied significance being that reality is, from one standpoint, inscrutable. These statements should not be taken to clash with what are known in logic as the laws of identity and contradiction, for those laws apply only to reality conceived as simple and static, and not as extremely complex and infinitely variable as here. The remaining three steps of the scheme are: (5) maybe, a thing is and is inexpressible; (6) maybe, a thing is not and is inexpressible; (7) maybe, a thing is, is not and is inexpressible. They are derived by combining the fourth step successively with the first three, all of which refer to the expressible aspects of reality. This relativistic view has become so essential a part of Jainism that it is often designated as "the doctrine of maybe" (*syādvāda*) or the doctrine of standpoints.

It may readily be granted that our knowledge of reality is relative; but the important question to consider is whether we can stop short at it, as Jainism does. The very notion of relativity implies an absolute standard by which we judge; and, if such a standard is granted, the knowledge that completely satisfies it becomes the final truth about reality, and not any other. The relativistic view will, in that case, become restricted in its application to the sphere of ordinary human experience and the truth of the *sapta-bhaṅgī* will reduce itself to a mere truism. To judge from the way in which *kevala-jñāna* or "perfect knowledge" is described—not merely as comprehending all things and all phases of them but also as supersensuous and unique,[12] such absolute knowledge seems to be accepted in Jainism, and is not merely the presupposition of its view of knowledge. But, if this final truth be explained as a mere putting together of the several partial truths, the characterization of knowledge as relative becomes meaningless for the reason already stated. Old Indian critics of Jainism express the same argument in a somewhat different form.[13] If all our knowledge concerning reality is relative, they say, the Jaina view that it is so must also be relative. To deny this conclusion would be to admit, at least, one absolute truth; and to admit it would leave the doctrine with no settled view of reality, and thus turn it into a variety of scepticism.

## II

As regards the practical part of the teaching, there are two points to be chiefly noted. It is pessimistic, though not ultimately so; and it is also severely ascetic. Most of the ascetic principles accepted here have been traced by modern scholars to Hindu sources;[14] only, in some cases, those principles have been carried to extremes in Jainism. The vow of non-violence (*ahiṁsā*) is an instance in point. No Jain will knowingly kill or harm even the tiniest of insects. But not all disciples are required to adopt so austere a standard of conduct. If they are not monks (*śramaṇa*) but laymen (*śrāvaka*), they may practise restraints in a less rigorous manner until they qualify for becoming ascetics in the complete sense of the term.

The goal of life, as already remarked, is to restore the soul to its pristine purity so that it may attain omniscience (*kevala-jñāna*). It is a discarnate state, and the soul has all perfections then—not only infinite knowledge, but also infinite peace and infinite power. As in Upanishadic teaching (p. 29), freedom here also means getting beyond good and evil by transcending both merit (*puṇya*) and demerit (*pāpa*). The discipline recommended for bringing about this consummation is threefold. It begins with faith in the teaching (*saṁyagdarśana*); and when right knowledge (*samyagñāna*) and right conduct (*samyak-cāritra*) come to support it, there results *mokṣa*, or nirvana as the Jains more usually call it. These three—right faith, right knowledge and right conduct—are termed the "three jewels" (*tri-ratna*). The cultivation of the power of mental concentration (*yoga*) plays an important part here, as generally in the other Indian doctrines.[15]

To understand how this discipline helps liberation, it is

necessary to recall that the link between the *jīva* and the *ajīva* is karma, by which term is meant, as we know, matter in an extremely subtle form. The soul, in its mundane condition, is permeated through and through by such matter; and its aim in life is to extricate itself from this variety of *ajīva*. The processes of bondage and extrication from it are thus pictured: There is first of all the influx (*āsrava*) of karma into the soul which results in bondage (*bandha*). This karma is being continually liquidated, as a consequence of its effects of joy and sorrow being experienced. But in the case of average men, other karma, good as well as bad, is finding its way into the soul equally continually owing to its willed actions so that it can never be said to be free. After death, this karmic accompaniment (*kārmaṇa-śarīra*) follows the soul in its new existence. It is thus that the beginningless and virtually endless cycle of transmigration proceeds. Man's hope of salvation rests on the fact that the process of the influx of new karma can be stopped; and it is as a means to this end that the discipline, in its triple form, as indicated above, is prescribed. As in the case of the forging of bondage, there are two steps in the freeing of the soul from it. The first is the stoppage of the flow of new karma, and it is called karma-check (*saṁvara*); the second is that of destroying the karma that has accumulated from the past, and it is described as the falling off of karma (*nirjara*). With the complete destruction of binding karma, one automatically attains liberation (*mokṣa*), which is a state of absolute perfection and implies, by the way, that although Jainism may deny the existence of a supreme God, it retains the idea of the divine as representing perfection. These five, viz. movement of karma (*āsrava*), bondage (*bandha*), karma-check (*saṁvara*), its falling off (*nirjara*) and liberation (*mokṣa*), together with *jīva* and *ajīva*, are sometimes spoken of as the seven principles of Jainism.

### C. BUDDHISM

The story of Buddha's life as familiarly known, is, for the most part, based on tradition long posterior to the time when he lived. According to this account, he was born at Kapilavastu, his father being the ruler of a principality. Like Vardhamāna, he was thus of royal descent. The date of his birth is now generally taken as 563 B.C. He is represented as a greatly accomplished prince. He was married at the age of 16, and a son was born to him in course of time. It was about this time that he began to reflect upon the vanities of life and upon the tragedy of death, disease and old age which afflict mankind. This is picturesquely represented in the story as his meeting an old man, a sick man and a corpse in succession. Those sights were followed by that of a recluse who had completely renounced the world; and it led to his resolve that he would free himself from all worldly ties and strive his utmost to discover the way out of life's unending misery. In pursuance of this resolve, he left the palace the same night, looking upon it as "a place of dust," and went away to a distant forest. There, in the company of five others, he practised severe penance, mortifying his body as it was the common practice at the time for intensely religious-minded people to do. He led this kind of life for six years; but not succeeding in his object thereby, he began a fresh course of self-discipline characterized by less severity. Then his companions left him, dissenting from his view. In this second attempt, he was successful and he became fully enlightened (*buddha*) and reached, as it is expressed, "the end of cravings."

He did not, however, remain content with this personal illumination, but decided to teach the way to it to others also. His first disciples were the five ascetics who had earlier parted from him, and were at the time in a place near Benares known as Sārnāth or the "Deer Park." It is in the first sermon which he delivered to them, after converting them to his way of thinking, that, as tradition has it, he dwelt upon the Four Noble Truths (*ārya-satya*) to which we shall refer later. He thereafter succeeded in converting many others, including his own family. His activities, however, were confined to a relatively limited region which comprised portions of modern Behar, the United Provinces and Nepal. He died in 483 B.C. at the age of 80 at Kuśinara on the day, it is said, which was the anniversary of his birth, as also of the attainment by him of complete enlightenment. This event took place between two *sāla* trees, a circumstance which is piously depicted in the sculptures and bas-reliefs relating to the closing scene of his life. Buddha is undoubtedly one of the great religious teachers of the world. In the third century B.C. the famous emperor, Aśoka, became a Buddhist; and it is commonly believed that through the impetus he gave to it, Buddhism began to spread not only in other parts of India but also beyond it.

## I

There is much difficulty in determining the original form of this creed, for, as already pointed out (p. 40), we have no record of it come down to us from the period in which it was first promulgated. The earliest works relating to it, which constitute its "canonical literature," may contain much that was actually uttered by Buddha; but there is no means of knowing for certain what those portions are. Hence there has been a good deal of difference of opinion among modern scholars regarding the exact character of his teaching. It is obvious, however, that Buddhism began as a religion and that it was forced, not long after, to become a philosophy since it had to defend itself against metaphysical schools of Hindu and Jaina thought.

A similar difficulty is experienced in defining the relation of early Buddhism to Brahmanism. That it should have been greatly influenced by the latter, the dominant faith of the land at the time, goes without saying. The points to be considered are the extent of the influence, and the precise form of Brahmanism which influenced it. It is now generally believed that primitive Buddhism represents a new expansion, not against, but within Brahmanism. The canonical literature, no doubt, now and again criticizes Brahmanism, but mostly on its ritualistic side. The conclusion to be drawn from it is that Buddha's teaching was a protest against the over-elaborate ceremonialism that, in one sense, had given rise to the Upanishadic doctrine itself (p. 18). An important consequence of this rejection of ritual was the emphasis placed on morality which, though by no means ignored in Brahmanism, was assigned a somewhat subordinate place in it (p. 37). The references to the Upanishadic doctrine, the other aspect of Brahmanism, are far fewer, showing that Buddhism did not diverge from it very much. There are, however, some differences, to the more important among which we may now draw attention.

The Upanishadic doctrine was, as we know (p. 18), intended for only a select few. The characteristic feature of Buddha's teaching, on the other hand, was that it admitted no esoteric truths, and was meant for all who were not satisfied with leading a life of natural inclinations. It was "a folk-gospel," as it has been described. Its message was for the plain man, and it accordingly gave rise to a general uplift of great significance. A second divergence was that, while Brahmanism relied overmuch on the instruction given by others, Buddhism laid particular stress on self-reliance and self-effort in knowing the ultimate truth. The disciple was asked to think for himself, and to accept others' opinions only after he had been fully convinced of their soundness. That is, it was not dogmatic even in the least. For the rest, early Buddhism was the same as Brahmanism of this type, and believed in the same cosmological and eschatological views, including the doctrine of karma. The main features of primitive Buddhism may be summarized as follows:[16]

We have seen that in the early Vedic period, man was regarded as distinct from the divine, and that this view had been gradually transformed by the time of the Upanishads into the view that he was himself essentially divine. It is this God-in-man that Buddha understood by ātman—neither body nor mind, but spirit. He also believed that, as spirit, it persists here as well as hereafter so that it is wrong to say, as is often done, that Buddha denied the self or identified it with the body and the mind. It, however, represented to him not man as he is, but as what he might or ought to be. In other words, it stood for the ideal self, to realize which there is an innate urge in man. His foremost task in life accordingly is to act in response to it; and the result of so acting, viz. the "waning out" of his lower nature, of the lust and hate in him, is all that is meant by liberation or nirvana, a word with which we have already become familiar in connection with Jainism. It is not the annihilation of the self, but only the extinguishing of selfhood in the ordinary acceptation of the term. Early Buddhism is thus a gospel of hope, and not a gospel of despair as it is commonly represented to be.

But what is the means to such liberation? The Upanishads, whose teaching is nearly the same, lay down a course of discipline for the self becoming Brahman. But, according to one of the two interpretations of them (p. 25), the lapse of man from his true spiritual state is conceived not as real, taking place in time, but as only apparent. The goal is not therefore anything which is to be reached in fact; it has only to be realized in thought. It thus lays little stress on "becoming," in the sense of attaining what has not yet been attained. The other interpretation of the Upanishads, according to which spirit is self-evolving, is, no doubt, very different in this respect; but there, it is the goal that is represented as important, and not so much the way leading to it, as here. For original Buddhism, it is man as an aspirant after perfection that matters more than man as having achieved it. Further, in the Upanishadic view, the immediate means recommended for attaining the ultimate goal, even when it is conceived as *growing into* Brahman, is *yoga* (p. 26); Buddha's emphasis, on the other hand, is throughout on *dharma* in its ethical sense (p. 37). It is described as "the lamp of life," and signifies perfect conduct or godly living, not a mere code of dogmas as it came to do afterwards.

## II

The original form of the creed, thus reconstructed, must contain elements that are hypothetical. It also seems to do less than justice to certain aspects of the teaching of the Upanishads. For example, it ignores that a dynamic conception of Brahman finds a conspicuous place in them; and it also minimizes the importance attached therein to moral purity in the scheme of discipline for the realization of the ultimate truth (p. 27). However that may be, the point for us to note now is that the teaching of Buddha was positive and constructive. But the negative and analytic view came in course of time to prevail; and, as a consequence of it, Buddhism gradually became thoroughly monastic in character. This transformation had already taken place by the time the systems proper took rise. It forms the chief teaching of the Pali Buddhistic literature

(p. 40), whose main features we are now to sketch very briefly. We shall be able to do this best by explaining what is meant by the Four Noble Truths which, according to the Pali canon, formed the subject-matter of the very first sermon Buddha delivered at Benares. The account that has come down to us of these Truths is now taken to represent, on the whole, a later stage of the teaching—the result of "monkish misapprehension." Their implication is that life is an evil; and their chief aim, to point out how it can be overcome. In these Truths, we have what corresponds to a physician's treatment of a disease—ascertaining the nature of the disease, discovering its cause and setting about its cure by adopting appropriate means thereto. They are:

(1) *Life is evil.*—The whole teaching, as shown by its implied comparison of life to a disease, is based upon a pessimistic view, betokening monkish influence. But even in this later form of the doctrine, evil is not to be taken as the final fact in life. Its pessimism means that life is full of pain and suffering, not in itself, but only as it is ordinarily lived, for the doctrine holds out the hope that they can be completely overcome in the stage of nirvana which can be reached here and now, if one so wills.

(2) *Ignorance is the source of evil.*—The origin of evil is in ignorance (*avidyā*), or not knowing the true nature of the self. We commonly assume it to be an integral something which is other than the bodily organism; and we believe that this self not only persists as long as the organism does but also survives it. According to canonical Buddhism, this is an absolute error, and there is no self other than the complex of the body (*rūpa*) and the mind (*nāma*). It is sometimes spoken of as consisting not of these two, but of five factors (called *skandhas*), one of which is the physical body (*rūpa*), and the rest represent different phases of mind (*nāma*) like cognition and feeling—a view which shows how the spirit of analysis came to prevail more and more. Even in this sense of being a mere complex, whether of two or of five factors, the self is not permanent. It is undergoing change almost constantly; and, in nirvana, it completely ceases to be. It is the clinging to this false self, as a result of our ignorance of its real nature, that explains all the misery of life as it is commonly lived.[17] Thus Buddhism,

which postulated a changing self as a protest against a static one as conceived by some at the time, came in course of time to virtually repudiate it. We should add that this principle of explanation was soon extended to other cases, with the result that all things, and not the self alone, were deemed to be mere aggregates (*saṁghāta*) of their respective component parts. A chariot, for example, is nothing more than an assemblage of the pole, wheels, etc. This is known as the doctrine of the non-substantiality (*nairātmya*) of things.

(3) *Evil can be overcome.*—It is possible to remove this evil, for it is caused, and whatever is caused is removable according to this teaching. Given the cause, the effect follows;[18] and, if the one can be removed, the other will necessarily cease to be. The fact that life's evil is caused is exhibited in the form of twelve links, known as the "chain of causation." The first of them is ignorance of the true nature of the self, which implies that, as in the case of the Upanishadic doctrine (p. 25), evil is radically of the metaphysical type. Of the remaining eleven, it will do to mention only three, viz. craving or thirst (*tṛṣṇā*), death and rebirth. That is, man's ignorance gives rise to a selfish craving for things; and unsatisfied cravings lead to rebirth after death. It is this recurring cycle of birth and death that should be ended; and the result is nirvana, which may accordingly be described as the cessation of ignorance, of craving or of birth and death. The goal of life is thus conceived here as purely negative while, in the original teaching, it meant the complete development of the higher self, through overcoming the tyranny of the lower. A person who succeeds in breaking through this circle of *saṁsāra* can, it was believed, attain the serene composure of nirvana in the present life; and he is, as in Jainism, called an *arhan* or "the worthy one." The principle underlying the chain of causation, which was originally formulated to account for the evil of life, was later extended to all things, whether psychical or physical; and they likewise came to be regarded as caused, and therefore as ultimately exterminable. This is known as the doctrine of the impermanence (*anityatva*) of things.

(4) *Right knowledge is the means of removing evil.*—As knowledge is the logical antithesis of ignorance, enlightenment about the true nature of one's self will remove evil. By this enlighten-

ment, we should understand an inner conviction (p. 26) which, to be effectively secured, requires a long course of previous moral training. Here we find the emphasis which, as we stated earlier, Buddha had once laid on right conduct. But in consonance with the general trend of the development of the doctrine, the emphasis is now shifted on to knowledge or wisdom (*prajñā*) and meditative practice (*yoga*) chiefly on the Four Truths. Even so far as it continues to emphasize conduct, an ascetic spirit comes to prevail though, as compared with Jaina teaching, it is mild. It certainly imposed on its advanced adherents strict rules of discipline; but, at the same time, it discouraged them from resorting to any form of self-torture in their enthusiasm for reaching the goal. It was "a middle path" that it commended—a path like that which Buddha himself is stated to have followed before he attained illumination. These three, viz. right conduct (*śīla*), right knowledge (*prajñā*) and right concentration (*samādhi*) are the most important elements in the discipline. It includes five more, and is therefore known as the Eightfold Path;[19] but it is not necessary to specify them here. This discipline, it should be added, is in its entirety intended for those who enter the order of ascetics. As in Jainism, it was less rigorous in the case of lay disciples.

III

We have now made a rapid survey of two stages in the history of Buddhism, and seen how vastly they differ from each other. One of the most noteworthy features of it in the next stage is its spread far beyond the limits of India, to countries like China and Japan. In those countries it has, with its emphasis on compassion, a feature which it shares with Jainism, greatly helped the growth of beneficence. Referring to Japan in this connection, a modern writer says that "it is still the greatest of the influences which make for mercy among a Spartan people." The break-up of the doctrine into numerous sects is another feature of the same kind. We read of many sects in India itself, so that its disruption is not all to be ascribed to its coming into contact with alien faiths in other lands. It will suffice for our purpose to draw attention only to a broad distinction that arose in the doctrine, viz. that between what are known as the Hīnayāna and Mahāyāna schools. Perhaps the distinction in some form is older than the present stage. The significance of these terms is not exactly known. They probably mean the "lower" and the "higher" path respectively. Their chronological sequence and their precise relation to the teaching of Buddha again are undetermined. In presenting these doctrines, we shall follow mainly the account given in Indian works, particularly those by Hindu and Jaina writers. There are a few beliefs common to both the Hīnayāna and Mahāyāna forms of the creed, and we shall refer to the most striking among them before considering the two separately.

It is known as the doctrine of momentariness (*kṣaṇa-bhaṅga-vāda*), because it avers that nothing that is, lasts for longer than one instant. We have seen that, in canonical Buddhism, all things had come to be conceived as impermanent. This view is now pushed farther, and attempts are made to show that the only distinction in the history of a thing is the one between origin and destruction, and that it does not continue to be even for a single moment after birth. If a thing emerges at this instant (say), it is no more at the next. It is not possible to refer here to the elaborate arguments by which this doctrine is supported. We shall only remark that reality according to it, whether material or spiritual, is a flux or a flow (*saṁtāna*) since none in the succession of states constituting it is static. Hence all our notions of stability are illusory. "No man can step into the same stream twice," it is said, because the stream in the two moments is only similar and not identical. Objects are ever changing. Even when a thing is not changing into something *else*, it is not constant but is reproducing itself and is therefore to be regarded as a series of like forms succeeding one another perpetually as in the case of a lamp flame.

Our previous account has shown that, although Buddhism regarded reality as but an aggregate, it did not deny either external objects or the self (*sarvāsti-vāda*). It recognized both, and was therefore fully realistic in its view of knowledge. This feature survives in Hīnayāna Buddhism;[20] but naturally it is modified in accordance with the new hypothesis of momentariness. Neither external reality, nor the self, consequently lasts longer than an instant. But everything, it is believed, may continue *as a series* for any length of time, the similarity of its several members, as already mentioned, giving rise in our mind to the illusion of sameness or identity. The flame of a lamp appears to be the same in any two moments; but really it signifies two separate states of it, which have no substantial identity. In other words, there are modifications but nothing that endures through them. Here we see the antithesis between Buddhism and Jainism which acknowledges identity as also similarity. Both doctrines accept change, but while it is partial in the one case, it is total in the other.

When we remember that Buddhism repudiates the idea of an enduring substance, we see that the self (ignoring for the moment the physical element entering into its make-up) should be conceived in it as a continuous stream of ideas. If so, it may be asked how the Buddhist can account for facts like memory, which involve reference to the past. The answer is that, when a particular idea constituting the self of a particular moment disappears, it does so after leaving its mark behind and that the self of the next moment is consequently informed by it through and through. That is, the self of a person at any instant, though not the same as it was at a previous instant, is not quite different from it. It is by this subtle, and not quite convincing, distinction that moral responsibility is maintained to belong to an individual for what he does. The criminal who is punished may not be the same person that committed the crime; but yet he merits punishment, it is argued, for, being a continuation of the criminal, he cannot be considered as another.

As regards external reality, which also is conceived as momentary, each member of the series constituting an object is called a *sva-lakṣaṇa*—a term which literally means "like itself" or "unique." It represents a bare particular. If it still appears as characterized in some manner, say *as* blue or sweet, that characteristic is purely an illusion. The predicates, which all represent universals or common features like qualities and actions, are called *sāmānya-lakṣaṇas.* They are really figments of the mind which appear transferred to the object—constitutives of our thought, and not of the external world on which it is directed. The contrast here again with Jainism, which regards such features as actually characterizing objects, is clear. The *sva-lakṣaṇas,* which are the ultimate basis of external reality, may be taken to stand for the data of sense like colour or taste; only we should remember that the momentary sensation is, to take particular instances, merely "blue" or "sweet" and not *something* that is qualified by "blueness" or "sweetness." The number of *sva-lakṣaṇas,* which are the ultimate facts of the outer world, is infinite. The conception of an external thing in this school accordingly is that it is a series of particulars or aggregates of them which are really devoid of all characteristics, although they appear to possess them.

So far we have spoken of Hīnayāna Buddhism. The Mahāyāna form of it is represented by two schools, both of which are idealistic. According to some, called the Yogācāras, knowledge points to no external object whatsoever. There is only the self, conceived as a stream of ideas much as in Hīnayāna Buddhism; but none of the ideas is here regarded as having any objective counterpart. Since the doctrine thus reduces all reality to thought, it is named Vijñāna-vāda or "the theory of the sole reality of ideas." One of the chief arguments in support of this view is based upon the inseparable connection that is observed to exist between knowledge and object. There is no knowledge that does not refer to an object; and there is no object that can be conceived except as known. This necessary association between them, it is said, shows that there is no need for treating them as distinct, and that the so-called object may well be regarded as an aspect or form of knowledge itself. The idealism of the school consists in this explanation of objects as but states or forms of the "mind," if we may use that word for the series of ideas which here constitutes the self. The assumption of these forms by the mind is due to the revival of former impressions (*vāsanā*) left on it by previous experience; and the diversity of perception is explained, not by diversity in the presented objects but by that in the nature of the revived impressions.

Such an explanation may sound strange, for it may be thought that the original impression at least must be due to an external object. But this objection is warded off by two arguments. First, it is denied that the impressions have any origin in time. They are literally beginningless. Secondly, it is pointed out that impressions are left on the mind not merely by valid knowledge caused, as it is commonly assumed, by a corresponding object outside it but also by error, for example, the fancied perception of a ghost. To suppose that every mental impression should be finally traceable to an external object, actually existing, is to beg the very question at issue. So, even if there were a beginning to any series of impressions it would not establish the existence of a *real* object corresponding to it at any time in the past.

This doctrine is analogous to what is described in modern philosophy as subjective idealism or subjectivism. The chief objection to it is that it places all experience on a level with dreams. In other words, it abolishes the distinction between truth and illusion, since in both alike there is no object outside knowledge. But it is hardly a defensible position. We infer the falsity of dreams by comparing them with waking experience. If the latter also is likewise false, we may ask by what experience it is shown to be so. Whatever the answer of the Yogācāra to this question may be, his position becomes untenable, for he will have to admit either that there is a higher kind of knowledge which is not false or that waking experience itself is true. Further, as a consequence of rejecting external objects, the subjectivist must deny the existence of all selves besides his own, for, if there is no reason to believe in external physical objects, there can be none to believe in other people except as part of his dream. The doctrine will thus be reduced to solipsism, or the theory that there is only a solitary self and that everything else is mere fancy. It is clear that such a theory, though it cannot be logically proved to be wrong, stultifies all the presuppositions of practical life and puts an end to all philosophical controversy.

The second development on the idealistic side is nihilism, the doctrine of the Mādhyamikas, which denies the reality not only of external objects but also of the self. It supports this conclusion by pointing out that the notion of things, physical as well as psychical, is riddled with contradictions and that they cannot therefore be accepted as real. Of the several arguments adduced in this connection, we shall refer to one that is based upon the Buddhistic view of causation. According to it, as we know, there is nothing that is uncaused; and the Mādhyamika points out that the notion of an object originating is inconceivable, whether we regard it as existent or not prior to origination. In the former case, it does not require to be produced; in the latter, it is impossible to produce it, for nothing cannot be made to become something. It means that the notion of causation itself is a delusion; and since, according to Buddhism, there is nothing that is permanent, we should perforce conclude that the whole universe is self-discrepant and illusory. Nāgārjuna, the greatest teacher of this school, says, "There is neither being, nor cessation of it; there is neither bondage, nor escape from it."[21] This doctrine is therefore known as "the doctrine of the void" (*śūnya-vāda*).

But it is necessary to add that the above explanation of all experience as a delusion is only from the ultimate standpoint. The doctrine grants a sort of reality (*saṁvṛti-satya*) to the subject as well as the object; and they are held to be real, relatively to the activities of everyday life. It does not deny that we know, feel and act; only it holds that the final significance of it is nothing, because all is void. For this reason, the name of "relativism" will bring out its character better than "idealism." But we may question, as we did in the case of Jainism, whether the Mādhyamika can at all speak of a realm of relativity when he recognizes no reality that is absolute. Moreover, the denial of the self or mind altogether is impossible, for to think of the absence of all consciousness is itself a state of consciousness and therefore points to the persistence or the irrepressibility of mind.

We have described the Mādhyamika school as maintaining that the ultimate reality is the void or vacuity-in-itself. Both the Hindus and the Jains have all along represented it so. But the majority of modern scholars who have studied this school of thought are of opinion that "the void" (*śūnya*) here means only that it is nothing, *as it were*, since it is altogether incomprehensible. This view is supported by the Mādhyamika definition of the ultimate reality (which is the exact opposite of that given in Jainism), viz. that it neither "is" nor "is not," nor "both is and is not," nor "neither is nor is not."[22] It excludes all conceivable predicates, including that of non-existence; and the ultimate has accordingly to be viewed as beyond all conception, and not as absolute nothing. Such an interpretation is, indeed, logically involved in the doctrine, since the negation of everything, without implying a positive ground (*avadhi*) is inconceivable. According to this interpretation, the doctrine ceases to be finally relativistic, for it accepts an Absolute, though it may regard it as altogether ineffable. It may be stated that there is evidence to show that the Yogācāras also admitted an absolute consciousness or universal self in addition to the particular egos and their respective ideas referred to in the account given above.[23] According to these alternative interpretations, the goal of life in Mahāyāna Buddhism is merging in the Absolute, not annihilation as it would otherwise be, and as it generally is according to Hīnayāna Buddhism.

Now as regards the practical discipline leading to the final goal. The Hīnayāna scheme is virtually the same as in canonical Buddhism. But the Mahāyāna form of it has modified it profoundly in two important respects. The attainment of liberation by the individual has ceased to be the ultimate aim; and the person that succeeds in acquiring enlightenment is expected to work for the good of his fellow men, instead of remaining satisfied with his own nirvana. Such a person is called a Bodhisattva (literally, "wisdom-being"). This ideal, with its emphasis on the welfare of others, far excels the other one of the *arhan* who is concerned chiefly, if not solely, with salvation for himself. Buddha is represented to have been a Bodhisattva in many of his former lives; and we shall indicate best the love and compassion which are the characteristic features of this ideal by citing the saying which tradition ascribes to him, viz. that he would willingly bear the burden of everybody's suffering, if he could thereby bring relief to the world. Secondly, while the Hīnayāna was atheistic and looked upon Buddha as essentially a human being, though divinely gifted, the Mahāyāna gradually came to deify him and adopted devout worship of him as a means to salvation. In these developments, Mahāyāna Buddhism has been considerably influenced by theistic Hinduism.[24]

Chapter Four

# NYĀYA-VAIŚEṢIKA

*

WE have alluded to two distinct streams of thought, one having its source in the Veda and the other which originated in opposition to it (p. 39). Of the several forms which the latter assumed, some in course of time became united with the former by accepting the authority of the Veda in certain important matters like *dharma*. As regards their general metaphysical position, they remained more or less true to their original character; but this difference on the theoretical side did not signify much, for the teaching of the Veda itself, not excluding the Upanishads, was, as we have seen (p. 19). comprehensive and included diverse types of thought like dualism and monism or realism and idealism. Of such heterodox doctrines that turned orthodox, the Vaiśeṣika is one. But it is not found treated of by itself except in a few works, and is generally found synthesized with another doctrine known as Nyāya. Whether the latter also was independent of the Veda, to begin with, is not quite clear. Probably it was not, the doctrine, as shown by the general sense of the name it bears, viz. "argument" or "conclusion," having come into existence in connection with the interpretation and justification of Vedic teaching. Its distinguishing feature is its belief in the utility of analysis and in the reliability of reason. Further, it aims much more systematically than the other systems at defending its standpoint against rival views. That is, it is both logic and dialectics. This science of philosophic method, as we may term it, became early in its history associated with the Vaiśeṣika whose main aim was metaphysical; and even in the earliest commentary we now have on the Sūtra of Gautama, the alliance between them is seen. Hence the doctrine has come to be known as Nyāya-Vaiśeṣika, and it is in this combined form that we shall deal with it here.

## *Nyāya-Vaiśeṣika*

The chief sources of information in regard to this system are (1) the Vaiśeṣika Sūtra of Kaṇāda which is in ten chapters, each of which is divided into two sections, and the gloss on it by Praśasta Pāda; and (2) the Nyāya Sūtra of Gautama which is in five chapters, each divided into two sections, and the commentary of Vātsyāyana on it. The work of Praśasta Pāda, unlike that of Vātsyāyana, is not strictly a commentary; but, taking as its basis the aphorisms of Kaṇāda, it deals with the various topics in its own way. It is still of much importance in understanding the doctrine in the earlier stages of its growth, and is of great authority. In the course of its history, an important change was made in the character of the combined system by Gaṅgeśa of Mithilā (1200 A.D.), the outcome of which was to emphasize the logical character of the system to the comparative neglect of its metaphysical and dialectical character. It is in this modified form that it has since been chiefly cultivated ; and it accounts for its utilization mostly as subsidiary to the study of other systems, particularly the Vedānta. Later manuals like the *Tarka-saṁgraha* of Annam Bhaṭṭa and the *Siddhānta-muktāvalī* of Viśvanātha Pañcānana are compiled on this basis.

### I

It is admitted by all that the outside world is known to us through the mind, which is assisted in its operation by the senses. This fact has led to a very important controversy among philosophers, viz., whether we can talk of the existence of external objects without reference to any mind. The Nyāya-Vaiśeṣika, like Jainism (p. 62), believes that the being of the external world, although necessarily known through the mind, is in no way dependent upon it. If all the minds in the universe should cease to be, even then the objective would, in its view, continue to exist. It sides in this respect with common sense. For this reason, viz. its belief in the independent existence of the external world, the system is described as realistic; and it is different from those systems which believe the reverse of this to be true, and are designated as idealistic. Another controversy of equal importance among philosophers is whether the ultimate reality is one or many. The present doctrine maintains that it is many, and is therefore described as pluralistic to distinguish it from others that are monistic. These many distinct entities, it is stated here, must be either atomic or all-pervasive. They are partless in both cases; and a corollary to this is that, if any object is made up of parts, it cannot be eternal. All finite objects are accordingly explained here as emerging from or, more correctly, as produced by a combination of atoms. The latter, viz. the pervasive entities, cannot so combine, and will not therefore yield any product.

We have stated that the doctrine believes in the multiple character of ultimate reality. We shall now briefly sketch this pluralistic view under the two heads of nature and spirit:

(1) *Nature:* Matter, time and space are all recognized here as independent entities. Of these, matter is really five-fold, its varieties being known as elements (*bhūta*). Of the five elements, which have already been enumerated (p. 24), all excepting *ākāśa* are, in their ultimate form, atomic. It is from these atomic elements ultimately that common objects like hills and trees or tables and chairs are derived. *Ākāśa* is infinite and all-pervading. But its conception here is peculiar, for it does not represent space as in the Upanishads; it is explained as a unique substance sometimes rendered as "ether" in English and has been postulated here solely to serve as the substratum of the quality of sound. Time and space are infinite and all-pervading, like *ākāśa*. Thus in the ultimate stage, the physical universe consists of an indefinite number of atoms of four types, and three infinite and pervasive entities—*ākāśa*, time and space.

The conception of atoms in this doctrine is partly like and partly unlike that in Jainism (p. 62). According to the latter, all atoms have taste, colour, smell and touch; but here they are regarded as differing in their qualitative nature from one another, and their division into four classes is based upon this difference. Air has only one quality, viz. touch; fire has two, viz. touch and colour; water has three, viz. touch, colour and taste; and earth has all the four including smell. Of these, one is regarded as the distinctive feature (*viśeṣa-guṇa*) of each of the four elements—smell of earth, taste of water, colour of fire and touch of air. Sound, as already stated, belongs to *ākāśa* and is explained as its special quality. Owing to these differences, the atoms of different classes can be easily distinguished. But it is not these classes of atoms alone that are distinct from one another; the various atoms that belong to one and the same class also are conceived to be so, though they are all qualitatively alike. Their mutual distinction is explained by assuming a unique *viśeṣa* or individuality in each of them—a conception which will become clear as we proceed. Of the two atomic theories, the Nyāya-Vaiśeṣika one appears to be the later, for it shows a more developed form; but it is by no means certain that it is based on the Jaina theory.

The way in which the existence of atoms is inferred is as follows: It is known from experience that finite wholes like a jar can be split up into smaller parts. This process of division cannot be carried on indefinitely, for then it will be impossible to account for the observed differences in their magnitude as all of them, small or big, would consist of an infinite number of atoms. If, on the other hand, we assume a limit to the division, the differences in magnitude found in objects like "a mountain and a mustard seed" may be explained by the difference in the number of atoms going to make them up. Of two things, the smaller in size will contain fewer ultimate parts than the bigger. It is the final constituent of material objects in this process of division and sub-division that is termed an atom (*paramāṇu*). Not being further divisible, it is taken as indestructible or permanent. It is clear from the above that the number of atoms in each of the four classes is indefinite, and that all of them are supersensible. Their magnitude is not finite, but infinitesimal or infinitely small. That they have differentiating qualities, such as colour or taste, has therefore been only inferred[1] from the nature of the common objects that are made out of them.

Now as regards the manner in which the concrete objects of common experience are derived from these atomic elements. Broadly speaking, two explanations may be given in all such cases. We may regard the derived things as mere aggregates of the atoms as Buddhism, for example, does (p. 76); or as new creations which, though dependent for their coming into being on the constituent atoms, are yet distinct from them. To a third view which also is possible, we shall refer in the next chapter. There are certain serious objections to the first of these views, viz. that objects are mere aggregates of their constituent parts. To mention one of them: The same number of atoms may conceivably constitute two objects, and yet each may have its own determinate character. To view them both as mere collections of atoms would be to leave unexplained this character, which makes each what it is. To introduce a qualification by saying, for instance, that the parts are differently disposed in the two objects would be to admit that they are more than aggregates. Hence the present doctrine favours the second view that the parts and the whole are entirely distinct. This means that, when an object is produced, what was not in existence once comes to exist anew, and that it may therefore well exhibit novel features. The theory is accordingly described as "the theory of not-pre-existent effect" (*asatkārya-vāda*). That is, it holds causation to be creative, and is therefore also characterized as "the theory of origination" (*ārambha-vāda*). Thus the doctrine asks us to believe that when a globe, say, is made out of two hemispheres, we actually have three things—the globe and the two hemispheres which pre-existed its production and still continue to be.

This may look like a quibble, but it is perfectly in accordance with the ordinary belief that the whole has a character of its own as distinguished from the parts. A jar, for instance, can be used for fetching water, unlike its parts. Yet the view that the material cause and the effect are entirely distinct is hardly convincing. This extreme position leads to the necessity of postulating a special relation, which is known virtually to no other system and is not recognized by common sense. If the constituent parts and the whole are absolutely distinct and if, as it happens here, they are never found apart when both exist, their relation stands in need of a special explanation. The system recognizes contact or conjunction (*saṁyoga*) as the relation between, say, a table and the paper that may be on it. But the same relation will not do in the present case for, while the table and the paper may be separated at our will, no separation of the whole from the parts in the same sense is possible, for it necessarily involves the destruction of one of them, viz. the whole. To separate the threads woven into a piece of cloth is *ipso facto* to destroy the cloth. It is consequently regarded as a more intimate relation than conjunction, and is given the special name of *samavāya* and treated as an independent category (*padārtha*). Its formulation is quite arbitrary, and is necessitated by the radical pluralism of the Nyāya-Vaiśeṣika; but its importance in understanding the system cannot be exaggerated. We shall have occasion to refer to it more than once in the sequel.

The Nyāya-Vaiśeṣika doctrine generally accords with common sense. It accepts, for instance, the independent existence of objects like tables and chairs on the strength of ordinary beliefs. But it does not follow those beliefs throughout, as is clear from its employment of artificial expedients like *samavāya* and *viśeṣa* which also it elevates to the rank of an independent category in explaining ultimate difficulties. It splits up objects into smaller and smaller parts; but, finding it hard to distinguish those parts from one another in the ultimate stage, arbitrarily postulates the characteristic of a *viśeṣa* in each of them. It only means that these ultimate parts are mere abstractions. The doctrine naturally finds it also hard to reconstruct concrete wholes out of such abstractions without assuming an equally arbitrary relation, viz. *samavāya*.

The manner in which the atoms combine to form wholes is thus described. Two primary atoms of the same kind produce the binary. The atoms in it are *conjoined* with each other; but the binary itself, which is different from them according to what has just been stated, is in *samavāya* relation with them. That is, the parts are conjoined; but the whole is inherent, as we may say, in the parts.[2] Three such binaries produce a triad, which has a finite magnitude and is sensible unlike the binary. The triad, which is identified with the mote in the sunbeam, has for its parts three binaries and is related to them through *samavāya*. It is out of such triads that the whole of the material universe, including the bodies of living beings, is created. At the end of a cycle, it is resolved into its constituent atoms in the reverse order; and when that process is completed, they remain isolated from one another till the next cycle begins.

It is in elaborating this cosmological scheme that the system postulates the existence of God as the all-knowing Being, who disposes the atoms in the manner required for the emergence of the world as we know it. He does not create the atoms, because they are eternal like him. In other words, he is only an efficient cause (p. 30) possessing the will and intelligence required for bringing about the desired result. The variety characterizing the created world is determined by the past deeds of the beings that are to inhabit it. The doctrine accordingly associates a purpose with creation, viz. the reaping of the fruit of their karma by created beings and, we should add, the affording of opportunities in the case of man to emancipate himself.[3] God is therefore not merely a creator; he is also the architect of the universe. Here we find two of the common arguments for the existence of God: (1) The cosmological, which reasons from the fact that the world is an effect to a Being who can bring it into existence; and (2) the teleological, which reasons from the evidence of design or purpose found in the world to a just and prescient agent. From the vastness of the universe and its extraordinary diversity, it is deduced that its author must possess infinite power as well as infinite wisdom. An interesting feature about this theistic conception is that the supreme power is identified with Śiva, one of the two Gods who, as we have seen (p.32), claimed the faith and devotion of the pious Indian in post-Vedic times.

(2) *Spirit:* Under this head, we shall consider the self or ātman and *manas*, which are the two remaining "substances" (*dravya*) acknowledged in the doctrine. The former is represented as eternal and all-pervading, its eternity being involved in the karma doctrine. We have pointed out (p. 47) how the karma doctrine implies the beginninglessness of the self; and any positive entity that is without a beginning is, in the Nyāya-Vaiśeṣika view, necessarily without an end. But there is nothing in the intrinsic nature of the self, as conceived in the system, which is spiritual as that word is ordinarily understood. The point in which it differs from other entities, whether atomic or all-pervading, is that it may come to possess knowledge, feeling and volition, while the rest can never do so. In other words, the self is the basis of psychic life, but that life is only adventitious to it. The necessary condition for the appearance of psychic features in the self is its association with *manas*. For these reasons, it would perhaps be better to describe the two together as really constituting the self in the common acceptation of that term. But we should remember that the conception

of *manas*, taken by itself, is equally non-spiritual. The true self is thus broken up here, we may say, into two "selfless elements."

The selves are many; and, although they are all-pervading, their capacity to know, feel and will is ordinarily manifested through the physical organism with which each of them is associated for the time being. The very disparity in the circumstances characterizing the lives of beings is regarded as an index to the fundamental distinction of their selves. This difference, being intrinsic, continues in the state of release also; and, though all other differences between any two selves disappear when both have been released, there will be the *viśeṣas* then, as in the case of atoms, to distinguish them from each other.[4] Every self has its own distinctive *manas*, which keeps company with it till it becomes free. It is atomic; but, unlike other atomic entities recognized in the system, it does not give rise to any new products.

In the empirical state or *saṁsāra*, the *manas* is generally[5] in operative contact with the self; and, according to the nature of certain other conditions that may be present then, such as contact of an organ of sense with an appropriate object, knowledge in one of its forms springs in the self and gives rise, in its turn, either directly or indirectly to love, hate, pleasure, pain and volition. All these six qualities are specific to the self as colour is of fire, or odour of earth. They are all perceivable, but only internally or through the *manas*. It means, we may add by the way, that knowledge, in this doctrine, while it can reveal other objects cannot reveal itself but requires another to do so. The *jñāna* which manifests another *jñāna* is termed "after-knowledge" (*anuvyavasāya*). To these six should be added two more qualities, *dharma* or moral merit and its opposite, *adharma* or demerit,[6] which are not however directly perceived or felt like the others but are only to be inferred from the effects, viz. pleasure and pain respectively which, according to the karma doctrine, they occasion. Their conception being moral, it would be better to postpone the further consideration of them to the next section, which deals with the practical teaching of the doctrine. Compared with the Upanishadic view of the self, this is a very poor one; and, when we remember that knowledge or experience here is neither the essence nor a constant feature of the self, but that it only appears when certain external factors—none of which is spiritual—co-operate, it will be seen that the system is not far removed from materialism (p.58) As in it, here also the coming together or co-operation of physical or, more correctly, non-spiritual factors is regarded as somehow giving rise to experience.

The existence of the self is taken as given in introspection or internal perception, such as "I know," and "I am happy." These perceptions cannot refer to the body or any other physical accompaniment of the self, for knowledge and feeling cannot characterize them. There are also, no doubt, perceptions like "I am stout" and "I am lean," where the "I" clearly points to the physical body; but such statements the doctrine explains as figurative, implying that the person who makes them is, at least, half-conscious that what is stout or lean is other than the true "I," though connected with it. This is shown by the expressions he uses at other times like "my body," signifying that the body is what he owns and is not himself. While one's own self may thus be taken as directly given, those of others must necessarily be regarded as matters of inference, for they are known to us only through the perception of their bodies and the way in which they behave.

The divine self also is classed under this head. Udayana, of the tenth century A.D., who has written a masterly treatise on the existence of God, implies in his prefatory remarks that the universality of belief in God is a sufficient proof of it. But he also gives more direct proofs to two of which, the cosmological and the teleological, we have already referred. Of the eight specific qualities that may characterize the individual self, four, viz. moral merit and demerit, hate and misery are, of course, not found in him. He has right knowledge which embraces all existence, universal love and right volition. According to some exponents of the doctrine, he has also infinite happiness or bliss.[7]

We have thus far explained the nature of the nine fundamental "substances" (*dravya*) recognised in the system. They are earth, water, fire, air, *ākāśa*, space, time, self and *manas*. We have also, by the way, alluded to several qualities postulated in it, viz. odour, taste, colour, touch, sound, knowledge, love, hate, pleasure, pain, volition, *dharma* and *adharma*. These qualities, however, are such as are peculiar to certain classes of entities (*viśeṣa-guṇa*). There are other qualities also accepted here, which are general (*sāmānya-guṇa*) in the sense that they may pertain to more than one class of substances. Thus "weight" (*gurutva*) for example is found in objects derived from earth-atoms, water-atoms, etc. We have also mentioned another of these, viz. "conjunction" (*saṁyoga*), which may be found between two substances,[8] and pointed out its distinction from *samavāya* which too, like it, is a relation. It is sufficient for our purpose to remember these fourteen qualities, or fifteen including "weight," which we mentioned only to illustrate general qualities; and we shall not tax the reader's mind by explaining the nature of the qualities remaining out of the total number which, as it seems, is arbitrarily fixed at twenty-four.

In consonance with the realistic and pluralistic spirit of the doctrine, these qualities are all regarded as separately real or as having their own being, although they are never found by themselves. Theoretically a substance may, provided it is a product, exist without a quality for a little while; but no quality can be discovered, except as characterizing some fundamental substance or some object derived from it. This one-sided dependence signifies that the relation between the two is *samavāya*. Just as the parts of a whole may exist by themselves, although the whole can never be found apart from them, so a substance may, subject to the above limit of time, exist by itself although no quality can do so.

The same relation, which is really a metaphysical fiction, holds between objects and movement or action (*karma*), the third of the categories postulated. Not all substances, however, can exhibit movement. It is only atomic and finite objects that can change their place, which is what "action" means here. The all-pervading primal entities cannot obviously do so, for there is no space left into which they may move. There is one important point to be noticed in connection with movement as understood in this system. We know that we can initiate movement. We can lift our arm, for example, and also communicate motion to a static object like a ball. On the basis of this experience manifestly, it is believed here that movement is always to be initiated by a sentient being and that no physical object can, of itself, move. It may, no doubt, receive motion from other physical objects, say, one billiard ball from another; but even then, when we trace its first cause, it will invariably be due to a conscious agent. Where there is movement and no such agent is apparently at work, as when the wind is blowing, the doctrine refers it to the action of some mythical being or of some supernatural agency. This view of movement is at the bottom of the cosmological argument for the existence of God alluded to above. The atoms themselves being incapable of movement, the creation of the world requires a competent conscious agency to initiate it in them.

Substance (*dravya*), quality (*guṇa*) and action (*karma*), together with *samavāya* and *viśeṣa*, constitute five of the six positive categories of the system. Of these, *samavāya* is conceived as one and eternal, whatever be the nature of the things it relates. The *viśeṣas* are many; and they are eternal, characterizing, as they do, eternal things like atoms of the same class or the selves which cannot otherwise be distinguished.

The remaining positive category may be described as "universals" (*sāmānya*), whose conception we may now explain. There are, in the first place, the diverse eternal substances which form the basis of the universe, viz. the four elements, selves and *manas*. To these we have to add the myriad finite objects derived from the former four. These fundamental and derived objects, though quite distinct from one another ontologically, are not without common features. It is by virtue of these common features that we divide them into groups as earth-atoms, water-atoms, selves, chairs, tables, etc. The common features, by virtue of which they are so grouped, are called universals.[9] They are revealed only through the corresponding particulars, and are never found by themselves. Yet they are regarded, like the particulars which they characterize, as real in themselves. In this respect, the present doctrine differs from Jainism (p. 65), according to which the particular and the universal together constitute reality; and either, taken by itself, is an abstraction.

The universals resemble qualities and action in being attributive, and are related to their respective particulars through *samavāya*.[10] In this respect also, the present doctrine differs from Jainism, according to which the relation in question is one of identity-in-difference. They are also regarded as eternal and independently real, and not as transient configurations of particular objects as in Jainism (p. 66), so that their place is among the fundamental aspects of the universe, like atoms and selves. The universals characterize not merely substances but also quantities and actions. It means that the red colour, say, seen in various objects is not one and the same but is many and that all of them share a distinguishing feature, viz. "red-ness", which is eternal and unchangeable. But no universal is found in any of the remaining categories—*samavāya*, because it is one, universals and *viśeṣas*, although they are many. The means of cognizing universals is perception, where the corresponding particulars are perceptible; elsewhere, it may be inference or others' testimony.

The system accepts, in addition to these six positive categories, a negative one also, called "non-existence" (*ahāva*); but it should be carefully distinguished from absolute nothing. The manner in which the doctrine is led to postulate such a category may be indicated as follows: Let us take the statement that a certain object is not blue. What does this exactly mean? There are two ways of understanding it. We may take it positively—as meaning that it has some other colour, say, green. Or we may regard its meaning as not extending so far, but as stopping short at the denial of the colour in question. When we say that an object is not blue, we of course imply that it has some other colour; but the literal meaning of the statement is merely the absence of blueness. We shall come across both these views of non-existence in the sequel; but, so far as the present doctrine is concerned, the idea of non-existence is of the second kind—the mere absence of something. That something, viz. blueness in the above example, is termed the correlate or counter-entity (*pratiyogin*) of non-existence. Because non-existence may thus be defined or particularized, it cannot be equated with absolute nothing. In fact, such absolute nothing, which means the negation of everything, lies outside human thought and is a pseudo-concept according to the Nyāya-Vaiśeṣika.

Non-existence is fourfold. It may be such as involves a reference to time—the denial of a thing with the suggestion that it has already been (*pradhvaṁsābhāva*) or that it will only hereafter come to be (*prāgabhāva*). Or it may involve a reference to space—the denial of a thing somewhere with the suggestion that it is somewhere else (*atyantābhāva*). Lastly, it may mean mutual exclusion (*anyonyābhāva*), as when we deny that the paper is the pen. The last is obviously eternal, owing to the self-identity or changelessness of things which, unlike Jainism (p. 65), the present system recognizes. As regards the channel through which we cognize non-existence, the doctrine holds that, as in the case of universals, it is perception where its correlate is perceptible and that, in other cases, it is either inference or verbal testimony. Thus the absence of a table is perceivable, because the table itself is so. Only we must, at the time, see the bare floor of the room (say) in which we expect it to be. The absence, on the other hand, of infra-sensible germs of a disease in a place can only be inferred or learnt through communication of the fact by another person.

We have stated above that knowledge arises in the self when certain conditions are fulfilled. These conditions are two in the case of perception in addition to the one already mentioned, viz. contact of the self with *manas*. The *manas* should come into contact with a sensory organ, and the sensory organ with an appropriate object. Thus perceiving colour means that the sense of sight and *manas* are both co-operating with the self. There are certain other circumstances also that are necessary, such as the presence of light; but we need not specify them, especially as their recognition is not peculiar to this doctrine. In other forms of knowledge also, contact of the self with *manas* is necessary; only the rest of the conditions vary. For instance, in inferring fire from smoke, it is necessary to recall past experience inductively relating them with each other.

The common idea of perception is that it is complex and points to objects as characterized in some way. That is, it involves a reference to an object, its characteristic such as colour and the relation between them; and all these three appear synthesized in it. The present doctrine accepts this view; but it believes that perception in this sense presupposes a stage of pure sensation in which these three elements, though presented, are not apprehended in the same connected way as in the other. They are felt then merely as something (*idam kiṁcit*). This stage is described as indeterminate (*nirvikalpa*) to contrast it with the latter determinate (*savikalpa*) stage. Unlike the later the former does not admit of definite linguistic expression. Nor can its existence be directly known. It can only be inferred from the principle, held in this doctrine, that the complex presupposes the simple. Since, according to the realistic postulate of the system, it is in the very nature of knowledge to point to an outside object, the reality of the object given in the indeterminate stage, however vague its apprehension may be, is taken to be unquestionable. The possibility of error arises only at the determinate level, where two or more things are apprehended as mutually related—a point to which we shall refer presently.

This view of perception assumes that objects are directly known. There is another view, which we shall mention in the next chapter, according to which objects are not known directly but only through psychic media which in some way resemble or symbolize them. When, however, the Nyāya-Vaiśeṣika takes objects to be apprehended directly, it does not mean that there are no illusions or doubt. Not all knowledge is therefore valid. For knowledge to be valid, it should present the object to the self as possessing that characteristic which it actually has. The implication of such a view is what is called the correspondence theory of truth. That knowledge is true which is faithful to its object. Erroneous knowledge, on the other hand, contains as part of its content one or more aspects, not actually given. But it is maintained that there is always some object or other presented and that error can never be wholly subjective, for, even when it later comes to be discovered, the feeling is that something, say a rope, was mistaken for another, a snake. What this theory of error really signifies is that there can be no hallucination with nothing at all to serve as its objective basis, as there may be according to one school of Buddhism (p. 80). In other words, the error is not in respect of the presented object as such, but is confined to its predicative (or attributive) elements. The subject of even an erroneous judgement is real; it is only the predicate that is not so.[11] Hence a thing is stated to appear in error in a manner which is different from what it actually is (*anyathā-khyāti*).

To give a simple example: When travelling in a railway carriage, a child may take the trees, which it sees outside, to be moving in the opposite direction. This is an error, but only so far as associating the trees with motion is concerned because it belongs to the train and not to them. Here, however, movement is actually given, though not where it is felt to be. It is not necessary that it should always be so. In the example already adduced, it is only the rope that is given and not the snake also. But the snake too should in itself be real, according to the doctrine, and must have been actually experienced somewhere previously. This conclusion may be conceded, although it is by no means necessary, as we have pointed out in considering the Yogācāra view of knowledge (p. 82). But the Nyāya-Vaiśeṣika does not stop at this; it goes farther and assumes that the very "snake" experienced before is, by a process into the details of which we cannot enter here, actually presented to the percipient at the time, so that even in this case the object for which the "rope" is mistaken is *given*. Whatever the justification for such an assumption may be, the essential point for us to remember is that error always has an objective basis, and that its erroneous character lies in transferring to what is actually presented some feature which does not belong to it, no matter whether that feature is now being, or has in the past been, experienced.

How is the validity of knowledge to be known? Indian theories of knowledge are divisible broadly into two classes—one maintaining the self-validity (*svatah-prāmāṇya*) of knowledge; and the other contending that it needs to be validated by an extraneous means (*paratah-prāmāṇya*). In the former view, whenever knowledge arises, the presumption is that it is right; and verification becomes necessary only when there is some circumstance throwing doubt upon it. In the latter case knowledge by itself guarantees nothing in this respect; and its truth or falsity is to be ascertained through some appropriate test. We shall deal with this point at some length in a subsequent chapter. For the present it will suffice to say that the Nyāya-Vaiśeṣika upholds the second view and that the truth or falsehood of knowledge is, according to it, to be determined by practical verification (*saṁvādi-pravṛtti*). If it is "water" for instance which we think we perceive, the validity of the perception is known by the successful quenching (say) of our thirst by it. If it fails to satisfy this or some other similar test, we conclude that it is invalid.

Thus the truth or falsity of knowledge is a matter of later

inference. It is true if it works; otherwise, it is false. It should, however, be carefully noted that this pragmatic criterion is here only a *test* of truth and does not, as in modern pragmatism, constitute its nature. Unlike the latter, the Nyāya-Vaiśeṣika lays full stress on the cognitive function of *pramāṇa*. Error implies ignorance of the true character of the object given, and the removal of that ignorance is the primary purpose of knowledge. The practical activity to which it leads, and which is here made the criterion of its validity, is only a *further* consequence of it. It implies a motive operating subsequently to cognition, viz. to attain what is liked or to avoid what is disliked. In the absence of such a motive, knowledge will not lead to any practical activity; but its logical quality is not thereby affected.

The Vaiśeṣika doctrine recognises only two *pramāṇas*, viz. perception and inference; but the Nyāya accepts two more, viz. verbal testimony and comparison. We may now give a brief account of three of them, leaving out comparison which, as understood in this doctrine, is not of much logical significance.

(1) Perception (*pratyakṣa*): We know how perception is explained here, and what constitutes its validity. It only remains now to refer to a certain important variety of it which is described as "extraordinary" or "transcendental" (*alaukika*) perception. It really falls beyond the scope of empirical psychology. A *yogin*, it is said, is able to directly perceive things which are not so perceivable by the average man, for example, atoms, moral merit (*dharma*), etc. He is supposed to have developed a mystical power which brings him face to face with such supersensuous entities. The conditions of developing this power, it is instructive to note, are identical with those for attaining salvation, viz. moral purity and proficiency in meditation. In fact, the theory is that the perfected saint alone is able to exercise his perceptual power in this extended and extraordinary way. Such knowledge, as we may expect, is necessarily valid. This is the intuition of the individual seer, to which we alluded in an earlier chapter (p. 44).

(2) Inference (*anumāna*): We have referred to the unsuccessful attempt of the Cārvāka to dispense with this *pramāṇa* (p. 57). We did not allude to the question of *pramāṇas* specifically in our brief sketch of Jainism and Buddhism. Both these doctrines

acknowledge the legitimacy of inference; but as there is nothing very special which requires to be noted here regarding the Jaina view of it, we shall pass on to consider the Buddhistic conception of it. Buddhism confines the legitimacy of inference only to cases where the existence of the cause is inferred from the presence of something which can be demonstrated to be its effect.[12] It is, for example, quite legitimate to deduce that there is fire where we see smoke, because we know that there is a causal relation between them and that hence the fire is a *sine qua non* of smoke. The first requirement here then is the perception of the causal connection between two things, viz. fire and smoke in our example. If now a person, who is aware of this connection, notices smoke somewhere, say, on a hill, and remembers the relation which perception has thus established, there arises in him the idea of fire on the hill. The present doctrine makes an important innovation here, whereby the scope of inference becomes greatly widened. According to Buddhism, the fact of smoke is connected with the fact of fire, for fire is the *necessary* cause of smoke. In the Nyāya-Vaiśeṣika, the element of necessity is not insisted upon in the same manner. Or rather, taking for granted the uniformity of nature, it believes that the required condition of necessity exists in cases where one thing, as a result of adequate observation, is known to accompany another invariably, although the inner connection between them is not demonstrable in our present state of knowledge.[13] Cloven hoofs and horns furnish an example of such invariable concomitance; and it is therefore quite legitimate, according to this doctrine, to deduce the presence of the one from the presence of the other.

Inference is two-fold—that which resolves a doubt in one's own mind (*svārtha*), and that which does so in another's (*parārtha*). The latter is necessarily couched in language, and its several stages are thus expressed;

> The hill is fiery.
> Because it has smoke.
> Whatever has smoke has fire, e.g., the kitchen.
> The hill has smoke, such as is always accompanied by fire.
> Therefore the hill is fiery.

There are two points worthy of notice here: First, the universal proposition in the third step is supported by a typical example to show that it has been derived through observation. Hence the Indian syllogism is not deductive merely, but is also inductive. Secondly, the fourth step, which may appear to be superfluous, is meant to indicate that neither the sign or the mark nor the inductive relation, by itself, leads to a knowledge of the signified but only a proper combination of them.

This syllogistic form, with its five members, is only for leading another to the conclusion in question; and the verbal form, in itself, constitutes no part of inference. It only helps to direct the mind of the listener to think in the required manner, and thereby gives rise to the same process of thought in his mind as the one in that of the speaker. So if the syllogistic *form* is described as *anumāna*, it is only by courtesy (*upacāra*). That is, the Nyāya-Vaiśeṣika, like the rest of the Indian systems, rejects the verbal view of logic which is common in the West. It was never forgotten in India that the subject-matter of logic is thought, and not the linguistic form in which it may find expression.

(3) Verbal testimony (*śabda*): Of the two systems of thought which we are now considering, it is the Nyāya alone that admits verbal testimony as an independent *pramāṇa*. Though accepting the authority of the Veda, the Nyāya explains its validity in its own way—by tracing it to the omniscience of God whom it views as its author. In this, it differs from the Mīmāṁsā; and the difference will be made clear when we come to deal with that doctrine. Further, the system does not restrict verbal testimony to the Veda, but also extends it to secular matters, defining it in general terms as the testimony of a trustworthy person (*āpta*)—one that knows the truth and communicates it correctly. Only the latter cannot always carry with it the absolute certainty which the Veda, by virtue of its source, necessarily does.

We have already dealt with the general nature of this *pramāṇa*, and the need for recognizing it (p. 44). We may now refer briefly to the significance of specific verbal statements or propositions. A word like *gauḥ* ("cow"), when uttered, calls up in the case of one that is acquainted with its meaning a picture of the animal "cow." In the case of others, it fails altogether to be significant and ends by creating merely an auditory impression. To be significant two or more words should be appropriately conjoined so as to form a sentence. Sometimes single words may convey information, but then one or more other words are always to be understood from the context. Thus the unit of significant *śabda* is a sentence. But what is the nature of the information which such syntactically conjoined words convey? It cannot be merely the meanings of the various terms, because they are already known and so are only remembered at the time. It is some particular relation among the things denoted by the actual words forming the sentence. When we say "The book is on the table," it is a specific relation between the table and the book that is made known to the listener. The relation in this specific form is not the meaning of any single word used in the sentence, the preposition "on" signifying only location in general; it is none the less known. Hence the import of a proposition is commonly stated to be relation (*saṁsarga*); and this holds good of the logically valid proposition as of that which is not.

## II

So far as the nature of the goal of life is concerned, the Indian systems may be divided into two classes—those which conceive of it merely as one of absolute freedom from misery, and those which take it as one of bliss also. The Nyāya-Vaiśeṣika is of the first type; and its conception of non-existence (*abhāva*) allows it to put forward such a view of the goal, for, according to it, the absence of misery is not *the same* as the presence of bliss. The nature of the self also, as understood in the system, fits in with such a view, for neither sorrow nor pleasure, though specific to it, is of its essence. Gautama accordingly terms it "escape" (*apavarga*). The underlying idea is that evil is as much a fact as good, and that we cannot have one of them without the other—a view which the materialist also, as we have seen (p. 59), holds, although he differs very much from the present doctrine in the conclusion he draws from it. The self must therefore be subject to both pain and pleasure or neither. The former is *saṁsāra*, characterized by tension of mind which is relieved only off and on by some evanescent pleasure; the latter is *mokṣa* or perfect repose, provided a state bereft of consciousness, as we shall see it is here, may be so described. If to avoid evil is desirable, then we must make up our mind to forgo the good as well. The recognition of the ultimacy of evil, it should be added, does not make the system pessimistic, for it admits the possibility of individuals passing beyond evil. That is, though evil is here taken to be a fact, it is not regarded as inevitable, for any person, who seriously wants to escape from it, can do so. This individualistic conception of freedom does not mean that we should grow indifferent to suffering in others, or reduce our efforts to alleviate it as far as possible. The intense need felt for overcoming it in one's own case should rather lead to a redoubling of one's efforts in that direction.

We have pointed out that *mokṣa* is a state beyond pain and pleasure. It is desirable to say a few words more about it. When a person, who has qualified himself for final release, departs this life, his self is believed to transcend not merely pain and pleasure but all its specific qualities. As a consequence, it will then be devoid of thought, feeling and will; and *mokṣa* thus becomes a condition of perfect gloom from which there will be no re-awakening. Such a state has rightly been condemned by the opponents of the doctrine as a remedy worse than the disease which it professes to cure. But it is only *mokṣa* as attained after death. If, instead of this theoretically final state, we take the one that precedes it in the present life in the case of a person who has acquired complete fitness for *mokṣa*, we see that the state is far from unsatisfactory. Not all the specific qualities will be eliminated then, but only the undesirable ones like hate and self-love. Such a person will continue to have right knowledge, right volition and right feeling; and he will necessarily be incessantly engaged in doing the right, or in contemplating the ultimately true. That is, his condition then will approximate to the perfection of divine nature as already described. Although the system does not acknowledge a special state which some doctrines designate as *jīvanmukti*, this exactly corresponds to it.[14] Judged from this positivistic standpoint the doctrine, though negative in its final significance and severely ascetic, has features which are not without a special appeal to a certain type of mind.

What is the means to the attainment of this goal? The answer to this question will be found in the Nyāya-Vaiśeṣika view that evil is due to the association of the self with the *manas* and the body. The physical body will, no doubt, be destroyed at death; but, according to the karma doctrine, it will be replaced by another when the self is born again. The *manas*, on the other hand, will remain the same throughout and be in contact with the self. Being eternal, it will continue to be, even after one has attained freedom; but its presence will be quite inoperative then, and pain, pleasure and such other features will no longer affect the self. Liberation consists in realizing this fact, viz. that, though the self is actually related to both body and *manas*, that relation is by no means necessary to it. As in the other doctrines, right knowledge is thus the means to liberation here also; and ignorance, the source of bondage. It is this ignorance (*moha*) that serves, by begetting hatred (*dveṣa*) and narrow love (*rāga*) as the root-cause of *saṁsāra* with its sorrows as well as fleeting joys. Like other forms of error, say that of the rope-snake, this ultimate error also is a misconception, because it represents a neutral self as involved in misery. Only we should remind the reader that, since the erroneous knowledge that gives rise to *saṁsāra* is immediate, it needs an equally immediate knowledge (p. 27) of the true nature of the self to overcome it.

We have seen that the self, in itself, is devoid of pleasure and pain; and it should therefore be beyond their causes according to the karma doctrine, viz. virtue and vice. These, or more strictly, their immediate effects of good and evil, are known as *dharma* and *adharma*, the remaining two of the eight qualities that are specific to the self. They abide in the self till they yield their respective fruits of happiness and misery, and it is for reaping those fruits that one takes birth. Even when the misconception to which this life is due is removed by right knowledge, activity will continue; but such activity, Gautama says, does not lead to re-birth or to the accumulation of *dharma* (*adharma* being quite unthinkable in such a case), because it is not the result of any self-interest or short-sightedness.[15] Such a person necessarily becomes free, when dissociation from the physical body takes place at death. It will be seen from the above description of *dharma* and *adharma* that their notion here is entirely moral (p. 37). This original conception has since been extended, and the terms have come to include the results of actions commended or condemned in the Veda. This extension of their meaning is due to the later admission, already mentioned, of the authority of the Veda by the system.

Now as regards the details of the discipline leading to the ultimate goal of life. Broadly speaking, this discipline is to be undergone in two stages: (1) The first is the cultivation of a spirit of detachment. It is advocated by all the schools, and we may look upon their respective metaphysical views as only assigning different reasons for it. In the case of the Upanishads, for example, the need for it is explained by the unity of all being; in the present doctrine, by the intrinsically detached character of the self. The training of this stage is predominantly moral, and signifies a complete overcoming of selfish desires and impulses. The important truth underlying this view is that much of the world's misery is traceable, directly or indirectly, to man's selfishness, as an individual or as a member of an exclusive organization; and that neither for the individual nor for society as a whole will there be any peace until it is completely overcome. (2) The above ethical qualification helps to secure the seriousness necessary for acquiring a knowledge of the ultimate truth, through study and reflection, and for effectively pursuing the philosophic ideal. Accordingly the discipline in the second stage is mainly intellectual. The final step here consists in meditation (*yoga*) on the ultimate truth which, if successfully practised, results in a direct experience of it, such as will terminate the original ignorance. The resemblance here generally to the course of discipline for attaining the goal of life, described in the previous chapters, is clear; only the content of the truth to be realized is different. It is not therefore necessary to dwell upon it further here.

Chapter Five

# SĀṄKHYA-YOGA[1]

*

THIS system of thought is one of the oldest, but its origin has for long been a matter of controversy. Some scholars, both old and new, explain it as derived from the Upanishads; but others maintain that it is an independent doctrine. Whatever be its origin, the system has largely influenced Indian thought as a whole; and its importance is next only to that of the Vedānta. As in the case of the Nyāya-Vaiśeṣika (p. 84), the present system also is a blend of two doctrines, viz. the Sāṅkhya and the Yoga, of which Kapila and Patañjali were respectively the first exponents; but the historical relation between the two doctrines is not definitely known. Their general metaphysical standpoint, and their conception of the ideal of life are the same; but there are also some more or less important features in which they differ. To one or two of them we shall refer later. The names by which these two doctrines are known are extremely common in Indian philosophical literature. Besides referring to schools of thought, they frequently mean methods of approach to the ultimate reality. The former, which is derived from a Sanskrit word (*saṅkhyā*) meaning "reflection," stands for the method of realizing the ultimate fact of philosophy through knowledge. The latter, (*yoga*), on the other hand, which signifies contemplation, stands for the method of realizing the same by means of steady and persistent meditation. This distinction, however, reduces itself to one of the precise place assigned to them in the course of discipline for achieving the ideal, since all the Indian systems, including the present one, alike prescribe both. While some lay greater stress on knowledge by making it the *proximate* aid to release, others do the same in regard to meditation.

It is somewhat strange that while the literature bearing on the other systems is quite extensive, that relating to the present one, especially the Sāṅkhya part of it, is very meagre. The oldest work now available on the Sāṅkhya is the *Kārikā* of Īśvara Kṛṣṇa who flourished about the fifth century A.D. It has been commented upon by several scholars including the great Vedāntin, Vācaspati. There is a Sāṅkhya Sūtra, which is ordinarily believed to be as old as the primary sources of the other systems; but it clearly shows dependence on the work just referred to, and modern research has found it necessary to assign to it a date not earlier than the fourteenth century A.D. The most important work of the other system is the Sūtra of Patañjali who, in all likelihood, is different from the celebrated grammarian of that name belonging to the second century B.C., and lived probably much later. It has an old commentary by Vyāsa who only bears the name of, but is not the same as, the renowned sage of antiquity. There are also other commentaries on it as, for example, the one by King Bhoja.

## I

This system, like the one treated of in the previous chapter (p. 85), regards both matter and spirit as ultimately real and also admits, like it, a plurality of selves which it usually terms Puruṣas. But it differs from the Nyāya-Vaiśeṣika in that it traces the whole of the physical universe, with all its variety, to a single source called Prakṛti. Puruṣa and Prakṛti, or spirit and nature, are thus the two basic conceptions of the doctrine; and we shall begin by describing their nature. To take up the latter first:

(1) *Prakṛti:* There are two ways of explaining the origin of the physical world. It may be traced, as in Nyāya-Vaiśeṣika (p. 86), to a plurality of ultimate reals which are supposed to be simple and atomic; or it may be derived from a single substance which is assumed to be complex and all-pervasive. If the former is the theory of origination (*ārambha-vāda*), the latter is the theory of evolution (*pariṇāma-vāda*), for in it the things of the world are looked upon as the result, not of new creation, but of transformation within the primal substance. The Sāṅkhya-Yoga adopts the second mode of explanation; and Prakṛti is the name which it gives to the principle or entity, out of which is evolved

the physical universe in its infinite diversity. Its resemblance to the conception of "That One," mentioned in tracing the growth of monism in the Veda (p. 15), is clear. Only while that principle is spiritual in its character, the present one is not so. This primal entity is not directly perceived by us; and its existence, like that of the atoms in the Nyāya-Vaiśeṣika view, has only to be inferred. Here, as elsewhere generally, the system bases its conclusions on reason and does not, like some others, invoke the aid of revelation in support of them.

Prakṛti, the First Cause of the universe, is thus one and complex; and its complexity is the result of its being constituted of three factors, each of which is described as a *guṇa*. By the word *guṇa* here, we should not understand what it is commonly taken to mean, viz. a "quality." It means here rather a "component factor" or a "constituent" of Prakṛti. But it should not be regarded as built up out of them, for, while it depends on them, they depend just as much on it, both being equally beginningless. These three constituents again, though essentially distinct in their nature, are conceived as interdependent, so that they can never be separated from one another. It means that they are not mechanically placed together, but reciprocally involve one another and form a unity in trinity. In other words, they not only coexist but also cohere. This intrinsic interdependence of the *guṇas* excludes the possibility of the breaking up of Prakṛti by their separation.

The three *guṇas* are named *sattva, rajas* and *tamas*. Each of them stands for a distinct aspect of physical reality: roughly, *sattva* signifies whatever is pure and fine; *rajas*, whatever is active; and *tamas*, what is stolid and offers resistance. The above description shows that the *guṇas* are not merely distinct but are also, in some measure, antagonistic in their nature. The antagonism, however, is not such as to preclude their acting together. They function as one; and their harmonious action is illustrated by the example of a lamp-flame—the result of co-operation between the wick, oil and fire which, in their separate nature, appear to be hardly fitted so to co-operate. In other words, the physical universe is an orderly whole; and there is no ultimate contradiction in it, though it may consist of opposing elements.

It is not only Prakṛti that consists of these *guṇas*; everything that emerges from it is also similarly constituted, for the doctrine maintains that effects are essentially identical with their material cause. In fact, it is by an analysis of the things of experience and a proper synthesis of their common and enduring features that the conception of Prakṛti has been reached, as the idea of gold, for instance, may be reached by an examination of the nature of things like golden rings and bracelets. The present view of causation then is the exact opposite of that to which we drew attention in the last chapter. It holds that nothing can ever come into being afresh or pass away finally. When therefore we speak of an effect as produced, all that we mean is that what was latent merely becomes manifest. The underlying idea is that the effect is always there, though in a potential form, and that it only becomes actual when certain conditions known as the efficient causes, like the activity of the potter in the case of a pot, are fulfilled. The material cause and the effect are not accordingly taken here to be quite distinct, as in the Nyāya-Vaiśeṣika (p. 88); they form, on the other hand an identity in difference, as in Jainism. This view is designated as "the doctrine of pre-existent effect" (*sat-kārya-vāda*) in contrast to the other, termed "the doctrine of not-pre-existent effect" (*asat-kārya-vāda*).

These *guṇas* or "cosmic constituents," as we may term them, are in a state of perfect equilibrium in Prakṛti, until it begins to differentiate itself; and the diversity of the things that then successively spring into being from it is due to the diversity in the proportion in which the *guṇas* enter into their make-up in the process of evolution. Though only three in number, they can thus account for a multiplicity of distinctions. Prakṛti is not only complex and all-pervasive; it also evolves or undergoes change perpetually. Naturally the things that develop out of it are also conceived as sharing in its fluid character. Thus the paper on which these lines are printed may appear to be static; but it is really changing every instant, though it at the same time maintains its identity as long as it lasts. It is necessary to add that evolution means change of form (*pariṇāma*), a conception which is unknown to the Nyāya-Vaiśeṣika, and not change of place (*parispanda*) (p. 93) which is what the latter means by "action" (*karma*). A plant, for example, may be shifted from one place to another; but it may also grow or wither where it is. The change, however, as conceived here, is not in one direction alone. The evolutionary process is periodical; and every period of evolution (*sṛṣṭi*) is followed by a period of dissolution (*pralaya*) when the whole diversity of the universe becomes latent or goes "to sleep," as it were, in Prakṛti. Cycle thus follows cycle; and, as in many other Indian doctrines, it is believed here that this series had no beginning and is not going to have an end. But even in the stage of dissolution, we must remember, Prakṛti does not cease to be dynamic, motion being conceived as original to it; only its component parts, the *guṇas*, constantly reproduce themselves then instead of acting on one another and giving rise to a heterogeneous transformation. In this spontaneous activity of nature, we find another important difference from the Nyāya-Vaiśeṣika, according to which matter has no activity beyond what may have been communicated to it from without (p. 93).

Now as regards the things that emerge from Prakṛti. The first of them is the "intellect" (*mahat*); and that, in its turn gives rise to the principle of individuality or "egoism" (*āhaṁkāra*). What exactly we have to understand from these terms will become clear soon. Meanwhile we may note that the nature of these entities, as indicated by their names, shows that Prakṛti adjusts itself first to the needs of Puruṣa by evolving the most important aids to life's experience, viz. the organ of thinking and the principle of consciously or unconsciously appropriating the thought or regarding it as one's own. From the second proceed two groups of principles: One of them consists of the further aids to conscious life, viz. *manas*, the five sensory organs which are well known and the five motor organs, viz. those of speech (*vāk*), handling (*pāni*), walking (*pāda*), evacuation (*pāyu*) and reproduction (*upastha*). The other forms the basis of the objective world, viz. the five elements. The former group is taken to proceed mainly from the *sattva* aspect of "egoism"; and the latter, from the *tamas* aspect of it. The third factor of *rajas* is not regarded as issuing in any separate group of principles,[2] but merely as co-operating with both *sattva* and *tamas*.

The elements are thought of as having two phases, the first in which they remain simple (*tanmātra*) and the second in which they combine to form the five gross elements as known to us. The simple elements are called "elemental sound" (*śabda-*

*tanmātra*), "elemental colour" (*rūpa-tanmātra*) and so forth, showing that the doctrine makes no distinction between substance and quality.[3] There is indeed no harm in speaking, for the sake of convenience, of either substance or attribute apart from the other; but to think of the two as really separate from or external to each other, as the Nyāya-Vaiśeṣika does (p. 93), is, according to the present doctrine, to indulge in an illegitimate abstraction. The so-called quality and substance together form a unity; and it is this concrete unity, and not either by itself, that any material thing represents. The resemblance to Jainism (p. 65) here is clear. The manner in which the simple or subtle elements combine to produce the gross is as follows: From elemental sound emerges space (*ākāśa*); from that and elemental touch, air; from these two and elemental colour, fire; from them and elemental taste, water; and from them and elemental odour, earth. These gross elements, to use common phraseology, are characterized by qualities in accordance with the nature of their constituent factors—*ākāśa* by sound; air by sound and touch; and so on. Here again may be noted a difference from the Nyāya-Vaiśeṣika which does not recognize the division of elements into two classes as simple and gross.

These, together with Prakṛti and Puruṣa, are the 25 principles of the Sāṅkhya-Yoga; and they may be shown thus in a tabular form:

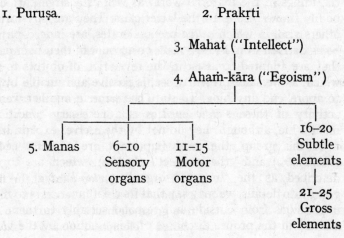

1. Puruṣa.

2. Prakṛti

3. Mahat ("Intellect")

4. Ahaṁ-kāra ("Egoism")

5. Manas

6–10 Sensory organs

11–15 Motor organs

16–20 Subtle elements

21–25 Gross elements

The above represents what we may describe as *primary* evolution. The common things of the world, such as trees and mountains as well as the physical bodies of living beings, are the result of a further or *secondary* transformation of the gross elements. We describe the latter transformations as "secondary" for, though these things also are the result of change, the change does not give rise to any new principle or category (*tattvāntara*) as, for instance, when the "intellect" (*mahat*) becomes "egoism" (*ahāmkāra*) or "elemental sound" becomes space (*ākāśa*). They are the result merely of disposing in different ways their constituent factors, viz. the gross elements, which endure as such in them. "It is just as in a game of dice; they are ever the same dice, but as they fall in various ways, they mean to us different things." These secondary changes take place, and may again be reversed, within the limits of a single cycle; the primary set of evolutes, on the other hand, continue throughout the cycle and disintegrate only at its termination. A tree, for example, may perish and break up into its constituent elements like earth, water, etc.; but the latter will not be further reduced to their sources, viz. the *tanmātras*, during the same cycle.

It is necessary to draw particular attention to one point in the above scheme whose knowledge is essential to understand the Sāṅkhya-Yoga explanation of experience, as will be set forth later. It is the distinction between the things in which *sattva* predominates and those in which *tamas* does. Most of the things of the material world as well as a large part of our bodily frame belong to the latter class. They are physical. The others also, in which *sattva* preponderates, are indeed physical, being derived from Prakṛti; but, on account of their finer nature, they are adapted to assist in the revelation of objects to spirit which, as we shall presently see, is passive and unable by itself to apprehend anything. To state the same in another way, the activity of these *sāttvic* entities is a necessary condition of mental life, although they do not by themselves explain it.

Of this group, the most important are *manas*, "egoism" (*ahaṁ-kāra*) and "the intellect" (*buddhi*), which are together described as the "internal organ" (*antaḥ-karaṇa*). Without going into details, we may say that its chief function is to receive impressions from outside and respond suitably to them. It is assisted in the proper discharge of this function by the various organs—sensory and motor—which belong to the same group. This whole apparatus, consisting of the internal organ and its several accessories, may be taken as roughly corresponding to the brain and the nervous mechanism associated with its function according to modern psychology. Both are physical in their nature, and both alike are indispensable to the self in acquiring experience. It is specific to each individual and, together with certain other factors, is here supposed to accompany him throughout worldly existence (*saṁsāra*). This relatively permanent accompaniment of Puruṣa is known as the "subtle body" (*linga-śarīra*). Unlike the physical frame which, by contrast, is called the "gross body" (*sthūla-śarīra*), it does not part from one even at death and, like *manas* in the Nyāya-Vaiśeṣika (p. 91), is cast off only when freedom is fully achieved.

It follows from the above account that the principles numbered 3 to 15 in the above scheme are to be understood in a double sense. They are not only cosmic in their significance as representing stages in the evolution of Prakṛti; they also have a reference to the individual's conscious and sub-conscious life. From the standpoint of the experiencing individual, the three *guṇas* are also described as being of the nature respectively of pleasure (*sukha*), pain (*duḥkha*) and bewilderment (*moha*), because they serve as the necessary means to arouse those feelings in him. For a person to feel happy, say, his inner or mental attitude should be predominantly *sāttvic;* or to feel miserable, the attitude should be *rājasic.* It is a mystery why the cosmic aspects should be designated as ' intellect," "egoism" etc., if they have no psychological significance. To a possible explanation of this discrepancy, we shall refer at the end of the chapter.

To sum up the conception of Prakṛti: The whole of the physical universe emanates from it; and, since it is conceived as ultimate and independent, the explanation *so far* may be characterized as naturalistic.

(2) *Puruṣa:* What prevents the doctrine from being a philosophy of nature, pure and simple, is its recognition of Puruṣa by the side of Prakṛti. Prakṛti does not exhaust the content of the universe; it leaves out the very element by virtue of which we become aware of the existence of the physical world. And it is that element of awareness or principle of sentience which

Puruṣa represents. While the doctrine thus differs from naturalism, it does not identify itself with absolutistic or idealistic systems, because it preserves to the end the dualism of Prakṛti and Puruṣa. No satisfactory explanation of experience is possible, according to the Sāṅkhya-Yoga, if we do not admit the equal and independent reality of both the material and the spiritual elements.

The existence of Puruṣa also, like that of Prakṛti, is reached here through reasoning. If the latter is postulated on the principle that effects presuppose a material cause which is immanent in them, the former is postulated on the principle that contrivances, exhibiting design, always have a transcendent reference or conspire to an extraneous end. The bodily organism, for example, with its many well-adapted parts suggests that it is meant to serve a definite purpose; and there are numerous other instances in nature with a similar teleology implicit in them. To judge examples like "a prepared bed" given in this connection, the end that is meant here is only such as benefits a sentient being. That is, the purpose implicit in nature is to be understood as some "value," though not necessarily a *human* value. The entity, whose ends such adaptations and contrivances serve, is Puruṣa. In other words, spirit is the principle for the sake of which nature evolves; and this, as already pointed out, is shown by the character of the first evolutes. Another argument to support the existence of Puruṣa is (to state it in quite general terms) the presence of the spiritual instinct in man, or the instinct which prompts him to strive for self-perfection; but imperfection is inevitable so long as he is in association with Prakṛti as it is conceived in the doctrine. This "impulse to *escape*,"[4] as it is termed, would be meaningless if there was no one to extricate himself from Prakṛti. Hence it is concluded that there must be an entity which is other than and wholly independent of Prakṛti. Both Prakṛti and Puruṣa alike are thus deduced from an investigation of the nature of common things; the only difference is that while the one is the result of arguing from those things to their source or *first* cause, the other is the result of arguing from them to their aim or *final* cause. The world is derived from a principle which is like it in its nature, but subserves the ends of another which is quite unlike.

Puruṣa is manifold in contrast to Prakṛti which is single; and the doctrine may for that reason be described as pluralism. The plurality of Puruṣas is sought to be deduced from the observed distinctions in men's temperaments. The mental or moral disposition of no two persons is identical; nor is their reaction to their social or physical environment the same. But it may be pointed out that this argument only shows that the Puruṣas are different in their empirical condition and not in themselves. In their liberated state, as we shall see, there is absolutely no difference; and to postulate numerical difference between entities, when there is no distinction whatever in their intrinsic nature, seems unwarranted. There is not here even an attempt made to justify this pluralistic view, as there is in the Nyāya-Vaiśeṣika by postulating *viśeṣas*—each unique to a self (p. 91). Granting that the existence of Prakṛti implies the existence of Puruṣa, the logical conclusion to be drawn from it is that that Puruṣa also is one and single—cosmic nature enshrining a cosmic self.

The conception is, in other respects also, the very opposite of Prakṛti. Puruṣa is not complex but simple; it is not dynamic but static, knowing neither change of place nor change of form. It is passive while Prakṛti is ever active, which means that it is to be identified more with feeling or the affective side of the mind than with any other. It cannot consequently either *know* or *will* anything in the familiar sense, unless it is assisted by the internal organ and its various subsidiaries. In itself, it is only an "enjoyer" (*bhoktṛ*), and not an "agent (*kartṛ*)—a mere looker-on or "witness" (*sākṣin*), as it is described; and, though it is of the very essence of sentience, all its psychic life is due to its association with the evolutes of Prakṛti like the internal organ in which, as pointed out above, the *sattva* element predominates. That which constitutes the activity of the subject, as commonly known to us, is due to the physical element which enters into its make-up. Like Prakṛti, however, it is supposed to be omnipresent; but the revelation of its presence during the transmigrating state (*saṁsāra*), for the reason just stated, never takes place outside the physical limitations like the body, with which it happens to be associated at the time.

The exact manner in which these two disparate entities are brought or *seem* to be brought together is a difficult point, and remains one of the perplexities in the system. But we do not propose to enter on any discussion of it here. Whatever the ultimate explanation may be, Prakṛti and Puruṣa virtually act as one; and we shall therefore take it for granted that, in some way, they co-operate. It is, indeed, a matter of ordinary experience that there is no spirit without a body or a body which functions as a living organism without spirit. This complex of nature and spirit—or perhaps, we should say, a compound of them—is not ultimate, according to the doctrine. It is only the empirical self, and is to be distinguished from the true or transcendental self, viz. Puruṣa; but, from the practical or everyday standpoint, the distinction is of little consequence. The Prakṛti element that most intimately enters into this combination is the internal organ. There are other elements too, like the sensory organs, but they are all in one sense or another subsidiary to it. The coming together of these is the necessary presupposition of all experience, for spirit without nature is inoperative and nature without spirit is blind. In the resulting union, each finds its complement; and the defects of both are made good as when a blind man and a cripple, it is stated, safely traverse a considerable distance, through co-operation, although neither by himself is capable of doing so.[5] And we may point out, by the way, that consciousness is not explained here to be a product of matter as in materialism (p. 58). Matter is merely the medium for spirit to manifest itself, not its source.

This association of the two is found not only ordinarily but also in *jīvanmukti* or "freedom while still alive," when a person has become fully enlightened and has transcended all the weaknesses of human flesh. Such a person, when he departs this life, must no doubt continue to be, Puruṣa being considered immortal; but it then remains as pure spirit, wholly emancipated from nature. That condition of isolation is described as "final aloofness" (*kaivalya*)—to distinguish it from *jīvanmukti* in which the Puruṣa remains associated with the body, senses and so forth, though no longer in bondage to them. As in Jainism (p. 61) then, perfection means here also not a *becoming*, but merely liberation from physical bonds. The spiritual goal is reached by merely throwing off the natural.

The self in the empirical sense is not a detached entity like the Puruṣa, but exhibits the result of innumerable forces that have acted upon it in the course of its beginningless history. It is consequently not passive and does not remain a mere spectator of whatever happens to be presented to it, but is active and meddles with the external object as it apprehends it. It does not however, as in the Buddhistic view (p. 79), import through such meddling any new features into its notion of the object presented; it only *selects* certain aspects of it and omits the rest. According to this theory of selective apprehension all the characteristics that can ever be known of an object actually belong to it; and, if only some of them are apprehended by a particular person at a particular time, it is entirely due to subjective limitations. Things are thus really richer in their nature than they are ordinarily perceived to be. Since the kind of the selection made in the case of any object depends upon the past life or character of the person in question, a thing that attracts one may completely repel another. One and the same damsel, to cite the stock example, delights her lover but is a source of constant annoyance to her rivals in love. The aspect under which an individual perceives the world is thus intimately personal to him; yet the doctrine does not maintain, as the Yogācāra school of Buddhism does (p. 80), that there is no external reality at all. The different world-views are, no doubt, relative to the individual; but they, at the same time, point to an objective universe which is common to all and is real in its own right.[6] The chief argument in support of this realistic position is that, although there are differences among men in their views of things, there are as certainly points of agreement also among them. If there are occasions when each can speak only for himself, there are others when one can speak for all.

Here is an important feature of the system, for it neither sides with the view that things are precisely as they are apprehended, nor with the other which holds that the mind makes its own things. It avoids either extreme, and attaches equal importance to the subjective and objective factors in explaining the fact of experience. It is an external world that we know just as truly as the view, which each one of us has of it, is his own. Men obtrude their personalities into their judgements, and subjective prejudices undoubtedly affect their knowledge of things; yet they never create the things they perceive. But our knowledge, though pointing to an external universe, is one-sided. This is a fundamental defect of human experience. It may not indeed amount to an error of commission (p. 97), as it is according to the Nyāya-Vaiśeṣika (*anyathā-khyāti*); but it is partial knowledge and, so far as it is not recognized to be so, it becomes an error, though only an error of omission (*akhyāti*). This incomplete knowledge, with its natural over-emphasis on a part of what is apprehended, accounts for the conflicts and inconsistencies of life, whether they be found in the same person at different times or between different persons at the same time.

If all knowledge be thus imperfect in its very nature, what is truth? The doctrine holds that it is complete and comprehensive knowledge, in which one part supplements and corrects another. It is knowledge which knows no preferences or prejudices, and lays appropriate emphasis on all aspects of the objects known. Here it may be asked whether such knowledge is at all attainable, so long as its means continues to be the internal organ, which is a product of Prakṛti and therefore consists not merely of *sattva* but also of *rajas* and *tamas*. In answering this question, it is necessary to remember that it is not the internal organ as such that limits our view of the world in the manner described above; for, in its intrinsic nature, it is essentially *sāttvic* and is therefore specially fitted to be the means of revealing correctly all that is. Actually, however, *rajas* or *tamas* predominates in it as a result of the past history of the person to whom it belongs; and it is the relative predominance of either which accounts for whatever limitations it may possess as an organ of knowledge. By subduing these impediments to clear perception through proper self-discipline and restoring the internal organ to its natural purity, man may completely transform his outlook upon life and the world. *Rajas* and *tamas* cannot, of course, be entirely eliminated; but when the internal organ is purified or "the heart is cleansed," their presence will become quite harmless.

But it should not be imagined that this complete knowledge is merely an aggregate of all possible views of the physical world. It is rather experience in which they have all been integrated and, according to the explanation given of it by Patañjali,[7] is best described as intuitive. It is designated as "truth-bearing," and is not tainted even by the least error.

It conveys truth, the whole truth and nothing but the truth. It overcomes the idiosyncrasies of individual attitudes but it does so by a synthesis, not by a mere summation of them. In this synthetic view, which represents the climax of philosophic thought, all things are seen as they actually are; and he who succeeds in acquiring it becomes a spectator of all time and all existence. So soon as this whole and disinterested truth about the world dawns upon one's mind, one sees through Prakṛti and realises its absolute distinctness from Puruṣa. And it is a knowledge of this distinctness (*viveka-jñāna*) rather than that of the world as it is, that is stated here to be the means to release.[8] In other words, to know Prakṛti is to see through the empirical self; and when its true character is realized, Puruṣa comes into its own. Such knowledge is attainable in the present life; and it is the attainment of it that is the chief aim of life, according to the Sāṅkhya-Yoga. The whole realm of nature is conceived in the system as leading up to this consummation. It is designed for this, and exists solely for it. The noteworthy point here is that the physical accompaniment of man as well as his environment is neither hostile nor indifferent to his attaining the ideal of freedom. Through them rather, Prakṛti is ever educating him into a fuller knowledge of himself with a view to securing that result. Nature therefore cannot, in the end, be said to enslave spirit. In fact, it behaves towards man as a "veritable fairy godmother."

We are now in a position to understand the exact place of Prakṛti in the doctrine. The whole course of its evolution is determined by a purpose, and this purposive interpretation of nature makes Prakṛti meaningless in divorce from Puruṣa. Vācaspati goes so far as to state that, during the period of dissolution, Prakṛti is as good as not existing because it then functions for the good of no Puruṣa.[9] The changes in it are due not to a merely blind or mechanical interplay of the *guṇas*. In the words of Īśvara Kṛṣṇa, "Puruṣa's purpose is the sole cause of Prakṛti's evolution."[10] It takes on form and structure, in accordance with the needs of the self. The organ of sight, for example, comes into existence because it is necessary if Puruṣa is to see, and not simply because its constituent elements happen to combine in a certain manner. The purpose of Puruṣa, conceived as the end of evolution, is, as we have already stated, interpreted in terms of values which, in the case of man, may be broadly divided into the temporal and the eternal. The former are common worldly or secular values (*bhoga*) like the acquisition of wealth and the enjoyment of pleasure; and the latter is self-realization or escape from Prakṛti (*apavarga*). But they do not constitute a duality of purpose, for the approach to the ideal is necessarily through worldly life, the duration of which is determined by the moral and intellectual equipment of particular individuals. Whether it is for a longer or a shorter period, all alike have to pass through the trials and troubles of common life before their mind is turned towards the final goal. The truth implicit here is that man does not seriously think of spiritual freedom until he has learnt by his *own* experience the futility of secular values or is satiated with their attainment. It is only then that he will be able to revalue the values of life.

Before considering the nature of the practical discipline prescribed here for reaching the goal of life, it is necessary to say a few words about (1) *jñāna* or knowledge, in general, as conceived in the doctrine and (2) the *pramāṇas* accepted in it:

(1) As we have already stated (p. 97), two views of perception are possible. It may be held that objects are known directly or that we can know them only indirectly, through psychic media which in some way resemble or symbolize the objects in question. The present doctrine adopts the latter view, which may be described as "the theory of representative perception." Our explanation of the empirical self as a complex of Puruṣa and the internal organ will help us to understand what exactly is meant by this theory here. Knowledge, according to the doctrine, is a state or modification of the empirical self. But as Puruṣa, in itself, knows no change whatsoever, this modification must be solely of the internal organ. Since the Sāṅkhya-Yoga is realistic, the cognitive situation involves, according to it, not only Puruṣa and some modification of the internal organ but also an appropriate object. Off these three factors, the internal organ mediates or serves as a connecting link between Puruṣa and the object; and it is supposed to do so, by taking on a "form" which corresponds to the object to be apprehended. This form through which alone an object can be known, is called its mode (*vṛtti*); and knowledge means that mode as informed or illumined by the light of Puruṣa. It is thus neither the mode (*vṛtti*) by

itself, nor the illuminating principle by itself that perceives, but a blend of both. The illumination is a constant feature of all knowledge, but the modes vary in accordance with the objects presented. The chief weakness of this theory is that, while holding that objects can be known only mediately, it describes knowledge as bearing the impress of them. If objects are not directly accessible to us at all, it is clear that we can never speak of the forms, which the internal organ bears, as *corresponding* to those objects.

(2) The Śaṅkhya-Yoga admits only three *pramāṇas*, viz. perception, inference and verbal testimony, all of which have already been explained. It remains now only to refer to one variety of inference, to which we have not hitherto alluded. There are two types of reasoning generally recognised in Indian philosophy. The first of them is what is familiarly known as syllogistic inference (p. 100), and is illustrated by the example of deducing the existence of fire from perceiving smoke. We shall have an instance of the second type if, from the observed fact that an effect like a jar requires for its production a competent agent like the potter, it is concluded that the world, assuming it to be an effect, should also have been brought into existence by a competent Being, God. It is described in Sanskrit as inference based, not on perception like the previous one, but on what is "seen from likeness" (*sāmānyatodṛṣṭa*), and corresponds to analogical reasoning as dealt with in modern works on logic. It means that, while the first type is applicable only to cases falling within the sphere of common experience, the second applies to those that lie beyond it. The Sāṅkhya-Yoga accordingly utilizes this variety of inference in transcendental matters, thus restricting the scope of Vedic testimony considerably (p. 44). It is, for instance, through such inference that the existence of supersensuous Prakṛti is postulated. The doctrine appeals to the authority of scripture only where not even this type of inference is possible as, for example, in the case of the *order* in which the various principles up to the gross elements emerge from Prakṛti.[11] In the view of some, like the Vedāntins, such an extension of the scope of inference is not legitimate, for it can, at best, indicate not the certainty but only the probability of the conclusion drawn. We shall refer to this point again in a later chapter.

## II

The knowledge that we now have of the nature of Puruṣa will enable us to see why the ideal of life in this system is conceived as escape or aloofness (*kaivalya*) from Prakṛti. That is its intrinsic character. In this respect the Sāṅkhya-Yoga resembles the Nyāya-Vaiśeṣika. Both are equally gospels of sublime self-isolation (p. 103), the only difference being that the self in that condition is here regarded as continuing to be sentient or rather sentience, while it is not so regarded in the other. But this distinction is merely a theoretical one since, owing to the lack of appropriate means like the internal organ and the senses, it then remains even according to the present doctrine without any knowledge of its environment or, for the matter of that, of itself as in the other.

In its general features, the discipline for reaching this goal is the same as in the other systems. It consists of the cultivation of detachment and the practice of meditation, in addition to acquiring under proper guidance a knowledge of the ultimate truth and reflecting upon it. The discipline is only briefly touched upon in works on the Sāṅkhya, but it is fully set forth in those on the Yoga. If the one system has enlarged upon the theory the other has done the same in regard to the practical side of the teaching. But it should be added that the aim of meditation or *yoga* according to the present doctrine, is very different from that of Upanishadic *yoga*. It is not union here, but separation. There, it is believed, the individual self unites with or merges in the absolute self by means of *yoga* (p. 26); but here, where no such self is acknowledged, it comes to be by itself, through extrication from Prakṛti. Thus *yoga* which means "union" there, comes to mean "disunion" (*viyoga*) here.

The discipline comprises what are described as the eight "limbs" (*aṅgas*) or accessories of *yoga*. They are "self-restraint" (*yama*), "observance" (*niyama*), "posture" (*āsana*), "regulation of breath" (*prāṇāyāma*), "withdrawal of the senses" (*pratyāhāra*), "steadying the mind" (*dhāraṇā*), "contemplation" (*dhyāna*) and "meditative trance" (*samādhi*), Its purpose as a whole, is to assist man in the ascent from the narrow personal view congenital to him to the larger vision which brings freedom with it. This eightfold discipline may be considered in two stages:

(1) The first is concerned with the right direction of the will, and represents the attainment of the good as distinguished from the true. More particularly, it relates to the cultivation of virtues comprised in the first two steps of the discipline, viz. "self-restraint" (*yama*) and "observance" (*niyama*). The former is chiefly negative and consists of non-injury (*ahiṁsā*), truth-speaking (*satya*), abstention from stealing or misappropriation of others' property (*asteya*), celibacy (*brahma-carya*) and disowning of possessions (*aparigraha*). The latter is positive, and includes purity (*śauca*), contentment (*saṁtosa*), right aspiration (*tapas*), study of philosophic texts (*syādhyāya*) and devotion to God (*Īśvar-praṇidhāna*). These together may be described as the ten commandments of the Sāṅkhya-Yoga. It is on this pre-eminently moral foundation that any *yogic* training should rest, if it is to be fruitful; and the mere practice of breath-control or of *yogic* postures is spiritually of little avail. Without such a foundation, there is no possibility of seeing the whole truth or of attaining final freedom. He, on the other hand, who lays that foundation securely, even though he may stop short at it, will have achieved much. The key-word to this stage of the discipline is impersonality. Man must overcome the egoistic impulses in him which are the source of so much evil in the world (p. 105). The impersonal attitude thereby attained is described as "dispassion" (*vairāgya*), and its cultivation is recommended in order to awaken the spiritual will. It is described as "lower" (*apara*) detachment to distinguish it from the "higher" (*para*), which does not appear till full enlightenment has come and unselfishness becomes spontaneous. In fact, as Vyāsa observes, this higher detachment is hardly distinguishable from complete enlightenment.[12]

(2) The next stage of the discipline, consisting of the remaining six items, is for the specific cultivation of the power of mental concentration. Its details being somewhat technical, we shall refer here only to its broad features. Of these six items, the first three are devised to secure control of the physical frame with a view to facilitate the control of the mind. They refer, as already noted, to right bodily posture, regulation of breath and the withdrawal of the senses from their respective objects. The succeeding three assist in getting a direct, but gradual, mastery over the ever fitful mind. Any object may be chosen

for meditating upon in this stage; only a gradation of them is recommended in order that the more subtle may come after success has been attained in contemplating the less. When such control over the mind has been established, the disciple turns to direct meditation on the Sāṅkhya-Yoga truth. This is the culminating stage of *yoga*, which leads to the "truthbearing" knowledge mentioned above. It should be practised in two grades: The first is calculated to transform that truth from being merely mediately known into an immediate intuition. The disciple in this form of *samādhi*, remains conscious (as shown by its description as *saṁprajñāta*) of having attained the discriminative knowledge which is the means to release; but, in the next step (*asaṁprajñāta*) he transcends it; and the condition has been described as "sleepless sleep." As in sleep, one becomes here oblivious of the world and even of his own existence as an individual; but yet it is not a blank, since Puruṣa exists then with its effulgence all unobscured. In this final stage, all operations of the internal organ are suspended and spirit returns to itself, so to speak. The disciple then becomes a *jīvanmukta*. Between any two such states of *yogic* ecstasy, he will live the life to which he has become accustomed through long self-discipline; but because he is virtually divorced from Prakṛti, he will then remain "far from passion, pain and guilt."

There is one point in the above account which requires a word of explanation. We have mentioned devotion to God as an item in the earlier stage of the discipline; but we have not, so far, referred to his place in the doctrine at all. Of the two systems which we are here considering, the Sāṅkhya in its classical form is definitely atheistic. It believes in the permanence and supremacy of spirit, but knows nothing of God. Here it shows its rationalistic bias, for no convincing logical proof, as is well known, can be given of his existence. The Sāṅkhya, no doubt, like the other Indian systems, is essentially a philosophy of values (p. 50). But according to its teachers, all that is presupposed by the reality of the higher or eternal values is the immortality of the individual spirit. This is well indicated by the manner in which the teleological argument, already referred to, is utilized here. It is regarded not as implying a designer, but as pointing to one who benefits by the design. The Sāṅkhya concludes from the presence in nature of means adapted to the accomplishment of ends, not to God as their author, but to the self for whom it supposes them to exist. It thus accepts design, but denies a conscious designer. The Yoga system, on the other hand, postulates the existence of God (*Īśvara*) over and above that of Puruṣa. The allusion to God appears in our account of the course of discipline because, as we remarked before, it is entirely taken over from that system. Devotion to God would consequently have no place in the discipline which is strictly in conformity with the Sāṅkhya teaching. Here is one of the important differences between the two doctrines to which reference was made in the beginning of the chapter.

But the conception of God (*Īśvara*) here is vastly different from that of the Upanishads (p. 30). To begin with, he is here *one* of the Puruṣas so that, though eternal and omnipresent, he is not all-comprehensive. There are other Puruṣas as well as Prakṛti to limit his being. Nor is it a conception resembling that of God in the Nyāya-Vaiśeṣika (p. 89), since he is not responsible, in the ordinary sense of the term, for the creation of the world which, as we know, is the spontaneous work of Prakṛti. All that he is stated to do is to prompt, in a way, the evolution of Prakṛti or to bring about its connection with Puruṣa needed for the evolution. The argument for his existence is that the gradation of knowledge, power and such other excellences which we notice in men necessarily suggests a Being who possesses those excellences in a superlative form. In thus interpreting the mere notion of a perfect Being as implying its actual existence, Patañjali is relying on what is known in Western philosophy as the ontological argument. It is that necessary Being which is called God. He is accordingly a perfect Puruṣa and has always been so. He embodies in himself all that is good and great, and the conception is personal. He is therefore unique; and even the liberated Puruṣas do not stand on the same footing, for he has never known, like them, the trammels of *saṁsāra*. On account of his perfection, he serves as a pattern to man in regard to what he might achieve. In this respect, he resembles a *guru* who ought, likewise, to be an embodiment of the ideal. It is devotion to God so conceived that is meant by the last of the ten commandments, and it signifies a complete surrender of oneself to him. The practice of such a spirit of self-surrender places the coping stone, as it were, on the discipline for the cultivation of unselfishness.

According to the training so far described for attaining spiritual aloofness, devotion to God occupies a subordinate place. Its practice has to be followed by the discipline of the remaining six "limbs" (*aṅgas*), beginning with bodily postures (*āsana*) and ending with mental concentration (*samādhi*). Patañjali recognizes not only this discipline for securing freedom, but also an alternative one of devotion to God (Īśvara) and communion with him which, without all the elaborate preparation of *yoga*, qualifies for release.[13] That is, apart from serving as an ideal, God, out of his abundant mercy which is one of his perfections, sympathizes with suffering men and helps them in attaining spiritual freedom, if they only trust in him and meditate upon him. It is described as the easier of the two paths, obviously for those who can rest in faith; and it corresponds to the "path of devotion" (*bhakti-yoga*) to which we alluded (p. 56) in connection with the Gītā. This duality of the discipline as well as the little importance which the path of devotion attaches to what is so essential to the Sāṅkhya, viz. knowledge of the ultimate truth, suggests that belief in a supreme God is not organic to the doctrine.

From what has been stated so far, it is clear that the conception of Prakṛti is entirely teleological. If it served only a single purpose, viz. securing for Puruṣa either empirical values (*bhoga*) or eternal freedom (*apavarga*) we might regard it as its very nature to do so, though even then its constant and consistent pursuit of that end would not altogether be devoid of reference to a mind behind it. But actually it serves both these purposes. It is thus not a static teleology that characterizes Prakṛti. This implies a capacity on the part of Prakṛti to choose between the two, according to the needs of particular individuals.[14] No doubt, these do not constitute a duality of purpose, for one of them, as we have stated, invariably subserves the other. But even so, they imply that Prakṛti is able to adjust its activities differently to meet the needs of different Puruṣas; and that, in the case of any single Puruṣa, it can replace one aim by the other at the psychologically appropriate moment. Now these adjustments are inexplicable without a mental or spiritual factor capable of exercising choice. There is, indeed, such a factor recognized in the doctrine, viz. Puruṣa; but it is conceived as external to Prakṛti and wholly passive. Here we see a contradiction in the doctrine—insentient Prakṛti being able to exercise choice. The analogy of the blind man and the cripple, by which this view is supported, is hopelessly inapposite, for there both are intelligent and can therefore well co-operate with each other; but here, because one of the two is not so, no such co-operation is possible. A ready way of avoiding this difficulty is to assume a transcendent God, who directs the operations of Prakṛti *ab extra* in accordance with the deserts of particular Puruṣas. But such an assumption is against the very fundamentals of the doctrine, at all events, of the Sāṇkhya phase of it.

Is there any explanation of this glaring discrepancy? It appears possible to explain it in two ways: The first is to assume a spiritual element immanent in Prakṛti as a whole, which prompts and completely guides its evolutionary course from within. It would not then be nature that "wills" the salvation of Puruṣa but spirit or, if we like to put it so, spirit together with nature that does so. This assumption would satisfactorily account for the rational order discoverable in nature. Life is a struggle to attain true freedom eventually; and, if man pursues lower values at first, it is due to his ignorance of the ultimate truth. But that would be the teaching of the Upanishads (p. 24) in one of its two forms (*Brahma-pariṇāma-vāda*); and the doctrine in its present form would then have to be explained as derived from it. The Śvetāśvatara Upanishad, in fact, describes God as "hidden in his own *guṇas*."[15] This integral view of ultimate reality found in the Upanishads, we must take it, has been meddled with here as a result of dualistic bias; and spirit has been separated from nature, rendering the whole doctrine unintelligible. Its failure to account satisfactorily for the co-operation between Puruṣa and Prakṛti is the natural consequence of this forced separation of the two. Such an explanation also throws light on the names given to some of the evolutes of Prakṛti like "intellect" (*mahat*), "egoism" (*ahaṁkāra*), etc. As cosmic entities, they would then represent the psychic organs of the *universal* self which is immanent in Prakṛti as a whole. But as the notion of such a self was dropped when the doctrine emerged from the Upanishadic teaching, their designations naturally came to be quite arbitrary and perplexing. The other explanation is to suppose that the system was originally purely naturalistic (p. 57), and that the notion of Puruṣa or spirit, for which there is really no need by the side of self-evolving and self-regulating Prakṛti, was imported into it on the analogy of other doctrines.

Chapter Six

# PŪRVA-MĪMĀṀSĀ

*

WE now enter upon the study of the systems that are primarily based on Vedic authority; and they are two—one upholding the teaching contained in the earlier portions of the Veda, particularly the Brāhmaṇas; and the other, that contained in the later portions of it, viz. the Upanishads. They are, for this reason, respectively called Pūrva-Mīmāṁsā and Uttara-Mīmāṁsā. The name "mīmāṁsā," given to these systems, means systematic investigation, and shows the important place assigned to reflection (*vicāra*), in India even in the doctrines based upon revelation. The ultimate appeal in them may not be to reason: but, at the same time, they do not signify a blind reliance on untested and unsupported authority.[1] They may consequently be taken as rationalistic in practice, though not in theory. Dr. Randle ascribes this feature of the orthodox schools of thought to the circumstance that they had to face in Buddhism "a vigorous opposition which pressed free enquiry to the extreme limits of scepticism" and that it had to be met with its own weapons, which were perception and inference. "The fortunate result of this," he adds, was that the trammels of authority did not prevent the orthodox thinker from following where the argument leads."[2] We shall be concerned in this chapter with the Pūrva-Mīmāṁsā or, as it is usually called briefly, Mīmāṁsā.

In its origin, the doctrine goes back to the Brāhmaṇa period. The works of that period discuss various questions relating to ritual—although, for the most part, only in their bearing on particular ceremonies—by means of which one might win some specific good or avoid some specific evil. The very word "brāhmaṇa," it will be recalled, stands for the considered opinion of a priest of recognized authority (p. 14). The results of these discussions were systematized and considerably amplified in later times as shown by the important class of literature known as

Kalpa Sūtras (p. 36) which, in the words of Max Muller, serve as "a kind of grammar of the Vedic ceremonial." But it remained essentially a system of ritual exposition. In still later times, owing obviously to the conspicuous development of other systems of philosophy, the Mīmāṁsā also came to be a fully fledged philosophic doctrine with its own ontology and epistemology in addition to being a systematization of ritual.

The literature of the system is vast. Its primary source is represented by the Sūtra of Jaimini (*circa* 300–200 B.C.), which consists of 12 chapters divided into 60 "quarters" (*pādas*) or sections. It considers about a thousand topics, so that it is by far the biggest of the philosophic Sūtras. It is also perhaps the oldest among them. The earliest commentary on it which has come down to us, is by Śabara Svāmin (400 A.D.); and it has been explained in two somewhat different ways by Kumārila Bhaṭṭa and Prabhākara, otherwise known as Guru. This has resulted in a schism among the followers of the doctrine, separating them into two schools. The period when these glosses were composed is not quite definitely known; but it is believed, with much probability, that both of those thinkers wrote in the seventh century A.D. Kumārila's work has been printed almost in its entirety; but the work of the other is available only partly, and even of that part a fragment alone has seen the light so far.

## I

This doctrine may be compared to the Nyāya-Vaiśeṣika in that it is pluralistic and realistic (p. 85). Like it, it believes in the existence of a plurality of souls, and a multiplicity of material ultimates underlying the physical universe. But there are also important differences between the doctrines, as we shall soon see. The two schools of Mīmāṁsā again, to which we have just alluded, while agreeing with each other in various respects, exhibit certain differences in fundamentals. But we shall confine our attention here to the doctrine as propounded by the more influential of the two thinkers, viz., Kumārila, and refer only to a few points in the other doctrine, which are unique in the whole history of Indian thought.

Of the seven categories formulated in the Nyāya-Vaiśeṣika (p. 94), the Mīmāṁsā accepts five, viz. substance, quality, action, universals and non-existence; and it rejects the remaining two—*samavāya* and *viśeṣa*, which, as pointed out before, are nothing more than arbitrary assumptions rendered necessary by certain postulates of that doctrine. In the place of the former is here postulated a relation which is of a quite different kind and points to a fundamental divergence from the metaphysical position of the Nyāya-Vaiśeṣika. The present doctrine holds that existents like substance and attribute or the particular and the universal are not totally distinct (p. 88), but distinct while being the same. If they were entirely different, it is argued, they should be separable; but they are not, as admitted even in the Nyāya-Vaiśeṣika. In this view then, such existents together form an identity in difference (*bhedābheda*), a conception which we have already come across in connection with Jainism (p. 65), and the Sāṅkhya-Yoga (p. 109). This relation is termed *tādātmya*. The word literally means "identity"; but all identity, according to Kumārila, is identity in difference. It is because they are identical that we are able to predicate qualities (say) of substances. We say, for example, "The rose *is* red." But they are not absolutely the same, since a quality is not a substance. It is not right, Kumārila says, to postulate absolute difference wherever the notion of *two* arises, or absolute unity wherever the notion of *one* does. Things may be distinct in so far as they are experienced thus: "This is one, and that is another"; but they may also, at the same time, be one in so far as they are experienced as "This is *not other* (*ananya*) than that." This way of viewing things, it is clear, compromises in a large measure the pluralism of the doctrine, and shows that it is not radically pluralistic as the Nyāya-Vaiśeṣika is.

As regards the first of these categories, viz. substance, the Mīmāṁsā admits all the nine which the Nyāya-Vaiśeṣika does (p. 92); and it adds two more to them. They are "darkness" (*tamas*) and "sound" (*śabda*). Of the latter, the first is explained in the Nyāya-Vaiśeṣika as mere absence of light and the second as a quality of *ākāśa*. Elaborate arguments are adduced here to justify their inclusion under the head of substance; but they do not seem to be more than curiosities of Indian speculation, and need not therefore be recounted here. Regarding the substances accepted in both the doctrines, it will suffice to refer only to two points:

(1) The first concerns the atomic theory. We know that the Nyāya-Vaiśeṣika postulates (p. 88) indivisible and supersensuous particles as the ultimate cause of all the material products found in the universe. Kumārila, while recognizing this pluralistic basis of the physical universe, maintains that there is no need to push our analysis of common objects so far and stops at sensible particles such as the motes seen in the rays of the sun, corresponding to the triads of the other systems. The Nyāya-Vaiśeṣika upholds its belief on the strength of inference which, it avers, is attested by the insight of seers (p. 99). But Kumārila, as a Mīmāṁsaka, does not, as we have seen, recognize the latter (p. 44); and he takes exception to the use of inference, for upsetting the result of well-established facts of perception.[3] We cannot employ logic, he says, to defeat common sense. Where a matter is really supersensuous, our source of knowledge, according to him, is neither inference nor the insight of the so-called seers, but revelation; and revelation, he adds, is silent about the existence of atoms such as are accepted in the Nyāya-Vaiśeṣika. The ultimate particles he postulates of the four elements—earth, water, fire and air—are not thus indivisible, and possess finite magnitude so that they are not strictly atomic at all. Kumārila differs from the view taken in the Nyāya-Vaiśeṣika not only in regard to the precise magnitude of the ultimate material of the world of common experience, but also in regard to the nature of the relation between these particles and the wholes derived from them. This relation is, on the analogy of that between substance and attribute, explained as an identity in difference (p. 88). Whole and parts are not accordingly absolutely distinct, but distinct while being the same.

(2) The second point is the conception of the self. Although in general agreement with the Nyāya-Vaiśeṣika view here, the Mīmāṁsā differs from it in some essential respects. The self is all-pervading and eternal in both the doctrines. In both again, it is directly cognized by *manas*. But the manner in which it comes to be known is differently conceived. In the Nyāya-Vaiśeṣika, it is perceivable not along with the objects perceived

but subsequently and as the result of a separate effort. If an observer knows an object at one instant he may, if he so wills, become aware of himself as knowing it at a later instant. The character of the former knowledge, if it refers to a table, say, is expressible as "This is a *table*" and that of the latter as "*I* see a table." If the observer does not care for such "after-knowledge" (*anuvyavasāya*) (p. 91), as it is termed, it does not arise at all, so that a person who apprehends an object need not actually realise that *he* is doing so. That is, consciousness of objects does not imply self-consciousness, according to the Nyāya-Vaiśeṣika. But here it does, and the self is taken to be revealed whenever any object is known. The knowledge, as it arises, of a table, for instance, is therefore expressible as "I see a table"—a form which, is it stated, involves two notions —the "I-notion" and the "table-notion." Just as the table is the content of the latter, the self is the content of the former.

Though the self is thus known invariably at the time when any object is known, it is not known, as one may wrongly suppose, as the *subject* or agent in the act of knowing but only as the *object* of its own notion. It is conceived here as both subject and object—subject in so far as it *knows*, and object in so far as it *is known*. This, it is pointed out, is evident from the familiar experience "I know myself." It may appear contradictory to say that one and the same self can be both the subject and the object of one and the same cognitive act, but such contradictions do not affect the reality of things, according to Kumārila. The ultimate source of our knowledge of reality, he says, is experience; and when it vouches for the existence of contradictory features in a thing, we are fully justified in attributing them to it (p. 65). How the self comes to be known as the subject also, we shall explain presently.

The specific qualities characterizing the self are the same as in the other doctrine (p. 91), excepting only that *dharma* and *adharma* are not among them here. To the Mīmāṁsā explanation of them, we shall advert later. Of the remaining six qualities, viz. knowledge, desire, hate, pleasure, pain and volition, the last five are taken to be internally perceivable as in the Nyāya-Vaiśeṣika (p. 91). The first, viz. knowledge, is disclosed, according to that doctrine, to introspection and is therefore directly known. Here, on the other hand, it is only to be inferred. This is the result of a difference in the conception of its nature, which we shall now proceed to explain.

The reader will recall that, according to the Nyāya-Vaiśeṣika, knowledge is a quality belonging to the self. Here the view is that it is an activity of the self. It represents a process in the self, and implies that the latter undergoes a change in knowing objects. This process directly leads to the revelation or manifestation of the object in question, so that what the Nyāya-Vaiśeṣika conceives as one or as occurring in a flash, is here thought of in two stages—as process and result. The reason for thus splitting up into two what is usually taken to be one is that knowledge, involving as it does a relation between two things, subject and object, affects both when it arises. To view it from the standpoint of only one of them and describe it as arising in the self would not therefore adequately represent its nature. The cognitive process is naturally supersensuous, taking place as it does in so subtle an entity as the self; but its existence can be inferred from the fact of the revelation of the object to which it leads. This is why *jñāna*, as a process, is stated to be inferable here. The result to which it leads, viz. manifestedness (*prākaṭya*), is directly known, but as characterizing the object manifested. As the term "subject" means one that knows or has knowledge, it or the "I" as the agent in the act of knowing can obviously be known only after knowledge is known. Hence the subject *as such* is also known through inference, and not, as in the Nyāya-Vaiśeṣika, through introspection. It is therefore objects alone that are *directly* apprehended, and not either the subject or knowledge. The relation between *jñāna* and the self, we may add, is one of identity in difference. In this respect, the present doctrine resembles Jainism (p. 62), although its conception of knowledge as a whole is very different.

Before leaving the topic of the self, we have to point out another difference from the Nyāya-Vaiśeṣika view of it. The latter recognizes a supreme self or God in addition to individual selves. This distinction is not acknowledged here. In fact, elaborate arguments are adduced by Kumārila to show that there can be no self of the kind, possessing omniscience and such other super-excellences. We cannot, for example, satisfactorily account for the presence, it is said, of misery in a world created by an omnipotent and benevolent God.[4] This difficulty is commonly explained in Indian doctrines by reference to the past karma of living beings; but the Mīmāṁsaka contends that, if karma is thus necessary for a satisfactory explanation of the problem of evil, even after recognizing God, it may well be taken to furnish its full explanation (p. 61). As a consequence of declining to acknowledge a Creator, the doctrine looks upon the world as having had no beginning and as going to have no end. It thus rejects the theory of cycles put forward in so many other systems. That is to say, the world is self-existent. Origin, growth and decay are features characterizing individual things in it; but the physical universe, as a whole, "was never other than what it is now."[5] There is clearly a touch of naturalism here. "Wherefore God?," the Mīmāṁsaka says, "The world itself suffices for itself."[6] But it should be added that, as we observed in connection with the Sāṅkhya system (p. 124), to deny the existence of God is not to discard the higher values; for the doctrine, unlike materialism, believes in surviving souls and in the theory of karma. Its belief in the latter, indeed, signifies a much greater emphasis on the ethical order of the universe than what we find in most theistic doctrines with their reliance on divine grace as a means of salvation.

Like the Nyāya-Vaiśeṣika, this system also postulates 24 qualities, but with a few modifications. Thus it omits from the list "sound" which it classes under substance; and, as already pointed out, also *dharma* and *adharma*. Of the new qualities introduced in their place, it will suffice for our purpose to say a few words about only one, viz. "potency" (*śakti*). By potency is meant the causal power characterizing things, like the burning capacity of fire. It cannot be perceived, but its existence can be inferred from the effect it produces. In doctrines like the Nyāya-Vaiśeṣika, this power is identified with the thing itself which serves as the cause. But the Mīmāṁsaka raises certain objections to it. For instance, such identification would mean the necessary manifestation or emergence of the effect wherever and whenever the thing in question is present. But this is not verified in experience. It may, for example, have been ascertained that the absorption of a certain substance by a living organism will destroy its life. If a suitable antidote, however, is administered in time, it may prevent death, though the poison itself, it is said, continues to be present—a circumstance which shows that the substance in question and its killing power are not identical. Opponents of this view ward off such objections by explaining the *absence* of counter-agents, like the antidote in the above example, as a condition necessary for the causal factor to operate at all. It is not therefore right, according to them, to represent the cause as functioning by itself or before all the needed conditions, both positive and negative, are fulfilled.

In respect of the remaining three categories, there is not much to add to what has been said in the chapter on the Nyāya-Vaiśeṣika. We may only observe that universals, as conceived by Kumārila, are of two kinds. A universal may be what is common to two or more objects; or it may be what endures through two or more phases of a changing object. The difference between the two kinds, as already pointed out (p. 66), is that in the one the attributive element, say "cowness," is the same, while the substances, viz. the individual cows, vary; and in the other, the substantive element is the same, while the attributes vary, as in the case of a tree passing through many stages in the process of its growth. Here we find the twofold view of universals—abstract and concrete—to which we drew attention in dealing with Jainism. The Nyāya-Vaiśeṣika which, unlike the present doctrine, refuses to take a dynamic view of things naturally recognizes only the former type of universals and not the latter (p. 94).

To sum up: The conception of a thing in the doctrine is that of a one-many. It continues to be the same, though it has many aspects which may vary. To speak of the qualities or aspects of things and of the things themselves as altogether separate in the manner in which the Nyāya-Vaiśeṣika does (p. 93), is to indulge in a pure abstraction. These qualities or aspects may coexist or succeed one another in time. A tree has its colour, its shape, etc., all at the same time; but it has also, in the process of its growth, passed through several stages and has been a tendril and a seedling. Whether the attributes are of the one kind or of the other, their relation to the substance is one of identity in difference. Further, in the case of two or more attributes characterizing a thing, say the whiteness and cowness of a cow, they are identical in so far as they are the same with the cow, but are different as a quality and a universal.

That is, there is substantial unity between them, and multiplicity as attributes. They are both one and different, but from different standpoints. To speak thus of a thing as a one-many, however, is only to characterize it from the positive side. Every thing has a negative side also in so far as it is distinguishable from others. A rose may have its own colour, fragrance, etc., as its positive characteristics; but it is at the same time distinct from a lily. Unless we apprehend a thing in both these ways, the doctrine holds, we cannot be said to know it fully. To be a thing, it must be definite; and a mere positive description is not adequate to define it, for a thing can be truly known as that which it is only by being distinguished from that which it is not. This is the meaning of Kumārila's saying "All things are positive from their own standpoint, but negative from that of others (*sadasadātmaka*)."[7]

The Mīmāṁsā, like the Nyāya-Vaiśeṣika (p. 97), rejects the theory of representative perception. It accepts six *pramāṇas* altogether, including perception, inference and verbal testimony. We shall draw attention to certain important features of testimony in general and of scriptural testimony in particular, as understood in the present doctrine, before explaining the nature of the new *pramāṇas* acknowledged in it. That the Mīmāṁsaka does not recognize what is described as "transcendental perception" in the Nyāya-Vaiśeṣika system, we have already mentioned (p. 44).

In a previous chapter (p. 98), we referred to a discussion respecting the nature of knowledge which occupies a large space in all controversial works on Indian philosophy. The discussion, to state it very briefly, relates to the question whether knowledge is *presumably* valid or invalid.[8] There are adherents of both these views among Indian thinkers. Thus the followers of the Nyāya-Vaiśeṣika maintain that the validity or invalidity of knowledge can be established only *ab extra* and that, by itself, it vouches for neither. To repeat the illustration already given, the only means of finding out whether there is water or no, when we think we perceive it in front of us, is by appealing to another experience. If it quenches our thirst, for instance, we may conclude that our knowledge is valid. In general terms, it is the successfulness of the practical activity to which knowledge leads that determines its validity. Here naturally one may raise the important objection that, if such be the mode of validating knowledge, its validity can never be finally established, for the knowledge which validates would itself require verification. The answer to this objection given in the Nyāya-Vaiśeṣika is that, although strictly speaking this method of verifying knowledge through successful effort (*saṁvādi-pravṛtti*) becomes an infinite process, one or two tests of the kind at the most are, in practice, sufficient and that often in matters of everyday experience no test at all is required. The answer, based as it is on a purely practical consideration, is hardly satisfactory from the logical standpoint. By the easy manner in which the followers of the doctrine are satisfied with the test, they seem tacitly to subscribe to the view that knowledge is presumably valid.

The Buddhists think that the presumption regarding knowledge is that it is false, and that we cannot take it as valid unless satisfactory evidence of it is forthcoming. It is this ultra-sceptical view that explains why even the realists among them deny being to so much that is given in common experience (p. 79) and is accepted as real by so many philosophers. The Mīmāṁsaka holds the exactly opposite view, viz. that knowledge by its very nature is valid. It comes into being solely with a view to acquaint us with objects, and to question its validity will therefore be to question the very purpose of its existence. Doubtless it, not unoften, strays from truth. But the reason for it is always found to be not in itself but in some outside interference. The interference may be due to some defect in the means to or conditions of knowledge such as the senses, the presence of sufficient light and so forth. It is only when we suspect some such interference that we come to doubt the validity of a piece of knowledge and set about verifying it. Another circumstance that throws doubt on the same is when one item of knowledge, hitherto admitted as valid, is discovered to be in conflict with another. Then, and not till then, do we try to find out which of them it is that is really valid. These two, viz. (1) suspicion of defect in the means to and conditions of knowledge or, to state the same more generally, in its source and (2) the contradiction of it by other knowledge engender doubt and suggest the need for investigation. In the absence of either of these reasons, knowledge is presumed to be true.

Here the Mīmāṁsakas show a clearer appreciation of the realistic position than the adherents of the Nyāya-Vaiśeṣika, who by holding that *all* knowledge alike needs validation, compromise their realism to a very considerable extent.[9]

The chief bearing of this discussion is on the validity of the Veda; and there is a radical divergence between the Nyāya and the Mīmāṁsā conceptions of it. To the Naiyāyika, the knowledge derived through the Veda is, by itself, neither valid nor invalid; and if he yet regards it as absolutely valid, it is because of the fact that God, the all-knowing and the all-beneficent, is its author (p. 101). This is in accordance with his theory of the extraneous validity of knowledge. In other words, there is nothing in the Veda *as such* to prevent our entertaining doubts about the correctness of its teaching. All verbal testimony, in fact all testimony, needs to be properly validated before being accepted (p. 98), although in practice we may not always resort to such proof. The Veda, however, is necessarily valid since it proceeds from God, who is both wise and good in the completest sense of these terms. According to Kumārila also, who recognizes no God, the Veda is valid, but because, as knowledge, validity is inherent in it. There is certainly such a thing as error; but neither of the two reasons for suspecting it is found in the present case. In the first place, there is no possibility of vitiation at the source, for the Veda, according to the Mīmāṁsā, is not the work of any person, human or divine, and has therefore no source at all. Nor is there any likelihood of our experience coming into conflict with its teaching for, by hypothesis, it refers to supersensuous matters exclusively (p. 44). That is, the Veda is taken to teach only truth because it is self-existent, and because the scope of its teaching is strictly confined to matters beyond the reach of common human experience. In this latter respect, it satisfies his definition of valid knowledge (*pramā*) which includes, as we shall soon see, the condition of novelty.

The outcome of this view is the division of the Veda into two parts, one of which (*vidhi*) refers to supra-mundane affairs and has to be understood *literally*, and the other (*artha-vāda*) which, roughly speaking, relates to matters of ordinary experience. The latter carries with it no logical significance in the strict sense of the expression, for it merely reiterates facts otherwise known to us already as, for example, when it says "Heat destroys cold." Where, however, statements in this part of the Veda contradict common human experience, it rightly holds that preference should be given to the latter. Only, since the Veda cannot give expression to what is false or irrelevant, such statements are not discarded but are interpreted *liberally*—as one might say in contrast, and related to some supersensuous matter taught in the context in question. Their purpose generally is to flatter man into the doing of good deeds or to frighten him out of evil ones. "The sacrificial post is the sun," for intance, is a saying which occurs in the Veda. Being a patent contradiction, the identity affirmed here between the post and the sun is explained as merely a glorifying of the post with a view to commend the sacrifice in the performance of which it is utilized.[10] In other words, the contradictions that may be found in the Veda are only apparent; and they cease to appear so, the moment we rightly interpret it.

It is chiefly in connection with determining what portions fall under these two heads that the Mīmāṁsā lays down canons of interpretation, which are of great value not only to those who want to understand the Veda aright but also to all who are engaged in the work of finding out the exact import of fixed texts like legal codes. This interpretative aspect of the Mīmāṁsā system or its treatment of the logic of language, as we might put it, is as important as the two already mentioned, viz. its ritualistic and philosophic ones. To state the purpose of revelation as interpreted according to these canons is, as has been recognized by Indian thinkers for a long time, to convey to us a knowledge of *dharma* and *mokṣa* which are the two supreme values of life (p. 44). Of these two values, the doctrine we are now considering is mainly concerned with the former.

Thus the central features of the Mīmāṁsā view of the Veda are (1) that it is self-existent or eternal, (2) that it is concerned essentially with supersensuous matters and (3) that it includes portions requiring to be interpreted not literally but liberally. This ingenious view is defended by a series of arguments into which it is not necessary to enter here. It will suffice to remark that they involve a good deal of scholastic subtlety and that the conclusion to which they lead is, on the whole, far from convincing to the modern mind.

We may now briefly explain the nature of the three new *pramāṇas* accepted by Kumārila:

(1) Comparison (*upamāna*): It will be remembered that this *pramāṇa* is recognized in the Nyāya also; but we did not explain it in dealing with that system, since it is not of much logical significance as conceived there (p. 99). Its conception here is different. It consists in cognizing anew in an object, not presented to the senses, similarity to an object which is being actually perceived. Thus when a person sees a gayal and is struck with its similarity to a cow which is familiar to him, he is able to conclude therefrom that the cow also resembles a gayal. This view supposes that the similarity in the two cases is numerically distinct. That is, it takes for granted that if A is similar to B, the similarity of A to B is not identically the same as the similarity of B to A. This *pramāṇa* is not perception, since the cow, in which the similarity with the gayal is found, is not perceived at the time of forming this judgement. It is not inference, for, if it were, it would mean that one of the two similarities involved was the sign or mark of another. But neither can serve that purpose, for the similarity of the gayal to the cow is not, as a mark should be, in the cow which is the "minor term" or the subject of the conclusion; and the similarity of the cow to the gayal remains yet to be known at the time. Nor is it mere memory, for the simple reason that the similarity in question, by hypothesis, has not been previously apprehended. We may point out, however, that though this *pramāṇa* is not syllogistic inference, it reduces itself to what in modern logic is described as "immediate inference by reciprocal relations."

(2) Presumption (*arthāpatti*) : This signifies the discovery of a new fact or the postulation of a new truth, as the result of a contradiction between two other truths that are known to be well established. To give an example, trivial in itself but typical: If we know for certain that A is alive but is not in his house, we conclude that he is elsewhere. This really means the construction of a suitable hypothesis to account for the apparent discrepancy between two well-attested facts. That the conclusion so formulated is correct is quite obvious. It is on this *pramāṇa*, for instance, that the Mīmāṁsaka rests his belief in the survival

of the self after death. The Veda promises rewards for the performance of various rites; but those rewards are often stated to be reaped in a future life, and not immediately after the sacrificial acts are over. Since the person who reaps the fruit of a good or bad deed cannot, according to the doctrine of karma, be other than the one that did it, the Mīmāṁsaka concludes that the self should survive the body.[11] Some Indian logicians, like the Naiyāyikas, bring this *pramāṇa* under what, in modern terminology, may be described as "disjunctive reasoning." It is deducible, according to them, from the disjunctive proposition "A person who is alive must be *either* in his house *or* outside it," since no third alternative is possible.

(3) Non-apprehension (*anupalabdhi*): We have, so far, referred to five *pramāṇas* which are the means of knowing positive facts. The absence of any one of them in regard to an object or an aspect of it justifies, it is maintained, the conclusion that that object or aspect of it does not exist, provided that it is fit for being apprehended only by the *pramāṇa* in question and that all the conditions of apprehension, such as the presence of sufficient light in the case of ocular perception, are known to be satisfied. Let us suppose that the required conditions are fulfilled in respect of a visible object, an umbrella in a room where it is expected to be found, and yet that it is not seen. We may then conclude, as in fact we actually do, that the umbrella is not there. When therefore all the five *pramāṇas* fail to present an object (though it may be practically far from easy to know when this happens), Kumārila holds that the absolute non-existence of it may be deduced. This is the significance of "non-apprehension'. as a separate *pramāṇa* for knowing what are called "negative facts" (*abhāva*).

It will be remembered that the Nyāya-Vaiśeṣika ascribes the knowledge of the non-existence of a perceivable object to perception, and that of all others to inference (p. 96). The eye which reveals an umbrella when it is presented to it, also reveals its absence when it is not so presented, assuming that every condition required except the presence of the object is satisfied. According to Kumārila, this view is wrong, for it is impossible to think of the *absence* of a thing as in contact with a sensory organ—a condition which is admitted to be essential to perception. The inconceivability of non-existence being perceivable necessarily excludes the possibility of its being inferable, since inference is eventually based upon perception. Hence the need, it is argued, for recognizing a sixth *pramāṇa*.

Here we may point out an important difference between the two schools of Mīmāṁsā. The recognition of this *pramāṇa* implies the recognition of "non-existence" (*abhāva*) as a separate category. But the Prābhākaras explain every form of non-existence in a positive manner (p. 95). Thus they represent a table as the "mutual non-existence" of the chair (say), and the piece of wood out of which it is made as its "prior non-existence." [12] They accordingly reject "non-apprehension," and accept only the remaining five *pramāṇas*.[13] As a consequence, they acknowledge but four out of the five categories admitted by Kumārila. They add four more categories, making a total of eight; but it is not necessary to refer to any of them, beyond saying that the one-sided relation of *samavāya*, understood very much as in the Nyāya-Vaiśeṣika (p. 89), is one of them. Its acceptance implies that the Prābhākaras regard substance and attribute, and parts and whole, as quite different and do not form an identity in difference (*tādātmya*) as Kumārila holds. Their view is consequently radical pluralism like that of the Nyāya-Vaiśeṣika.

We have so far dealt with valid knowledge. But as not all knowledge is valid, we should indicate how the Mīmāṁsaka explains error. But before doing so, it is desirable to state briefly how Kumārila defines truth. According to him, knowledge, to be valid, should not only correspond to the given object as in the Nyāya-Vaiśeṣika (p. 97), but should also contain an element of novelty. That is to say, it must be in the nature of a discovery, and signify an addition to our knowledge—a point to whose bearing on the teaching of the Veda we have already referred more than once. The result of so defining truth is to exclude from the category of *pramā* all knowledge pointing to what has been known before, including memory which presupposes former experience. This does not, however, mean that such knowledge is not serviceable or that its object is false, but only that the doctrine attaches no particular epistemological significance to it.

Kumārila's explanation of error is nearly the same as that given in the chapter on the Nyāya-Vaiśeṣika. He admits that in error, knowledge partly strays from reality and so far misrepresents it (*anyathā-khyāti*). This admission that knowledge may arise without a corresponding object, even when that object is no more than a phase—a quality or relation—is, however, not very satisfactory from the realistic standpoint, for it throws suspicion on the trustworthiness of knowledge as a whole. One never knows in that case when it points to an existent object, and when not. To avoid this unwelcome position, Prabhākara devises a unique explanation of error which, whatever may be said of its ultimate value, saves knowledge from such suspicion. He substitutes for Kumārila's positive view of error a negative one (p. 118). That is, he explains error as one of omission (*akhyāti*) and not as one of commission (*anyathā-khyāti*).

The position of the Prābhākara school is briefly as follows: It maintains that knowledge never involves a reference to anything that is not actually given. One of the illustrations given in explaining this position, is a conch that is seen yellow by a jaundiced person. For the sake of simplicity, we shall make a slight alteration in it by supposing that the conch is seen through a sheet of yellow glass instead of by the jaundiced eye, and that the fact of the existence of the glass is for some reason or other lost sight of. Here we have, according to this view, the perception of the conch *minus* its true colour, viz. white, and the sensation of the yellowness alone of the glass. They are two acts of knowing; but they quickly succeed each other, and we therefore miss the fact that they are two. Each of them is valid so far as it goes, for neither the yellowness nor the conch as such is negated afterwards when we discover the error. But we overlook at first that they stand apart, and it is only this deficiency in our knowledge that is made good later when we find out our mistake. Thus the discovery of the so-called error only means a further step in advancing knowledge. It confirms the previous knowledge and does not cancel any part of it as false, so that to talk of "rectification of error" here is a misnomer. In fact, there is no error at all in this view, in its usual sense of a single *unit* of knowledge. In other words, it holds that the mind may fail to apprehend one or more aspects of what is presented, but that it never *mis*apprehends it and that all errors are therefore errors of omission.

A similar explanation is given in the case of a rope mistaken for a snake, or a piece of shell mistaken for silver; only the two *jñānas* involved in it are not both perceptual. One of them is the perception of the object presented, say shell, but as characterized only by features which it has in common with silver; and the other is the recollection of silver as a result of perceiving such features, but the fact that it is recollection is lost sight of at the time. Hence there is a failure here also to notice that there are two *jñānas*—perception and memory; and it is this deficiency in our knowledge which, as in the previous case, is made good later.

There is no need, on this view, to verify any knowledge. All knowledge is true in the sense that no portion of what it reveals is contradicted afterwards; and to question whether it agrees with reality in any particular instance is therefore to question its very nature. But truth being commonly distinguished from error, it is necessary to give some explanation of the distinction. The so-called error may be partial knowledge; but we cannot characterize it as such, for human knowledge is always partial in one sense or another. So another explanation is given, and it is indirect. Though all knowledge alike is incomplete inasmuch as it fails to grasp the features of a given object in their entirety, error is so from a specific standpoint, viz. a pragmatic one. It is *relatively* incomplete and its relative incompleteness is determined by reference to an extrinsic standard, viz. the fruitfulness of the activity prompted by it. In other words, that knowledge is true which works; and that which does not, is erroneous. Its success or failure is not regarded here as its test merely as in the Nyāya-Vaiśeṣika (p. 99), but as constituting its truth or error. Yet it should be noted that the explanation does not make the doctrine the same as modern pragmatism for, unlike it, it recognizes the absolute validity, epistemologically speaking, of knowledge so far as it goes. In fact, Prabhākara's view represents a position which is the very reverse of modern pragmatism for it denies error, in the logical sense, completely. The adoption here of the pragmatic criterion is only for the purpose of accounting for the commonly accepted distinction between truth and falsehood.

This theory merits commendation for its simplicity as well as for its complete consistency in explaining the logical character of knowledge. But it is far from convincing. The indirect manner, for instance, in which it explains the familiar terms "true" and "false" is hardly satisfactory. Further, a purely negative explanation cannot account for error which, as a judgement, presents the two elements in it as synthesized though they may be actually unrelated. There is only a single psychical process, and the resulting knowledge includes a reference to a positive element, viz. the relation between those elements which is not given. Error is therefore misapprehension, and not mere lack of apprehension.

## II

The most important point for us to consider on the practical side of the teaching is the conception of *dharma* in the two schools. Its importance becomes all the greater since, in the absence of any recognition of God, the many changes constantly taking place in the world, if they are not to be explained on a merely naturalistic basis or as entirely fortuitous, should be accounted for solely by the operation of *dharma* and its opposite *adharma*. As understood here, the term *dharma* stands, generally speaking, for Vedic rites or duties of a religious kind.[14] But it should be remembered that ethical conduct is not excluded, because moral purity is taken to be a necessary condition for a fruitful practising of ritual. The Vedas, as we have already stated (p. 37), will not cleanse the morally impure. Thus *dharma* may be more than morality but is not less. Nor should we think that these activities are non-social or purely individualistic for, though many of them may be primarily intended to secure some good here or hereafter to the agent, they include others which, as pointed out in an earlier chapter by citing the instance of the five daily sacrifices (*mahāyajñas*) (p. 39), stand for the practice of such important virtues as hospitality to guests. But *dharma* is conceived to yield its result mediately and not directly. The reason for this is that ceremonial acts signified by this term, being obviously transient, can have no direct causal connection with their result which does not accrue immediately. Hence it is assumed that the acts give rise to some unseen effect or invisible potency (*apūrva*), which lasts till the appropriate fruit is reaped. Similar effects, but of an undesirable kind, are assumed also in the case of *adharma* or prohibited acts like killing (*pratiṣiddha-Karma*). These unseen effects, which mediate between good and bad acts and their respective results of pleasure and pain, are supposed to abide in the self until they bear fruit.

The two thinkers agree in holding that it is the Veda, and the Veda alone, which determines what *dharma* is. They differ, however, from each other in the view they take of its exact nature; and the difference is of great consequence from the ethical standpoint. Before explaining it, it is necessary to draw attention to a distinction of importance in the actions prescribed in the Veda. Broadly speaking, there are two kinds of deeds included under *dharma* as taught in the scriptures. We have already dwelt at some length upon one of them (p. 38), viz. the "general" and the "specific" as they are called, which are both obligatory (*nitya-karma*). The other type of action, to which we have made a passing reference, is the optional (*kāmya-karma*), which one may or may not do (p. 37). According to Kumārila, although it is the Veda that formulates what is *dharma*, it appeals in commending it to man's innate desire for his own good by pointing to some welcome result such, for instance, as the attainment of heaven. It means that the Veda cannot, and does not, generate desire. Its purpose is only to communicate to man a knowledge, otherwise unattainable, of certain means to certain ends; but it leaves the question of choosing those ends entirely to him. A lamp we hold in our hand when walking in darkness, shows the character of the ground we have to traverse; but it leaves the choice of the path we pursue to ourselves. The promise of rewards, however, is restricted to the optional deeds, and no fruit is specified in the Veda as regards the obligatory ones. Even in the latter case, Kumārila assumes that a welcome, though negative, result affecting the agent is implied, viz. the prevention of some future or the destruction of some past evil. In other words, he is of opinion that no voluntary action is at all conceivable without an appropriate motive.[15]

The Prābhākaras, on the other hand, contend that to appeal to a desirable result in order to make *dharma* acceptable is to divorce it from all that it stands for, and therefore affirm that the ideal of *dharma* should be pursued for its own sake. The Veda gives us no end, but merely prescribes what is to be done. It is entitled to command action without commending it. Here we have the true imperative of obligation (*niyoga*); and it is this "ought," and not the ceremonial act that is meant by *dharma*. That is to say, *dharma* is an intrinsic value in this school and not merely an instrumental one—a good in itself, and not what leads to it as in the other. It is easy to understand the application of this principle to obligatory duties for which the Veda, as just stated, assigns no specific fruit. But the school maintains the same standpoint even in the case of optional deeds. The reference to the fruit, such as the attainment of heaven, found in the Veda while prescribing them is explained as intended merely to define the class or type of persons to whom the behest is addressed and not as implying any emphasis on the result as such. Whatever good may result from such acts is looked upon as a mere consequence of them, and not as a motive to their performance. To express the same in terms of modern ethics, it is not at all necessary in conceiving of the right to separate it absolutely from the good. The two may well be associated with or related to each other, and yet right may be right in itself.[16]

It is clear that, though there are points of difference, more or less important, the conception of *dharma* here resembles that of the "categorical imperative" put forward by Kant in the West. In both alike, deeds are to be done from a sense of duty and not from inclination. It is necessary to add that Prabhākara's teaching is not the same as that of the Gītā, for the latter commends the performance of duty as a means to an end (p. 55), though that end, viz. the purification of natural impulses, is very different from yielding to selfish inclinations.

To judge from the character of its teaching as set forth above, the ultimate ideal of life, according to the Mīmāṁsā, should be to reach heaven or achieve some equally desirable end in the coming life, which is other than *mokṣa* as taught in the Upanishads. Such an ideal appears to have been advocated in it for a long time. A comparatively late, but quite authoritative, writer says in so many words that the Mīmāṁsā has nothing to do with *mokṣa*.[17] The same is also implied in the subordinate position assigned to the Upanishads in some old works on the Mīmāṁsā. This subordination is variously explained. For instance, the Upanishads, according to some Mīmāṁsakas, speak of the self so much, not because it is of importance by itself but because, being the agent in the doing of sacrificial deeds, it is so intimately related to *dharma*. They accordingly protest against placing self-knowledge above action, as the Vedāntins generally do. But the influence of the Upanishads gradually asserted itself; and the old ideal ceased to be conceived as ultimate, and was replaced by that of *mokṣa* (p. 50). It is not possible to say when exactly this change came about; but it is found not only in Kumārila, but also in the standard works of the school of Prabhākara. Here we find a parallel to the synthesis of ritualism with the Upanishadic view of liberation, to which we alluded in dealing with the Kalpa Sūtras (p. 39). The probable conclusion to be drawn from it is that there was all along a Vedic school of thought which insisted on the exclusive importance of rites or, to state it otherwise, the ultimacy of the ideal of *dharma*, but that it was finally superseded by the view of the supremacy of *mokṣa*.

The conception of *mokṣa* here much resembles the conception of the same in the Nyāya-Vaiśeṣika (p. 103). It is final escape from all the ills of life. The only divergence between the two schools, which may be noticed here, is that some among the followers of Kumārila seem to have maintained that it was a state not merely of absence of suffering but also of positive bliss[18]—a view which appears to be more in consonance with the general spirit of his teaching. As regards the discipline, however, there is an important difference from the Nyāya-Vaiśeṣika, since the emphasis here is on *karma* rather than *jñāna* or self-knowledge as there (p. 104). A consequence of it is the rejection of *saṁnyāsa* which occupies a very important place in the other doctrines, not excluding the non-Vedic schools. Briefly the discipline consists in giving up optional and prohibited deeds, which are the direct cause of future births, and confining oneself to the doing of the obligatory ones, whose purpose is the removal of evil and whose neglect will therefore mean its persistence in one form or another. When thus the source of all future births is cut off, there results automatically, at the end of the present life, the restoration to the self of its intrinsic condition, which is *mokṣa.* The ideal signifies, so far as its achievement in this life is possible, the leading of an unselfish life fully occupied with the performance of social and religious duties as either directly taught or implied in the Veda.

Chapter Seven

# VEDĀNTA: ABSOLUTISTIC

*

THE indefiniteness of the teaching of the Upanishads, to which we drew attention in the first chapter (p. 19), explains the necessity that arose for its systematization. Such an attempt can be traced already in the later Upanishads,[1] but it became more and more deliberate afterwards. It is the result of the final systematization of this teaching that is called "Vedānta." The term occurs in the Upanishads; but while it there means only "the final portion of the Vedas," it has since come to signify the settled conclusions of the Veda taken as a whole. Accordingly the Vedānta, in its later forms, stands for the teaching not merely of the Upanishads, together with the earlier portions of the Veda, but also of other parts of the sacred literature such as the Bhagavadgītā and the Viṣṇu Purāṇa which are regarded as reiterating and amplifying the Upanishadic doctrine. The doctrine thus combines in one harmonious whole the results attained by all previous orthodox thinkers, and is therefore looked upon as the most perfect expression of Indian thought. We have already stated (p. 19) that a synthesis of the teachings on the practical side of the two main divisions of the Veda had been effected by the close of the Vedic period. The present synthesis, we should add, goes farther and includes their teaching on the theoretical side also.

The systematization was, in all likelihood, effected in more than one way; but the only attempt that has survived is represented by the Sūtra of Bādarāyaṇa, or the Vedānta Sūtra as it is commonly called. It is in four chapters, each divided into four quarters (*pādas*) or sections. In the current view the Upanishads, the Bhagavadgītā and this Sūtra constitute the triple basis of the Vedānta. It is greatly to be regretted that the Sūtra is not clear in its teaching. In fact it is, in its cryptic form, more ambiguous than the Upanishads or the Gītā; and this has led to several interpretations being put upon it. The consequence is that the divergences of view, originally prevalent, have reasserted themselves and continued in more or less the same form even after the composition of the Sūtra. But we must not conclude from this that the various schools of Vedānta are altogether at variance with one another. So far as their practical teaching is concerned, the agreement is quite conspicuous. It is not so on the theoretical side; but even there the different schools concur about several points such, for instance, as the eternity of the self and the need for acquiring right knowledge (*jñāna*) for attaining *mokṣa*.

Broadly the schools of Vedānta may be classed as either absolutistic or theistic—the former representing Brahman, the ultimate reality, as an impersonal principle and the latter as a personal God. Each of these, it should be added, includes different types of teaching. The chief of them, taking both kinds into consideration, are three known as Advaita, Viśiṣṭādvaita and Dvaita, predominantly associated respectively with the names of Śaṁkara, Rāmānuja and Madhva. We shall confine our attention mainly to these three schools which are all living creeds to-day, and shall devote the present chapter to the absolutistic interpretation of the Upanishads.

## I

The vagueness of Upanishadic teaching is particularly in reference to the relation of Brahman to the individual soul on the one hand, and to the physical universe on the other. Though, as pointed out already (p. 19), statements about their identity are many and prominent, those distinguishing them are not altogether wanting. The first problem to solve for any one attempting to systematize the teaching of the Upanishads is accordingly to harmonize these two sets of statements. The most obvious way of doing so is to attach equal value to both classes of statements and hold that the soul and the world are both identical with and different from Brahman. That was the view, for instance, maintained by Bhartṛprapañca (p. 23) who flourished before Śaṁkara, and commented like him on the Vedānta Sūtra and the Upanishads. Brahman, according to him, is one; but its unity is such as includes variety. Its conception is thus of a one-many. The variety is due to the infinite number of selves that it comprehends as well as the numerous distinctions of the physical universe. But the variety is only implicit in it, and becomes explicit in the process of creation (*sṛṣṭi*). Creation therefore means not the origination of new things, but only the articulation of the distinctions already subsisting in Brahman. In other words, this school resembles the Sāṅkhya, except in so far as it regards the evolving principle as being not the insentient Prakṛti, but the sentient and all-comprehensive Brahman (*Brahma-pariṇāma-vāda*). The individual soul, when it wins liberation, is not consequently lost in Brahman. It continues to retain its individuality, although that individuality must necessarily be very much transformed then.

The means to liberation in this view is neither adherence to moral and religious duty alone nor acquisition of right knowledge alone, but a combination of both. The former helps the cultivation of detachment by purging man of his selfish impulses (*āsaṅga*), and the latter leads to liberation by dispelling his ignorance (*avidyā*) regarding the ultimate oneness of reality. This view of a double discipline for attaining *mokṣa* exalts karma to the rank of a direct means to salvation, and thus makes it co-ordinate with philosophic knowledge. This is the doctrine, in its chief form, of the combined pursuit of the good and the true (*jñāna-karma-samuccaya*), as we may put it, for achieving self-perfection. Other schools of Vedānta also utilize karma as a means to release, but they assign to it as we shall see, a relatively subordinate place in the scheme of discipline. We may consequently conclude that in their attitude towards karma, Vedāntic systems like that of Bhartṛprapañca come nearest to the Mīmāṁsā (p. 149).

Such a view results in a doctrine which, so far as its theoretical teaching is concerned, is by no means unknown in the history of human thought. Roughly speaking, it may be described as Hegelian in its spirit; and it seems once to have been largely prevalent in India. But the advent of Śaṁkara thrust this view quite into the background; and it could never be resuscitated afterwards, although several attempts were made to do so by thinkers like Bhāskara (850 A.D.) and Yādava Prakāśa (1100 A.D.) Śaṁkara's objection to it is that, in its solution, viz. that Brahman and the *jīva* or the universe are both identical and different, the doctrine merely restates in a new form the problem to be solved. It holds that creation means only the potential becoming the actual; but this distinction between the potential and the actual is purely verbal, and does not really solve the problem of causation. The view of this school is that sameness (*abheda*) and difference (*bheda*), so far from being incompatible, are intelligible only if taken together (p. 131), while Śaṁkara maintains that, being mutually contradictory, they cannot be predicated of one and the same thing. It makes the nature of the thing self-contradictory; and self-contradiction, according to him, points to falsity. In other words, if unity and diversity be each an abstraction taken separately according to the one school, their combination *also* is so according to the other. Reality is what transcends both and, at the same time, explains them. To cite an illustration which is as old as the Upanishads: It is like the sun which explains the phenomena of day and night, but at the same time transcends them in that it knows no night, nor even day in our sense of the term.

Śaṁkara recognizes, as we stated in speaking about the Upanishads (p. 23), that there are two streams of thought in the Upanishads; but he thinks that one of them, viz. that which affirms the reality of diversity, is only a concession to empirical modes of thought. All diversity being thus only conditionally true, the only teaching of the Upanishads, according to him, is that of unity. Since, however, there can be no unity apart from variety, he does not describe his teaching as monism but only as "non-dualism" (*advaita*). Strictly speaking, it is therefore wrong to say, as it is now too common to do, that Śaṁkara teaches bare unity. If he did, his Absolute would be "pure nothing." But as Vācaspati says, he only denies the many but does not affirm the one.[2]

Great men, it has been stated, are of two classes. Some are absorbed so intensely in the solution of theoretical problems that their outer life becomes quite unimportant; but there are others who enter fully into the practical struggles of the age in which they live, and yet succeed in making a contribution of permanent significance to the history of human culture. Of these two classes, Śaṁkara belongs to the second. He was a great reformer; and the direction which he gave to his generation in matters social and religious, continues to guide the life and regulate the conduct of millions of people even now after the lapse of many centuries. He was, at the same time, a great thinker also who, though not claiming to have done anything more than elucidate what was already there in the Vedas and Vedic tradition, was virtually the originator of a new movement in philosophy.

It is a great pity that the exact period when such a great thinker lived and worked is not known. Usually he is assigned to about the close of the eighth and the beginning of the ninth century (788-820 A.D.), and the date may be taken as correct within the limits of a hundred years. In all his works, he subscribes himself as a pupil of Govinda who himself, according to tradition, was a pupil of Gauḍapāda. Unlike Govinda, Gauḍapāda has left behind him a work, known as his *Kārikā*, probably the first systematic treatise on Advaita, as understood in the school of Śaṁkara. It is described as a commentary on the Māṇḍūkya Upanishad; but really it is much more, and contains the basic principles of the doctrine as later expounded by Śaṁkara. Śaṁkara is stated to have died at the age of 32. The vastness of the work he did in this short period shows that it is not length of life that explains the work a man does so much as the depth of conviction by which he is actuated. Many works, both in verse and prose, are ascribed to him; but it is almost certain that several of them were not written by him. All that we can definitely say is that most of the commentaries ascribed to him, like those on the Vedānta Sūtra, and on nearly all the classical Upanishads, are by him. The *Upadeśa-sāhasrī*, which is an independent exposition of the advaitic doctrine, and probably a few other works of the same type are also his.

As shown by his criticism of Bhartṛprapañca, Śaṁkara regards all diversity as being an illusion (*mithyā*). But it is very important to grasp correctly the significance of so describing it. Śaṁkara's conception of the real (*sat*) is that of eternal being, and Brahman is the sole reality of that type. Similarly, his conception of the unreal (*asat*) is that of absolute nothing. The world, in all its variety, is neither of the one type nor of the other. It is not real in this sense, for it is anything but eternal.

Nor is it unreal in the sense defined, for it clearly appears to us as no non-entity can. Nobody, as it is stated in advaitic works, has ever seen or is ever going to see a hare's horn or a barren woman's son. They are totally non-existent. Further it possesses, unlike non-entity, practical efficiency or has value, being serviceable in life. This is the reason why the world is described in Advaita as other than the real and the unreal (*sadasadvilakṣaṇa*) or as an illusory appearance. The serpent that appears where there is only a rope is neither existent nor non-existent. It is psychologically given (*prasiddha*), but cannot be logically established (*siddha*). In other words, the things of the world, though not ultimately real, are yet of a certain order of reality. They are appearances, in the sense that they depend for their being upon some higher reality. The "serpent," for example, points to the existence of the rope; and the dependence is one-sided, for while the disappearance of the rope necessarily means the disappearance of the serpent, the reverse does not hold good. All admit that the name (*nāma*) with which we label a thing is conventional; the "what" (*rūpa*) of it also is the same according to Śaṁkara (p. 24). The only true reality is that which underlies this conventional particularity of common things.

While this is the general conception of the physical world in Advaita, that of the individual self is very different. Before explaining this difference, it is necessary to draw attention to an important distinction between two types of illusion in common experience. A person may fancy that he sees a serpent at a distance, while closer scrutiny reveals to him that it is only a rope. The latter or correcting knowledge, like practically all knowledge of the kind, affirms the existence of something; but it contradicts the object *as which* (i.e., serpent) that something appeared before. He says to himself or feels when he discovers his error: "It is a rope, not a serpent." Again a person looking at a white conch through a sheet of yellow glass, of whose existence he is not aware, takes it to be yellow (p. 144). But a suitable change in his standpoint will disclose to him that the yellowness belongs to the glass and not to the conch. Here also, as in the previous case, the later knowledge affirms the existence of some reality; unlike it, however, it does not deny the object as which it appeared, viz. the conch, but only an *aspect* of it—its yellowness. He still sees it as a conch, but only adds that it is white and not yellow. The illusion in the first case consists in mistaking a given object for another that is not given; in the second, it consists merely in attributing to an object which is given, a feature that does not really belong to it, though it also is presented at the time. But for the interposition of the sheet of glass (*upādhi*) to which the yellow actually belongs, there would be no illusion at all in the latter case.[3]

Now these types of illusion serve to illustrate the difference in the manner in which, according to Śaṁkara, one and the same Brahman comes to appear both as the world and as the individual self (*jīva*). It gives rise to the illusion of the world, as the rope does to that of a serpent in our first example. The ultimate truth, as realised by a *jīvanmukta*, denies the world while affirming the underlying reality of Brahman which is given in all presentations as positive being (*sat*) and with which we may therefore be said to be constantly, though not consciously, in touch. The individual self, on the other hand, is not illusory in this sense. It is Brahman itself appearing through media or limiting adjuncts (*upādhi*) like the internal organ (*antaḥ-karaṇa*) which, we may state by the way, are all elements pertaining to the physical world and, as such, are illusory. Or, to state the same otherwise, the individual self when seen *sub specie aeternitatis*, is Brahman itself. When this fact is realized in one's own experience, what is denied is not the *jīva* as a spiritual entity, but only certain aspects of it, such as its finitude and its separateness from other selves. Its conception may thereby become profoundly transformed, but the important point is that it is not negated (*bādhita*) in the same way in which the physical world is. It is, on the other hand, reaffirmed, though only as Brahman. We cannot therefore say that the individual self is false (*mithyā*), as we may that the world is false. We can only say that it is not truly the agent, the enjoyer, etc.

This difference in the explanation has a vital bearing on the Advaita doctrine, and Śaṁkara consequently lays particular emphasis on it. It brings out clearly what is meant by the identity of the *jīva* and Brahman which is of fundamental importance to the doctrine. The *jīva* is not false or illusory as the world is; for, if it were, there would be none to be saved and the whole teaching of the Upanishads would then be nullified. Salvation implies survival. The liberated *jīva* is not thus lost in Brahman. But, at the same time, it should be remembered that it would not be quite correct to say that it is preserved, for it is only as Brahman that it continues to be, losing its limitations which are all false. These limitations, which are really of its empirical adjuncts, appear transferred to it as, in our second example of illusions, the yellowness of the glass appears transferred to the conch. We may thus take the ego as an appearance of Brahman in the second degree, and not in the first as the physical world is. The notion of the ego is accordingly that of a complex (*viśiṣṭa*), and points not only to an element which is identical with Brahman but also to limiting adjuncts like the internal organ.

We now know the advaitic world-view in general. Brahman is the sole reality, and it appears both as the objective universe and as the individual subject. The former is an illusory manifestation of Brahman, while the latter is Brahman itself appearing under the limitations which form part of that illusory universe. There are certain important concepts of Advaita, whose nature we should next consider; but before doing so, it is desirable to refer briefly to the explanation given in it of causation.

So far, we have come across two views of it, viz. the theories of creation (p. 87) and of evolution or transformation (p. 109) advocated respectively in the Nyāya-Vaiśeṣika and the Sāṅkhya-Yoga. The advaitic view, as may be expected, is that the conception is wholly empirical and is without any ultimate significance. It will be better in explaining this position to begin by pointing out that of these two views of causation, the advaitin prefers the latter. That is, he is totally averse to admitting that anything can come into being anew. If the pot were once non-existent, and therefore altogether unrelated to the lump of clay from which it is made, it might as well be produced out of anything; and there would then be no need to seek for particular material causes, as we actually find it necessary to do, to produce particular effects. Hence the material cause and effect cannot be two separate things, but should form an identity in difference. This view, however, is only provisionally correct, according to Advaita, that is, so long as we restrict our attention to the empirical sphere.[4] Finally, however, Brahman is the source of all; and neither the pot nor its material cause, which as parts of the empirical world are false, can be in actual relation with it. The relation between the lump of clay and the pot, which are equally appearances, may be actual; but that between Brahman and the pot or the clay should necessarily be false. The causal relation holds between one phenomenon or appearance and another, but not between phenomena and reality. This is the meaning of saying that, according to Advaita, the conception of causation is empirical and has no ultimate significance. Belief in it, no doubt, forms an important implication of all practical life, but it is not logically defensible. It may appear that, while the notion of effect may be illusory, the notion of cause is real so far at least as Brahman, the ultimate source of everything, is concerned. Strictly, however, this way of putting it also is wrong, since the concept of cause is relative and cannot be retained when the concept of effect has been set aside. In this view then, Brahman, though it is the ground of the entire realm of causes and effects, transcends that realm; and the principle of causation does not accordingly apply to it.

The above view of causation is known as *vivarta-vāda* or "the doctrine of false transformation or of apparent change." The pot, in our example, is only an appearance or change, *as it were,* of its ultimate source, viz. Brahman, as the illusory serpent is of the rope. It is desirable to distinguish further between actual and apparent change. Actual change (*pariṇāma*) signifies that when a particular thing is destroyed, it does not disappear entirely. A rope when pulled to pieces remains as fibres. A pot, when broken, exists as potsherds. In apparent transformation (*vivarta*), on the other hand, the disappearance is complete. When the illusion of "serpent" is overcome, there will be nothing *of it* left. It remains only to add that the *jīva* is not an effect in either of these senses. It is not a real transformation, nor even an illusory appearance of Brahman, so that no principle of causation is at all involved there. If we yet speak of the individual self as born, we only mean that its adjuncts like the physical body come into being and not the spiritual element in it. Hence the *jīva* is described as beginningless (*anādi*). It is, as already indicated, Brahman appearing in an empirical dress.

To take up now the consideration of the important concepts of Advaita. They are four in number—one being a concept of nature, as we may term it; and the remaining three, concepts of spirit.

(1) *Māyā*—We have stated that the external world is unreal, but it is not therefore to be taken as chaotic. From the empirical standpoint, it is a cosmos; and Śaṁkara speaks of it in more than one place as exhibiting spatial, temporal and causal order.[5] That it is incessantly undergoing change is obvious. The change, however, is not total, and involves a persistent element. These two circumstances suggest that it is a unity in diversity. And, if it be so, it admits of being thought of in two stages—one in which the diversity is latent and the other in which it is manifest. Utilizing the terminology of the Sāṅkhya-Yoga, we may designate the former phase of it, in which the element of unity is prominent but not that of diversity, as Prakṛti. The latter phase, in which that element is obscured by diversity, is what we all know to be the every-day world. But this physical world does not exhaust the universe. There is a spiritual element also in it which is the self or ātman. So far, the explanation is similar to that given in the Sāṅkhya-Yoga (p. 114). At this point, however, a divergence appears between the two doctrines; and it is in regard to the relation between spirit and matter, constituting the universe as known to us. We shall now explain the exact nature and consequences of this divergence.

The Sāṅkhya-Yoga, it will be recalled, fails to explain this relation satisfactorily (p. 116). The Advaita definitely denies that there can be any relation at all between two such disparate entities as spirit and matter. But at the same time, it cannot be forgotten that our investigation of experience leads us to the conclusion that they are not only together but are often identified with each other as implied, for example, when a person says "I am walking." Here the act of walking is obviously a feature characterizing the physical body; and yet it is predicated of the person's self which is spiritual. The only explanation conceivable is that their association must be a mere appearance or, in other words, that the relation between them is ultimately false. Śaṁkara treats of this point in his celebrated preamble to the commentary on the Vedānta Sūtra, which is very brief and is written in what may be described as his "shorthand style." "The self or the 'I-element'," he says there, "is so opposed to the not-self or the 'Thou-element' that they can never be predicated of each other." A necessary corollary to this conclusion is that one of the relata is unreal. Both, of course, cannot be regarded as unreal, for in that case, since all the three elements—the two relata and the relation—become false, and since the idea of falsehood necessarily points to a standard of truth, we shall have to postulate another reality from the viewpoint of which we declare them to be false (p. 81). The advaitin therefore takes for granted that it is matter which is false. The other alternative would result in materialism, whose untenability we have already seen (p. 59).

This is the reasoning by which the Advaita arrives at the result, already mentioned, that the physical world is only an appearance; and in this consists its fundamental difference from the Sāṅkhya-Yoga. It follows that its causal phase, viz. Prakṛti also is false or, in advaitic terminology, "other than real and unreal" (*sadasadvilakṣaṇa*). It is called Maya in this doctrine; but the term Prakṛti may be applied to it, so long as we do not forget that it is here neither real nor independent of spirit as in the Sāṅkhya-Yoga. That is to say, if Maya explains the world, we have to seek for the explanation of Maya itself beyond it. It may be unique in that it is neither real nor unreal, but it is not ultimate; and that entity which explains it is spirit. We find it sometimes stated in modern works on Advaita that the principle of Maya is inexplicable, and that the doctrine therefore confesses its inability to explain the nature of the world. But it should be clear from the above that it is not "inexplicable" in this sense, but that it is only not *self*-explanatory. We may add, before leaving this topic, that the evolutes of Maya here are more or less the same as those of Prakṛti in the Sāṅkhya-Yoga.[6]

(2) *Brahman*—We began by representing Prakṛti as the source of the physical universe, and have arrived at the conclusion that that source, being unreal, necessarily implies a

ground, viz. spirit. This spirit, which is the ultimate basis of everything, is what Brahman or the advaitic Absolute signifies. Whatever reality the world manifests is derived from it. Hence in negating the world, we are only denying its existence apart from or independently of Brahman. To state the same in alternative phrase, the world is not a part or phase of Brahman but an appearance of it. We may accordingly say that the world is an *actual* change of Maya or that it is a change, *as it were*, of Brahman. The point of this distinction is that while Maya is conceived as really undergoing change in the process of manifesting the world, Brahman in the same process is conceived as remaining changeless. We may, for this reason, look upon Brahman also as the cause of the universe, though only in the sense in which a rope is the cause of the serpent in our example of illusory experience. Just as there would be no serpent without the rope, there would be no world or Maya without spirit. In fact, spirit is the only reality, all else being either Maya or its transformations. Although the universe cannot be explained without it, Brahman in itself is devoid of unity as well as diversity, which are the characteristic features of the empirical world. It transcends all empirical attributes as taught in the famous Upanishadic formula "Not this, not this" (*neti neti*). Hence it is regarded as devoid of qualities or featureless (*nirguṇa*).

Here naturally arises the question whether such an entity is not a sheer abstraction. Śaṁkara recognizes the force of this objection. It is, indeed, the very objection he seems to have raised against a certain other monistic view (*sattādvaita*)[7] of Upanishadic teaching which was in vogue in his time, viz. that Brahman is universal Being. Śaṁkara's monism differs from it in that it views the ultimate reality not as objective, but as identical *at bottom* with the individual self (*ātmādvaita*). This altered conception secures the maximum certainty to the reality of Brahman, for nothing can possibly carry greater certitude with it than one's belief in the existence of oneself (p. 22). "A man," it has been said, "may doubt of many things, of anything *else;* but he can never doubt of his own being," for that very act of doubting would affirm its existence.[8] It is thus eventually through something in ourselves that, according to Śaṁkara, we are able to judge of reality and unreality. Such a view does not mean that the self is known to us completely. Far from it. But, at the same time, it does not remain wholly unknown, being our own self—a fact which distinguishes the advaitic ultimate from not only the universal Being referred to above, but also (to mention a Western parallel) the thing-in-itself of Kant. We should also remember in this connection that what is meant by speaking of Brahman as featureless is that it transcends the distinction between substance and attribute, and not that it is a substance bereft of attributes.

(3) *Saguṇa-brahman:* We thus see that Brahman and Maya may each be represented as the cause of the universe, though in different senses. If now we choose to look upon them as *together* constituting the source of the world, their blend or combination becomes what is known as the qualified (*saguṇa*) Brahman, comprehending all the diversity of experience, including the experiencing selves. In this sense, Brahman may, like Maya, be conceived in two stages—as cause and effect. In the former, diversity is latent, while in the latter it is manifest. But, mingled as Brahman thus becomes with the falsity of Maya, it perforce descends to the phenomenal level, and is consequently designated the lower (*apara*) Brahman to distinguish it from the higher (*para*). It then forms the cosmic parallel of the individual self or the ego. Each is Brahman itself with an unreal adjunct; only the adjunct is all-comprehensive in one case, while it is finite in the other. The finite adjunct of the individual self is sometimes designated as *avidyā* to contrast it with the cosmic Maya of the qualified Brahman. In this view, Maya is the whole of which the many *avidyās*, associated with the individual selves, are parts or phases. Just as the whole universe is the effect of Maya, the portions of the universe which constitute the accompaniments of an individual self, like the physical body and the internal organ, are regarded as derived from the *avidyā* of that particular self. Whatever distinction there appears to be between the ego and the qualified Brahman or between one ego and another, is entirely due to these differing adjuncts. In themselves, the egos are not distinct from one another or from the qualified Brahman. This identity of denotation of the two terms (p. 21), *jīva* and the qualified Brahman, while their

connotations are different, is the advaitic interpretation of "That thou art" (*Tat tvam asi*). It does not mean, as it is so often represented to do, that man and the qualified Brahman or God (to use a term which we shall soon explain) are *as such* one. Such an attitude is as blasphemous, according to Advaita, as it is according to any religion or purely theistic doctrine.

The qualified Brahman, if personified, becomes the God or Īśvara of Advaita. Like it, God also may be represented as the cosmic parallel to the finite individual self, the distinction between them being entirely one of adjuncts. The consequence of this distinction is that God remains untouched by any of the evil consequences of association with a finite adjunct, such as narrow love and hate. It is attachment which implies preferences and exclusions; but God, being equally attached to all, is really detached. There is a Sanskrit verse which says: "One should give up attachment; but if that be not possible, one might cultivate it, but it should be equal attachment for all."[9] In the language of popular religion, God is represented as the creator of the universe, and Maya as the power (*śakti*) that helps him in creating it. In this form, he becomes the material as well as the efficient cause of the universe (p. 30), and is sometimes spoken of as the great Magician who brings forth out of himself the whole spectacle of the universe. The point of the comparison with a magician is that he is in no way deluded by that spectacle as others are, for there is in his case a never-failing realization of its actual character; and this is the reason why, as we stated above, evil does not touch him. What, however, is really ultimate, we must not forget, is the Absolute, and neither the qualified Brahman nor God. These conceptions are like stepping-stones to the weaker among the disciples in rising to a true conception of the ultimate reality.[10]

(4) *Jīva:* We have already spoken of the *jīva* or the ego in its relation to Brahman and the world, and there is not much to say about it now. Like the qualified Brahman or God, the ego also is complex in its character, being a blend of the self and the not-self. The latter element is *avidyā*, which corresponds to Maya in the case of the qualified Brahman. It is, as we might put it, the individual's share of Maya or Maya in

miniature. But this description applies literally only to the state of deep or dreamless sleep. In the state of dream, the *jīva* is associated not with *avidyā* as such, but chiefly with its off-shoot of the internal organ (*antaḥ-karaṇa*); and, in the state of waking, with the physical body also which is likewise derived from *avidyā*. Though both the *jīva* and God are alike complex in character, there is, as we have seen, a vast difference between them. The two elements in it are wrongly identified with each other implicitly, if not explicitly, in the one case, while they are not in the other. From this wrong identification arise all the confusions and troubles of life. It is in this complex form that the self functions as a subject, so that the illusion or false identity of the self and the not-self is prior to all forms of experience. Indeed, it is a necessary precondition of it. It is this complex entity again, which presupposes *avidyā* or ignorance, that transmigrates—a fact which implies that liberation, which depends upon the overcoming of ignorance, is transcending the notion of the ego. Thus, paradoxical, as it may seem, man, truly to be himself, must get beyond himself.

The above explanation will enable us to understand the advaitic conception of the *sākṣin* or "witness," which much resembles that of Puruṣa in the Sāṅkhya-Yoga (p. 115). It is the *jīva* viewed in its *true* character—not as one with or even as related to any of its adjuncts, but as aloof from all of them. It is thus pure consciousness, the "seeing light," and is virtually the same as Brahman. We may describe it as the transcendental ego to distinguish it from the *jīva* or the empirical ego. When we say that it is consciousness, the *sākṣin* should not be confounded with knowledge as it is familiar to us. The latter (*vṛtti-jñānā*), being a state of the *jīva* or subject, necesarily appears under the limitation of the fitful internal organ and therefore changes with it; but the former, being consciousness in itself (*svarūpa-jñāna*), never does, for all change as understood here is *for* consciousness and not *in* consciousness. When therefore we speak of knowledge as arising or disappearing, we mean only the changes in the internal organ which is wrongly identified with the witness. The witness is thus the implication of empirical thought. It is involved in all such thought, but is not identical with it. Its existence is deduced from the principle that what knows must be other than what is known—a principle which shows that self-consciousness, as explained by thinkers like Kumārila (p. 133), is a contradiction in terms. Nothing, it is said, can be the subject as well as the object of one and the same action. The eye can see other things, but not itself. The finger's end can touch other objects, but not itself. It is, no doubt, true that we speak of knowing ourselves; but then we mean only the *jīva* which includes non-spiritual or *knowable* elements like the body and the internal organ. In reality, it is not the "I" but the "me" that we know. The true self cannot be known; but it does not therefore remain unrealized, for it is self-revealing. In fact, it can never be wholly suppressed.

The advaitin accepts the theory of representative perception, and his explanation of the process of perceiving is much like that given in the Sāṅkhya-Yoga (p. 120). He also, like the other Vedāntins, believes in the self-validity of knowledge following the lead of the Mīmāṁsakas; but in his view of error, he entirely differs from the doctrines we have so far considered. He accepts an objective factor or counterpart in all knowledge *completely* corresponding to its content, and error is no exception to this rule. That is to say, all knowledge as such points to an object beyond it. But the object of illusion, he holds, is of a different status from that of valid knowledge, for it is sublated afterwards unlike the latter. The illusory serpent is sooner or later discovered to be merely a rope; but empirical objects like tables and chairs or mountains and rivers are not sublated in the same way. Ordinarily speaking, they exist prior to their being known, and continue to do so afterwards. An illusory object, on the other hand, endures only as long as its knowledge lasts. It comes into being along with its knowledge, and disappears along with it. The two are thus coterminous. But though illusory objects cannot be accepted as real because of such sublation, they are not unreal, for they clearly appear to us to be out there; and the totally non-existent cannot obviously make itself known. That is, they cannot be viewed as either real or unreal (*sadasadvilakṣaṇa*). Hence the advaitic theory of error is described as "the apprehension of the inexpressible" (*anirvacanīya-khyāti*)-where the word "inexpressible" stands for what cannot be expressed in terms of being or non-being.

There are thus two orders or being, of which we may take the real serpent and the false as examples. If to this we add what forms the common ground of them both, viz. Brahman, we have the three orders of reality usually mentioned in advaitic works. Of them, Brahman is real in the only true sense of the term (*pāramārthika*). Objects like the rope are empirically so (*vyāvahārika*) because, although by no means permanent, they endure in some form (say, as fibre if not as rope) so long as we view them from the standpoint of common experience. The being of the serpent, seen where there is only a rope, is described as illusory (*prātibhāsikā*); and its distinguishing mark is that it vanishes entirely, when the illusion is dispelled. The distinction between the latter two kinds of reality may be explained in a different way also. The illusory object is given only in individual experience. When one is mistaking a rope for a serpent, others may be seeing it as a rope. Hence such objects may be described as "private." The empirical object, on the other hand, is "public" inasmuch as its existence, speaking in the main, is vouched for by others also. The description of the illusory object as "private" does not mean that it is subjective as in the Yogācāra doctrine (p. 166) for, as we have just stated, it is other than knowledge.

From this view of error, we can find out the advaitin's conception of truth. According to the description just given, knowledge is true when no part of its content has to be discarded as false or, in other words, when it is not contradicted by the rest of our experience, but harmonizes with it. This signifies that it is non-contradiction or coherence with other knowledge which makes it true, and not correspondence with reality. The rejection of the correspondence hypothesis does not mean the denial of the view that knowledge points to an object outside corresponding to it. It only means that since *all* knowledge, as pointed out above, equally satisfies the condition of agreement with an objective counterpart, correspondence cannot be regarded as a distinguishing mark of truth. But coherence, while it may ordinarily serve as the mark of truth, cannot finally be regarded as sufficient, since there may be more than one set of such truth. The world of science, for instance, forms one truth-system; and the world of art, say, that of Shakespeare's *Othello* or of Scott's *Ivanhoe*, is another. They are relative, and what is true in one of them may not be true in another. The ultimate truth should include all such truths, and explain them either directly (e.g., in the case of the world of science) or, at least, indirectly by serving as their eventual basis (e.g., in the case of the world of art) as the rope explains the false serpent. It should therefore satisfy not only the criterion of coherence, but should also be comprehensive. That truth is the unity of all existence: "All this, verily, is Brahman." (*Sarvam khalvidam Brahma.*)

But it should be added that this is only to express the nature of ultimate truth from the empirical standpoint, for the notion of coherence implies the reality of diversity, while, according to Advaita, all variety is finally false. From the ultimate standpoint, the truth must thus be the ground of which the whole of this diversity is an appearance, viz. Brahman. At this point, the distinction between truth and reality disappears like all other distinctions; and it may be viewed as either, according as we choose. In the terminology of the Upanishads (p. 22), it is being (*satya*) and, at the same time, knowledge (*jñāna*). The difference in name is due to the difference in our approach to it. In itself, the Absolute transcends being as well as knowledge, as familiar to us, while explaining them both. The unity of all existence, postulated above as the highest of empirical truths, thus reduces itself in the end to the sole reality of spirit—a result which is the same as the teaching of "That thou art" and "All this, indeed, is Brahman." The only difference between them is that while the approach to the absolute reality is from the objective side in the one case, it is from the subjective in the other. Though truth in the ultimate sense cannot therefore be coherence, it may be characterized as non-contradiction (*abādhita*) since it is impossible to disaffirm or deny spirit, such denial itself being thought or a revelation of spirit.

The advaitin believes in all the six *pramāṇas* which we have so far mentioned; and, since his view of them is almost the same as that of Kumārila, no further reference to it is necessary. There is, however, an important difference between the two in regard to their attitude towards the Veda which, as we know, is a variety of verbal testimony; and it will suffice to refer to it here. It concerns the grounds on which the validity of the Veda is upheld. The advaitin, unlike the Mīmāṁsaka, holds that the Veda has had an author, viz. God; but it is not his work in the accepted sense of that word. Like everything else, the Veda also disappears at the end of a cycle; and God repeats it at the beginning of the next cycle, just as it was before, so that it may be regarded as eternal in the sense in which a beginningless series of like things is. It is therefore really independent of God (*apauruṣeya*) in so far as its substance as well as its verbal form is concerned, although its propagation at the beginning of each cycle is due to him. It thus secures self-validity for the Veda, without subscribing to the palpably unconvincing theory of the Mimāṁsā that it is self-existent and eternal. We may add that, in this view, the advaitin differs from the Nyāya also, for the latter ascribes the authorship of the Veda to God in the ordinary sense of the term. This advaitic view of the Veda, which stands midway between the Nyāya and the Mīmāmsā views of it is, we may note, common to all the schools of Vedānta.

## II

The goal of human life, according to Advaita, can be directly deduced from its explanation of the character of the individual self. The individual self is Brahman itself, and its supposed distinction from it is entirely due to the illusory adjuncts with which it identifies itself. Man's ultimate aim in life should accordingly be to know and realize this truth. Since the various accompaniments of the self are all false and the identification of the self with them is erroneous, the means of getting rid of them is right knowledge. As in the other doctrines, the achievement of the goal here also means bringing about a change; only the change is, in the present doctrine, conceived to be, not in the realm of being but in that of thought.[11] That is to say, man has to alter totally his standpoint towards himself and the world in order to become free. Final freedom does not therefore mean any actual change in the nature of the self. To give a familiar illustration: In a lunar eclipse, the moon is actually obscured by the shadow of the earth; and it remains eclipsed until this obscuration is removed by a change in the relative position of the heavenly bodies concerned, and the sun's light again fully falls on it. Here the change is real. In a solar eclipse, on the other hand, nothing at all happens to the luminary; and it continues to be, during the eclipse, as it was before. It is only the position of the observer with reference to the sun and the moon that gives rise to the wrong notion of the eclipse. When there is an appropriate shifting of that position, the eclipse perforce ceases to appear. Similarly in the present case also, the identity of the self with Brahman is not to be newly attained; it is already there and has only to be realized in one's own experience. This does not mean that there is no need, according to Advaita, for undergoing any practical discipline to realize it; but it is a point to which we shall immediately return.

In common with the other systems, the discipline here also consists of two parts—the first, meant for cultivating detachment (*vairāgya*) and the second, for acquiring knowledge (*jñāna*) of the ultimate reality and transforming that knowledge into direct experience. The former part of the discipline signifies adherence to duty in the manner taught in the Gītā (p. 54), that is, with no desire for its worldly fruit but with a view to perfecting character (*karma-yoga*). This preliminary stage of training is as essential to the achievement of the goal in the doctrine as in any other. No doubt we have stated that the attainment of the goal here implies only a change of standpoint, and not any actual change in the nature of the self. Yet it is wrong to think that the Advaita therefore commends or countenances idle quietism. Our common dualistic convictions about life and the consequent egoistic tendencies in us are so firm-rooted that no genuine effort to know the ultimate truth of oneness is possible until they are radically transformed; and such transformation can be effected only by long and continued performance of duty in a spirit of absolute disinterestedness. A mere intellectual apprehension of the advaitic truth is of no avail in this regard. Only while ethical activity is conceived in some other doctrines as contributing directly to final freedom, here it is taken to do so indirectly. By helping to purify the affections, it enables man to rise above his common egoistic attitude and fits him to pursue seriously the ultimate truth. To state the same in traditional terminology, karma is not here conceived as the cause of *mokṣa* or even of *jñāna* which is its means, but of a true *desire* to know (*vividiṣā*). Morality is accordingly described here as a remote or mediating cause (*ārādupakāraka*) of *mokṣa.* The purpose for which the doctrine commends eithical activity may thus be different from what it is in other doctrines and it may also recognize, as we shall presently see, a stage in the spiritual advancement of man when duty *as such* ceases to have any significance. But there is no question about the necessity for whole-hearted adherence to it in the earlier stages of life's discipline. "Though knowledge alone can in the end lead to *mokṣa*," Max Muller says, "virtue is certainly presupposed."

Success in this part of the training is indicated by the appearance in the disciple of the following traits which are described as "the fourfold aid" (*sādhana-catuṣṭaya*) to the study of Vedānta. They are (1) ability to discriminate between the transient and the eternal, (2) absence of desire for securing pleasure or avoiding pain here or elsewhere, (3) attainment of calmness, temperance, the spirit of renunciation, fortitude, power of concentration of mind, faith or the "will to believe" and (4) desire for true freedom. In one word, this part of the discipline qualifies for *saṁnyāsa.* As to whether one should *formally* become an ascetic before entering on the next stage of the discipline (*jñāna-yoga*), there is a difference of opinion among the advaitins; and some hold that it is not absolutely necessary to do so.[12] The above aids are mostly negative, but we must remember that their final aim of self-realization is quite positive. The narrow self is suppressed, but only to win the wider one.

The second part of the discipline is threefold as set forth (p. 26) in our treatment of the Upanishads—formal study (*śravaṇa*), reflection (*manana*) and meditation (*dhyāna*). It will suffice here to refer to only such important points concerning them as have not already been mentioned:

(1) Formal study (*śravaṇa*): This signifies learning from a proper preceptor (*guru*) that the ultimate teaching of Advaita is the sole reality of Brahman. The unity taught here, no doubt, includes both man and nature; but as the first and foremost interest of man is man himself and not nature, the truth as

embodied in "That thou art," or the fundamental identity of the individual and the absolute, is given prominence in the teaching. The disciple has accordingly to concentrate his attention on this aspect of the doctrine, and look upon the other, relating to nature, as more or less secondary.

(2) Reflection (*manana*): As a result of the above teaching, the disciple comes to know the unity of the individual and the ultimate reality. But this knowledge, being only communicated by another, cannot be fully convincing, especially as it is so much at variance with the verdict of common experience (*asam-bhāvanā*). Hence the present step of personal reflection, which is intended to assist the disciple in convincing himself, from examples taken from ordinary life, of the correctness of advaitic teaching. But in the very nature of the case, the arguments based on such examples are only analogical (*sāmānyato-dṛṣṭa*) for, while they are drawn from the realm of common experience, Brahman by hypothesis transcends it. They can thus only give support to, or indicate the probability of, Vedāntic truth (p. 121), and cannot demonstrate it independently of revelation. In other words, this type of argument is utilized here not as a *pramāṇa* but as only an accessory to it (*yukti*). This may appear to make the advaitic truth rest, in the end, on dogma. Such a view, however, would not be correct, as will become clear from what we shall say later regarding the place of reason in advaita taken as a whole.

(3) Meditation (*dhyāna*): The object of this stage is, as often remarked before, to transform into direct experience the mediate knowledge of ultimate reality acquired by the study of the Upanishads and by reflection upon their teaching. It is accordingly vision that is sought now, and not mere knowledge. In spite of the intellectual conviction attained, old habits of thought (*viparīta-sambhāvanā*) incompatible with it may now and again assert themselves. The present step is intended to overcome them. It consists in meditating upon the central point of advaitic teaching; and when that process is crowned with success, there dawns of itself upon the mind of the contemplative the truth of the statement "That thou art." The intrinsic bliss of the self also is released, as it were, in its wholeness at the same time.

We may now consider briefly the place of reason in Advaita.[13] There is no doubt that the advaitic truth should, in the beginning, be learnt from a teacher who is well conversant with it. But this does not mean that reasoning is discarded. Its need is fully recognized, as shown by the position assigned to reflection (*manana*) in the scheme of discipline. In fact, the belief is that the ultimate significance of the scripture will not become completely known until one has benefited by using one's reason in the manner stated above.[14] But it may be thought that the doctrine, however important the place it assigns to reason may be, is essentially dogmatic, because its truth is primarily to be known through revelation. That such a conclusion, however, does not follow will be seen when we remember the exact function of revelation. The aim here, as in the case of other Indian doctrines, is not merely to grasp the ultimate truth intellectually but to realize it in one's own experience. The scripture as such, being a form of verbal testimony, can however convey only mediate knowledge. To attain the ideal therefore means to advance farther than merely comprehending the scriptural truth. Scriptural knowledge, accordingly, is not sufficient, though necessary; and like reason, it also therefore becomes only a subsidiary aid to the attainment of the goal. The Upanishads themselves declare that when a person has seen this truth for himself, he outgrows the need for the scriptures. "There a father becomes no father; a mother, no mother; the world, no world; the gods, no gods; the Vedas, no Vedas."[15] Thus we finally get beyond both reason and revelation, and rest on direct experience (*anubhava*). Hence if Advaita is dogmatic, the dogma is there only to be transcended.[16] Further, we should not forget that revelation itself, as stated in an earlier chapter (p. 45), goes back to the intuitive experience of the great seers of the past. It is that experience which is to be personally corroborated by the disciple.

When this truth is realised, one attains *mokṣa* which, as we have seen, is not merely knowing Brahman but *being* Brahman. The person who has reached this stage is a *jīvanmukta* or a "free man," although he may continue to be associated with his several physical accompaniments. He is in life and yet lifted out of it. He will necessarily continue to work and help others, but the service which he renders will be the natural expression of his felt conviction regarding the oneness of all. Or, to state the same otherwise, the constraint of obligation is replaced in that stage by the spontaneity of love. This is the meaning of saying that duty *as such* ceases to be significant to a knower, and not that he grows indifferent towards the world. The kind of life which Śaṁkara led is a sufficient refutation of such a negative view. When a *jīvanmukta* casts off the physical body at death, he becomes freed in the final sense of the term (*vidheha-mukti*). This is the logical position of Advaita, and is staunchly adhered to in it. But in accordance with the teaching of the Upanishads (p. 29), it also recognizes what is termed "gradual or progressive liberation" (*krama-mukti*) in the case of those who advance on right lines but do not, in this life, aim directly at right knowledge. After death, they progress from one higher life to another until they acquire direct experience of the ultimate truth, and are finally liberated.

Chapter Eight

# VEDĀNTA: THEISTIC

*

ALTHOUGH the Upanishadic doctrine does not exclude belief in a personal God, it is not prevailingly theistic. Indian theism has a separate history; and we have seen that it had already developed in two main directions before the beginning of the Christian era, viz. Śaivism and Vaiṣṇavism. The revival of Hinduism under the Gupta kings (*circa* A.D. 400) to counter the success of Jainism and Buddhism meant, in reality, the resuscitation of these two creeds.[1] When their influence was specially strong in the South, Śaṁkara reinterpreted the Upanishads, thus restoring to India its old philosophic thought; and there naturally arose thereafter a desire in some thinkers to amalgamate the theistic creeds with the Upanishadic doctrine, introducing such changes in the new interpretation of the latter as were necessary for that purpose. It is the outcome of this desire that we have to take into account now. But we shall confine our attention to one aspect of it only, viz., the amalgamation of Vaiṣṇavism with the Vedānta; or, in other words, we shall deal here with the doctrines of Rāmānuja and Madhva. There was a corresponding effort made in regard to Śaivism also then; but the resulting types of it are substantially the same as the doctrines we are going to deal with in the present chapter or those we have already considered in the last, so far as they are theistic. The Śaivism of the South, called the "Siddhānta," for instance, is realistic and pluralistic like the Vaiṣṇavism of Rāmānuja and Madhva, while what is now known as "Kashmir Śaivism" is monistic and corresponds, more or less, to the view of Bhartṛprapañca referred to above.

We have traced the growth of Vaiṣṇavism till the time of the Gītā, and there is not much to say here about its subsequent history. The only point requiring notice is the development in the intervening period of the conception of the unity of the three chief Gods, including Brahmā. At one stage in their history, probably after they had triumphed over their common rivals of Jainism and Buddhism, these theistic creeds which were sectarian from the beginning (p. 33) seem to have developed a sharp antagonism. As a reaction against it arose the belief, doubtless under the influence of monistic philosophy, that the distinction of the three Gods is but an abstraction and that all of them are but phases of the one supreme God (Īśvara). We may refer, as a conspicuous instance of this catholicity of view, to Kālidāsa's description of Brahmā in one of his two epic poems and of Viṣṇu in the other. He speaks there of the two Gods in almost identical terms, and of each as the triune God. As a consequence of this belief, the selection for worship of any one of these deities has come to be looked upon by many as purely a matter of choice. It means only that it is the individual's patron deity (*iṣṭa-devatā*) and does not signify the rejection or setting aside of the others. It shows that the worshipper loves and reveres that particular deity more, and not the others less. This doctrine of *Trimūrti* ("Trinity"), as it is called, did not abolish the belief in the exclusive supremacy of these Gods, taken separately. The Vaiṣṇava systems we are now to treat of, are of that type.

## A. VIŚIṢṬĀDVAITA

It is Vaiṣṇavism in this form that Rāmānuja attempted to synthesize with the Vedānta. We should not, however, think that he was the very first to do so. He had predecessors in the field like Yāmuna Muni; but their efforts do not appear to have resulted in any systematic doctrine. Rāmānuja had the necessary genius for the work, and he succeeded eminently in his aim. This was about 1100 A.D. He has left behind him a new commentary on the Vedanta Sūtra known as the *Śrī-bhāṣya* and other works like the commentary on the Gītā, and the *Vedārtha-saṁgraha* which is an independent treatise explaining in a masterly way his philosophic position, and pointing out the basis for it in the Upanishads. Of the thinkers that followed him, we need mention only Vedānta Deśika (1350 A.D.), one of the most learned scholars which medieval India produced. He was a prolific writer, and the Viśiṣṭādvaita doctrine owes not a little of its vogue among scholars as well as the common people to his exposition of it.

## I

The chief difficulty in interpreting the Upanishads, as we know, is in reconciling statements that identify Brahman with the individual soul and with the physical universe with those that distinguish it from the same (p. 152); and we have so far considered two ways of doing it, viz. those of Bhartṛprapañca and Śaṁkara. The manner in which Rāmānuja harmonizes them is unique. He points out that, as shown by common linguistic usage, we often identify things that are distinct. Thus we say that the rose *is* red.[2] The "rose" which is a substance and "redness" which is a quality cannot be the same; but yet we speak of them as if they were, because usage permits it. Similarly one may say "I *am* a man," identifying a surviving soul with the mortal human form in which it appears. Such usage, however, is not found in the case of all distinct things. We cannot, for example, speak of a man and his coat or his staff in this manner, but have necessarily to say that he *has* a coat on him or a staff in his hand, thus indicating clearly their distinction by our mode of speech. Contrasting these two forms of usage, Rāmānuja comes to the conclusion that the relation in the two former cases should be different from and more intimate than that in the latter which is obviously mere conjunction (p. 88). It is found only between (1) substance and attribute, using the latter word as Rāmānuja does, in a wide sense and (2) body and soul, that is, between two substances of which one is necessarily spiritual. This intimate relation is termed by him *apṛthak-siddhi*, which literally means "inseparability." It connotes that one of the two entities related is dependent upon the other in the sense that it cannot exist without the other also existing, and that it cannot be rightly known without the other also being known at the same time.

The relation between Brahman and the soul or the world is of the second type, so that they are the body of which the soul is God. That is, God is the central principle of both the individual soul and the physical world. Neither can exist or be thought of without him. Hence rightly though the three entities are all real and distinct from one another, they are not on the same footing. Thus the final Upanishadic teaching, according to Rāmānuja, is that while Brahman, the soul and the physical world are all different and equally eternal, they are at the same time quite inseparable. The point to be emphasized here, because it is often missed owing to the description of the doctrine as "Viśiṣ*ṭādvaita*" (commonly, but erroneously, rendered as "qualified monism") is that the three entities are different, although they stand in a peculiarly close relation to one another. What is meant by describing the doctrine as *advaita* ("monism") is not that the complex of these three elements is a synthesized unity of differences but only that Brahman as embodied in or inspiring the souls and matter is one. The latter, viz. souls and matter are not identical with it or with one another. If we like, we may interpret the term "Viśiṣṭādvaita" as signifying that there is nothing outside this embodied whole.[3]

Such an explanation of the term is adopted not only when the whole realm of reality is concerned, but also in all cases involving this peculiar relation. Thus a blue lotus is a "unity" in the sense that the material substance of the flower, which is characterized by two qualities that are different from it as well as from each other, viz. "blueness" and "lotusness," is one. Similarly a person, who was once a youth and is now old, may be regarded as one when we mean by it the soul as embodied previously in a youthful, and now in an aged, bodily frame. The distinction between the two instances, it will be observed, is that in the one the dependent elements co-exist, while in the other they succeed each other. To put the whole matter briefly, it is the qualifi*ed* or the embodi*ed* that is one, while the factors qualifying or embodying it are quite distinct, though inseparable, from it.

There is no doubt that Rāmānuja has here hit upon a very plausible way of interpreting co-ordinate propositions, and has thereby successfully got over the difficulty which the Upanishads present. Where they distinguish the world or the self from Brahman, they give expression to what is a matter of fact. Where they identify them, they only mean that they are inseparable in the sense explained just now, and not that they are identical. It may be doubted whether it is altogether sound to draw a metaphysical conclusion from forms of linguistic usage—to take "the grammar of language for the grammar of reality." But even if we waive that consideration, it is difficult to believe that the view is consonant with the spirit of the classical Upanishads taken as a whole. In all of them, there is but one section[4] which seems directly to support it, viz. that in which God is described as other than, and yet as the "inner controller immortal" of, both the individual soul and the world. But this support weakens considerably as the teaching here is of Yājñavalkya whose conception of the ultimate reality, as set forth in other portions of the same Upanishad, is monistic in the commonly accepted sense of the term. The section in question may, after all, signify nothing more than the transcendent and immanent character of ultimate reality—a belief in which is a common-place of later Vedic thought (p. 16).

Rāmānuja acknowledges only two categories which he names (*a*) substance (*dravya*) and (*b*) non-substance (*adravya*) or attribute. Of the remaining categories accepted in the Nyāya-Vaiśeṣika (p. 94), he brings "movement" (*karma*) under the latter head, explaining it in terms of conjunction (*saṁyoga*) and disjunction (*vibhāga*). Universals like "cowness" are not, according to him, independent eternal entities; they only stand, as in Jainism (p. 66), for configurations or unique dispositions of the parts constituting the particulars in question. Though resembling one another, they are quite distinct. He does not admit *samavāya* and *viśeṣa*. He also dispenses with non-existence (*abhāva*), regarding it as expressible in terms of positive entities much in the manner of Prabhākara (p. 143).

(*a*) By "substance" is meant what undergoes change or "what has modes" (*avasthāvat*), as Vedānta Deśika says. This category is of six kinds, but we shall deal here only with three of them, viz. Prakṛti, *jīva* and God;

(1) Prakṛti is conceived very much as in the Sāṅkhya-Yoga (p. 107), the only important differences being (i) that it is not regarded here as independent of spirit and (ii) that *sattva*, *rajas* and *tamas* are taken to be its attributes and not its constituents. That it is not independent of God is shown by our description

of it as the body or garment of God. The latter variation on the Sāṅkhya-Yoga doctrine, viz. that Prakṛti is not the same as, but is the substrate of, the three *guṇas*, may be stated to be the result of Rāmānuja's recognition of the distinction between substance and attribute which the other doctrine does not accept (p. 112). The whole of the physical world, in its infinite variety, evolves out of it under the guidance of God. The relation between Prakṛti and its evolutes or modes is *apṛthak-siddhi*, for, so long as they exist, they are inseparable from it in the sense explained above. Rāmānuja designates this as *sat-kārya-vāda*, but it is not so in the sense that the effect was already there before it became manifest as the Sāṅkhya-Yoga teaches (p. 109). It is *sat-kārya-vāda* in the sense that it is *sat* itself, or the already existing, that is conceived as effect by reason of the transformation which takes place in its modes. The point to be particularly noted is that the material cause is not taken here to be the substance, as such (say, "clay"), but as characterized by a mode ("lump"); and the effect is the same substance as characterized by another mode ("pot").[5] The nature of the evolutes and their order of emergence from Prakṛti are, for all practical purposes, the same as in the Sāṅkhya-Yoga.

Before proceeding further, it is necessary to refer briefly to another of the substances, which is called *dharma-bhūta-jñāna*. It belongs to God and the individual souls, and is entirely dependent upon them. It has been described as "attributive intelligence" since the latter, viz. God and the soul, which are independent relatively to it, are also, as we shall see, of the nature of intelligence. It is reckoned as a "substance" (*dravya*) since it can assume different forms, and thus satisfies the definition of that term as given above. It is luminous and glows with its own light; but what it illumines is always for another and not for itself.[6] It thus stands, in its nature, midway between dead matter and spirit. Unlike the former, it has the power to reveal the objects, with which it comes in contact; but it cannot know them, as the latter can. Pain, pleasure, desire, hate and volition are all looked upon as only its variant forms. They are not regarded here as experienced, as in some other doctrines, but only as modes of experience. This entity of "attributive intelligence" is all-pervading in the case of God, and accounts for his omniscience. In the case of the liberated souls too, it is all-pervading; but during mundane life, it is more or less contracted. Hence its functions are not only greatly restricted then; they also come to depend upon extraneous aids like the organs of sense. Its expansion to the full is thus a mark of salvation.

(2) The *jīva* is different from God, but not independent of him. It is described as a *prakāra* of God, by which is meant that it is an accessory to him, and not that it is a mode in the sense of being a transformation of him. Like Prakṛti, it is coeval with God but not identical with him. It is looked upon as God's "body" inasmuch as God is immanent in, acts upon and guides it from the inside. It is atomic but, since it has as its invariable accompaniment *dharma-bhūta-jñāna* which can stream forth to any distance, it is able to apprehend things even though they be far off. It is self-revealing, being of the essence of sentience, and knows no change except through changes in its *dharma-bhūta-jñāna*.[7] The souls are many; and, if unity is predicated of them anywhere in the Veda, it is because all of them alike are of the nature of sentience and therefore form one and the same class. They are intrinsically happy but transmigrate and are subject to suffering, as a result of their past karma. The *jīvas* are of three kinds—those that were never in bondage, like Garuda, and have therefore always been free; those that have passed through the ordeals of life and have, through successful self-discipline, become free; and those that are still in the process of transmigration.

(3) God is the immanent principle of Prakṛti as well as of individual souls. The exact significance of representing them as his body is that they are sustained by him, are altogether subject to his control and entirely subserve his purposes. Or, as Rāmānuja puts it, God exists for himself, while eventually matter and souls exist for his sake. The same observation, we may state by the way, applies to the individual soul and its body also. In other words, God together with the souls and matter is an organic whole, just as the soul with its physical body is an organic unity. The implication is that the relation of body and soul is more intimate than mere *apṛthak-siddhi*, which may be found in inorganic wholes also like a rock (say) with its colour or form where there is no question, for instance,

of the one controlling the other.[8] God, like the individual soul, is of the essence of intelligence, self-revealing and knows objects through *dharma-bhūta-jñāna*. But unlike it, he is free from all defects and is possessed of all auspicious qualities. He is omniscient, omnipotent and omnipresent. He is also all-merciful; and it is through his grace, as we shall see, that man attains salvation. He is the author of the universe. But he is not merely its efficient cause as in the Nyāya-Vaiśeṣika (p. 90). He is also represented as its source or material cause, since there is nothing external to him from which it could come into being. Thus God here, as Brahman in Advaita (p. 164), is the *sole* cause of the universe. As cause, in this comprehensive sense, God has as his body the souls and matter in their unmanifest form; and as effect, he has them as his body in their manifest and diversified form. This should not be regarded as implying that he is affected by the evil, viz. suffering and change found in the world, for that evil belongs specifically to the souls or matter and does not so much as touch the Supreme who is absolutely distinct from them.

(*b*) The second category of attributes, in the comprehensive sense ascribed to it in this doctrine, may be defined as what is necessarily dependent upon the first. They are ten in number: the five sensory qualities like colour and sound, the three *guṇas* of *sattva*, *rajas* and *tamas* which qualify Prakṛti, conjunction (*saṁyoga*) and causal potency (*śakti*) which, as in the Mīmāṁsā (p. 135), is taken to characterize everything that can produce effects. Thus Rāmānuja rejects not only some of the categories, but also several of the qualities recognized in the Nyāya-Vaiśeṣika. For example, the specific qualities of the self like pain, pleasure, love and hate, as we have seen, he regards as different modes of but one of them, viz. knowledge. According to the Nyāya-Vaiśeṣika, they are distinguished from knowledge (p. 91) and are explained as the known or experienced; but here that objective view of them is discarded.

We have already explained Rāmānuja's view of knowledge—how it is related to the soul and how it operates. Two other important points about it remain to be noticed now:

(1) All knowledge, according to him, points to a complex or qualified object, and it does so even at the so-called indeter-

minate (*nirvikalpaka*) level (p. 96). It follows from this that, since experience is our sole guide in determining the nature of reality, it is wrong to postulate anything which is altogether featureless. This is Rāmānuja's criticism of the attributeless (*nirguṇa*) Brahman in which the Advaita believes. As regards the negative statements in the Upanishads, like "Not this, not this" (*neti neti*) to which the advaitin points in support of his belief, Rāmānuja says that such statements negate only some attributes and not all of them. When a person states, for example, that there is nothing in a house, he only denies something relevant to the context, say, grain or precious metals and not everything. Similarly here, what the Upanishads mean is that there is no evil feature whatsoever in Brahman and not that it has no qualities at all.

(2) There is no error in the logical sense of the term, according to him; and all knowledge is true necessarily, though it may not be true enough. In this he is avowedly adopting the position of the Prābhākara school of Mīmāṁsakas (p. 144). When a torch held in the hand is turned round rapidly, we see a circle of fire. This is an illusion, and Rāmānuja says that it is quite correct so far as it goes. He means that it is right in comprehending the fact that the point of the torch occupies every possible position on the circumference; it only omits to note that the occupation takes place successively and is not simultaneous, as it should do to form an actual circle. In explaining some other types of error, like shell-silver and the dream-elephant, Rāmānuja differs slightly from Prabhākara; but it is not necessary to refer to those differences here. Like Prabhākara again, he accounts for the familiar distinction between truth and error on a pragmatic basis.

Unlike the advaitin (p. 168), Rāmānuja admits only three *pramāṇas:* perception, inference and verbal testimony. Of these, it will suffice to say a few words as regards the last, in so far as it stands for the Veda. Rāmānuja assigns equal importance to both its sections—that relating to ritual and that relating to Brahman, the highest reality. The two together embody a single doctrine, the only difference being that while the second portion deals principally with the nature of God, the first treats of the modes of worshipping him. Here we see an important difference between him and Śaṁkara for, according to the latter, the two sections of the Veda are addressed to two different types of people—the earlier one, to those who are trying to fit themselves for acquiring Brahma-knowledge; the later, to those who aim at Brahma-realization (p. 170). We should also state that the present doctrine draws upon the Purānas for support to a larger extent than the Advaita does. To these we must add what is known as Āgama, which Rāmānuja places on the same footing as the Veda, but to which Śaṁkara declines to ascribe unqualified authority (p. 34). In this connection, we may also point out that, according to Rāmānuja, every word eventually signifies the supreme God, as every thing eventually points to him as its final essence. Hence language is richer in content for a knower than it is for the ordinary man. All words are signs to remind the wise man of God, as all objects are for him windows through which to see God. The principle thus enunciated helps us to understand what, according to Rāmānuja, the meaning of the Upanishadic statement "That thou art" (*Tat tvam asi*) is. Here the word "That" finally denotes God having the entire universe as his body; and "thou," God having the individual soul as his body. The import of the proposition, as a whole, is accordingly the identity of the embodied in both, viz. God—a point which has already been explained.

## II

The ideal is the attainment of the world of Nārāyaṇa, and the enjoyment there, under his aegis, of perfect freedom and bliss. The means to it is of two kinds—one called *prapatti*, which is meant for all and whose source is to be traced mainly to the Vaiṣṇava faith; and the other called *bhakti*, which is based upon the teaching of the Upanishads and whose adoption is restricted to the higher castes. The former is absolute self-surrender, coupled with complete trust in the mercy and power of Nārāyaṇa; and one variety of it is believed to bring release at once. But it should be sought formally and with the assistance of a proper preceptor. This means to salvation, because it represents a certain mental attitude, is explained as a form of *jñāna;* and Rāmānuja maintains that in recommending *pra-*

*patti*, he does not swerve from the teaching of the Upanishads that knowledge is the chief, if not the sole, means to salvation. The latter or *bhakti* involves a course of training in three stages, known as *karma-yoga*, *jñāna-yoga* and *bhakti-yoga*. These terms, as used here require some explanation.

(1) The first of them bears the same significance as it does in Advaita (p. 170). It stands for doing the duties of one's station in life in the spirit of the teaching of the Gītā, or with absolutely no thought of reaping from them the fruits with which they are commonly associated. The only points that require notice in respect of it are two: First, of the two motives for performing *karma* referred to in our explanation of the Gītā teaching (p. 56), the present doctrine naturally stresses the one that is based on theism, and commends the doing of duty solely to please God. The other aim of cleansing the heart is not ignored; only it is looked upon as the necessary result of so dedicating all one's deeds to God. Secondly, the word *karma* is used here to include much more than Vedic ritual, for example, worship of idols as taught in the Āgamas, repeating sacred formulae etc.

(2) The second term, viz. *jñāna-yoga* is here interpreted in a special way although, as in the other doctrines, it is laid down that it should normally follow *karma-yoga*. Its aim is to help the disciple to realize the true nature of one's own self in relation to God, on the one hand, and, on the other, to its physical vesture or, to state the same somewhat differently, to Prakṛti as a whole. It therefore consists in meditating upon the self, first as essentially spiritual and therefore other than matter with which it happens to be associated; and secondly, as entirely subordinate to God. The underlying idea of thus explaining *jñāna-yoga* is that self-realization is not by itself the goal of man as in Advaita (p. 169), but only a precondition to it, viz. God-realization.

(3) The third term, *bhakti-yoga*, means constant meditation on God. The word *bhakti* here does not have its popular meaning of blind faith. It stands for loving meditation for its own sake, based upon the highest knowledge, and is the same as *upāsanā* (p. 26), which is so prominent a feature of the practical teaching of the Upanishads. This meditation is here acknowledged to lead only to "firm recollection" (*dhruvānusmṛtiḥ*) and not to an

actual perception of the ultimate as in some other systems. It is, however, more than ordinary recollection, and is characterized by vividness and intense love for the object meditated upon. It is described as "memory resembling direct knowledge," and is attainable in the present life. The actual goal is reached after physical dissolution; and then the soul, thus qualified, has a direct vision of God as its own ultimate essence. But since the soul's intelligence becomes all-pervading in that state and renders the operation of the sensory organs unnecessary, it is not perceptual knowledge as commonly understood and can only be described as a unique form of direct experience. Rāmānuja does not accordingly recognize *jīvanmukti* as Śaṁkara does. It remains to add that even this approach to liberation depends for its ultimate success on absolute self-surrender (*prapatti*); and no one who does not completely surrender his will to the Supreme and earn his grace, at one stage or another, has any chance of reaching the goal of life. So great is the influence of the old Vaiṣṇava creed on the doctrine. It envisages the possibility of achieving the goal by *prapatti* without resorting to *bhakti*, but not that of doing so by *bhakti* alone.

A few words now need to be added regarding the place of *karma* in the discipline, or, what comes to the same, the place of *saṁnyāsa* in it. That it is incumbent on every person to carry out the duties of his station in life to the best of his ability till the first of these three stages of discipline is passed is clear. Śaṁkara too admits it. The distinctive teaching of the present doctrine is that it insists on their performance in the succeeding stages also. That is, indeed, the implication of the view that both the "works" and "knowledge" sections of the Veda are addressed to one and the same type of persons. The reason for such continued adherence to *karma* is, first, to prevent the evil that will result from the neglect of duty, whatever be the degree of spiritual advance one has made; and, secondly, fully to secure the grace of God which is necessary before one can attain freedom. It is this gracious attitude of God that is conceived as *dharma* here, and not the good deeds themselves (p. 146) or their immediate effect of moral and religious merit (p. 104), as in the other doctrines. *Adharma* is the opposite of this. The significance of this emphasis on *karma* is that householders also can strive for, and attain salvation. If *saṁnyāsa* or the relinquishment of the obligations of the householder is commended in the Upanishads, it only means that its assumption is a help to the early attainment of salvation, and not that it is either a necessary preliminary to it (p. 171) or that duties enjoined in the Veda may be neglected.

### B. DVAITA

This doctrine resembles Viśiṣṭādvaita in being theistic and in identifying the supreme God with Nārāyana or, as he is generally designated here, Viṣṇu. But it is more explicitly pluralistic. Its general metaphysical position is well indicated by the statement cited by Madhva, "Diverse and of diverse attributes are all the things of the universe."[9] Thus not only are the individual souls distinct from one another and from matter, material objects too are so. The doctrine is also realistic, and postulates the existence of objects quite apart from knowledge. Like the other schools of Vedānta, it also claims to be as old as the Upanishads, and holds that Madhva was only its great exponent in later times. He was born in a village near Udipi in the South Kanara District about the end of the twelfth century, and is believed to have lived to a green old age (1199–1278 A.D.). His influence was in the beginning naturally confined to the Western part of the Indian peninsula, but it has extended very much farther since. He was named Vāsudeva by his parents; but, after he renounced the world and assumed *saṁnyāsa*, he came to be known as Pūrna Prajña or "the completely enlightened." He, however, calls himself Ānanda Tīrtha in all his writings. He has left behind him commentaries on the chief Upanishads, the Bhagavadgītā and the Vedānta Sūtra, besides several other works. The chief characteristic of his style is brevity; but there are commentaries on them, that well explain all points which his aphoristic style may render obscure. Of the writers of these commentaries, the greatest was Jaya Tīrtha, who was a soldier as well as a thinker, and who was a successor of Madhva in the pontificate established by him at Udipi. Another Dvaita thinker to whom we may refer here is Vyāsa Tīrtha, who has written standard treatises on the doctrine which indicate his vast learning and his great dialectical skill.

## I

The principal features of the doctrine, as just stated, are its belief in a personal God who is identified with Viṣṇu, a deity worshipped from Vedic times, its realism and its pluralism. Of these, we shall refer to its realistic character later, and consider the other two features now. Its pluralistic view is based on common experience which, it is added, is supported by the Veda. The latter part of this statement will be seen to be quite justifiable if we take the earlier sections of the Veda, viz. the Mantras and the Brāhmaṇas; and it is contended that the Veda, being revealed, cannot be self-inconsistent and should therefore teach the same truth in the Upanishads also. In support of this contention are cited the few passages of dualistic import which, as already pointed out (p. 19), the Upanishads contain. We shall see later in what manner the far greater number of passages in them of monistic significance are interpreted in this system. The belief in God, unlike that in variety or difference, is based entirely on scripture, for he is taken to be beyond the reach of the unaided faculties of man. He is the efficient cause of the world, of which the material cause or source is traced to Prakṛti, conceived more or less as in the Sāṅkhya-Yoga (p. 126). According to Rāmāṇuja, who is equally great as a theistic philosopher, we know, God is the material cause also; but then he is to be viewed as embodied in the individual souls and matter in their subtle form. Such association with them, as Dr. Bhandarkar observes, was regarded by Madhva as too intimate to be consistent with the transcendent majesty of God. It may appear from what we have said so far that the Dvaita resembles the Nyāya-Vaiśesika. It does so to a large extent; but, as we shall see, it also differs from that doctrine vitally in certain details. We have already indicated two instances of such difference—the tracing of the physical world to a single source, Prakṛti, instead of to an indefinite number of atoms (p. 86), and the resting of its belief in God not on reason (p. 90) but on revelation.

As the conception of "difference" (*bheda*) is very important in this doctrine, it is necessary to explain it at some length. We may begin by stating why some thinkers, like the advaitins in particular, reject it. The notion of difference, they say, is relative, and is not therefore intelligible without reference to the things that are different. The idea of difference between A and B (say) presupposes a knowledge of these two entities; but that knowledge, since it points to them as *two*, already involves the idea of difference. There is thus mutual dependence between the notion of difference and that of the things which differ, and neither can therefore be fully understood without the other. The advaitins accordingly regard the idea of "difference" as self-discrepant, and dismiss it as but an appearance (p. 154). There are other arguments also adduced by them in this connection, but it will do for us to confine our attention to this one.

In meeting the above argument, the dvaitin points out that the difficulty of mutual dependence arises because of the assumption that difference is something in addition to the terms it relates. The fact however, according to him, is that it is nothing but the particular thing itself, or, as it is said, its very essence (*sva-rūpa*). In the above example, A is exactly what we mean by its difference from B; and B, its difference from A. Hence there are not *two* factors at all to be known—A *and* its difference from B, or B *and* its difference from A—to lead to mutual dependence, as stated by the critic. Now the question will naturally arise as to how, in that case, we can talk, as we often do, of "the difference *of* A (from B)" as if the two, viz. "difference" and "A" were distinct. The dvaitin's answer to this question is that the identity between a thing and its difference from another is a special kind of identity, in that it allows itself on occasions to be expressed in a form that seems to differentiate between them. He describes it as "an identity associated with *viśeṣa*" (*saviśeṣābheda*). The conception of *viśeṣa*, on which this view is based, is of great consequence in the doctrine, like that of *apṛthak-siddhi* in Viśiṣṭādvaita; and we shall, after dealing with it under the head of the Dvaita categories, refer to this topic of "difference" again. It will suffice for the present to remark that the final outcome of the Dvaita argument in this respect is that when we speak of difference between two or more things, we only mean that each of them is itself. Everything is unique, and it is this very uniqueness that constitutes its difference from other things.

*Bheda* or difference, whose notion is so fundamental to the view taken of reality, is explained as fivefold: God and soul, the different souls, God and matter, soul and matter and matter itself in its various forms are all absolutely distinct. This does not, however, necessarily imply the independence of the objects distinguished. The physical body, for example, is dependent upon the soul to which it pertains, although quite different from it. Particularly is this so in the case of God and the world. The difference between the two does not mean that the world has nothing to do with him, and can exist in spite of him. That is taken to be independent here which can, of its own accord, be, know and act.[10] Such an entity is God alone. Everything else exists, knows and functions finally at his will. Nor does difference in the case of God imply that he stands outside the universe as a mere spectator. He is immanent in it, and controls it from inside. It is on this basis of God's complete supremacy or, to state it differently, on the basis of not numerical but teleological unity that the Dvaita sometimes explains Upanishadic statements of monistic import like "All this, indeed, is Brahman" (*Sarvam khalvidam Brahma*).

In the recognition of "difference" as a final fact lies the distinction of the present doctrine not only from Śaṁkara's Advaita but also from all forms of monism. But at the same time, we should remember that, as just pointed out, it is not pluralistic in the ordinary acceptation of the term, for there is only one *independent* entity, and not many as, for example, in the Nyāya-Vaiśeṣika. Madhva goes so far as to ascribe even the being of everything else to God.[11] Although he seems to mean by it only that they are absolutely dependent upon his will and not that their being is derived from him, it is clear that there is nothing except God, which, according to Madhva, can be said to exist *in its own right*.

The doctrine acknowledges ten categories (*padārtha*). They are substance, quality, action, universals, *viśeṣa*, the specified (*viśiṣṭa*), the whole (*aṁśin*), potency, similarity, and non-existence. Several of these categories we have already considered in one connection or another; and their conception here is not very different. Of the remaining ones, it will suffice to deal only with substance and *viśeṣa*. But before doing so, we should mention one general point, viz. the Dvaita idea of the relation between a substance and its attributes. Madhva holds that this relation may be of two kinds. Some attributes last as long as their substrate does, for example, the weight of a material object; others do not. In the former case, he argues that the relation is always one of identity. In the latter case, on the other hand, he maintains that the relation is identity *and* (not *in*) difference. That is, the relation is identity so long as the attribute continues to characterize the substrate; but difference, when it ceases to do so. A thing may be white for some time, and then change its colour. The whiteness is identical with it as long as it characterizes the thing, but not afterwards, for, if it were so, that thing too should then disappear as the quality of whiteness has done. A consequence of this view of the relation between substance and attribute is that the essential characteristics of an eternal entity come to be viewed as eternal like it. Attributes characterizing temporal things are temporal and, even during the periods the things last, they may or may not be identical with them.

(1) Substance (*dravya*). The substances are twenty in number; but we shall confine our attention, as we did in the case of the other two schools of Vedānta, to three only of them, which form the chief subject-matter of all philosophy and religion.

(i) *God:* God, to whose pre-eminent position according to the doctrine we have already referred, possesses all excellences. He is unknowable in the sense that he cannot be exhaustively known even with the aid of revelation, and not in the sense that he is altogether beyond the reach of mind as Brahman is in Advaita (p. 166). He is, we may say, apprehensible but not comprehensible. God transcends *sattva*, *rajas* and *tamas* which are not qualities of Prakṛti here as in the Viśiṣṭādvaita, but are its first products. He has, however, his own attributes such as infinite power and infinite mercy, in addition to being the essence of knowledge and joy. The conception is personal; but the personality, it is added, is of the absolute kind. As already stated, God is not only the creator and destroyer of the whole universe; he also entirely controls it, in each and every one of its aspects. This is very well indicated by the statement, which Madhva cites in his works, viz. that "the individual self, matter, time and all exist only by his grace and would at once come to nothing, if that grace were withdrawn."[12] From this standpoint there are only two categories, as he himself elsewhere says—the dependent (*asva-tantra*) and the independent (*sva-tantra*). But though everything thus exists and functions for him, he, being intrinsically perfect, has nothing to gain through them. The multifarious activity of the universe is but a revelation of this perfection; and the entire creation is meant only to afford an opportunity to all for self-realization through proper self-discipline. Although one, God may assume any form he likes as, for example, when he incarnates as an *avatār* (p. 35). He is, again, as in Rāmānuja's doctrine, the ultimate significance of all words.

(ii) *Souls:* They are infinite in number, each being fundamentally distinct from others as shown by the difference in their experiences. Each has its own imperfections, such as ignorance and suffering. Each is atomic. They are different from God, and not only from one another; but the difference is not absolute as in the case of matter, for they have features like sentience and bliss (though qualified) common with God. It is on this principle of similarity that Madhva sometimes explains Upanishadic statements like "That thou art" (*Tat tvam asi*). They do not, according to him, imply identity of essence as in Advaita (p. 164), but mere resemblance. The souls are of three classes: first, those that are bound but may become free; secondly, those that are confined eternally to migration from one life to another within the mundane sphere; and lastly, those that are doomed permanently to the misery of hell. The recognition of the last two classes of souls is a peculiar feature of the doctrine, and shows that Madhva does not subscribe to the ideal of universal redemption, admitted by many among Indian thinkers. This is rather a strange conclusion to reach for a doctrine which is so thoroughly theistic and, as we shall see, places so much reliance on divine grace. It not only means that the element of evil will ever persist in the universe, but also restricts the scope of human freedom and the power of divine grace.

(iii) *Prakṛti:* This is the ultimate source of the physical universe. It is eternal but insentient. The three *guṇas* of *sattva, rajas* and *tamas,* as already stated, are regarded as its first products. From them emerge in succession the "intellect" (*mahat*), "egoism" (*ahaṁ-kāra*), *manas,* the sensory organs and the five elements much as in Sāṅkhya-Yoga (p. 110). The Dvaita view of causation differs not only from the Advaita view of it but also from those held in the Nyāya-Vaiśesika and the Sāṅkhya-Yoga (p. 158). The effect produced is regarded as neither existent only, nor non-existent only, before its production (and presumably after its destruction) but both existent and non-existent (*sadasat-kārya–vāda*). It exists then as the cause, but not as the effect. That it should exist as the material cause is shown by the fact that certain effects can be produced only from certain causes, for example, cloth from threads and pots from clay. There is no contradiction, it is pointed out, in this double predication, for the two predicates, "existent" and "not-existent," are not affirmed from the same standpoint. While a thing may exist as the cause, it may not exist as the effect. Even after it has been produced, it is existent as well as non-existent; only it then exists as the effect and not as the cause. We have thus far spoken of the material cause (*upádāna-kāraṇa*). The Dvaita, like the other doctrines, recognizes also the efficient cause (*apādāna-kārana*) and the relation between it and the product is, of course, absolute difference.

(2) *Viśeṣa:* This, as we have stated, is of great importance in understanding Dvaita ontology aright. Let us consider, for instance, the nature of the relation between substance and attribute, an object and not its provisional quality which we have already considered, but its permanent one, say, a coin and its weight. Three explanations of it are possible. The two may be taken as identical, or as altogether distinct; or they may be regarded as both identical with and, at the same time, different from each other. According to Dvaita, none of these explanations is tenable; and in each of them, it points out, lies implicit the notion of *viśeṣa*. On the reasoning set forth in the previous chapter (p. 153), the last of these is really no explanation at all. We may, therefore leave it out, and consider only the remaining two.

The first explanation identifies the coin with weight, but we often speak and think of the weight *of* the coin which clearly signifies a distinction between them, and is therefore opposed to the assumption of identity between them. To explain the discrepancy, the upholders of the view must assume something in the coin or in its weight or in both which, though there is no actual difference between them, justifies our distinguishing them as above. It is this "something" which the Dvaita terms *viśeṣa*. If we adopt the second view that the coin and its weight are altogether distinct, we shall have a triad—the two relata and the difference which qualifies them. Now if, as is taken for granted here, substance and attribute are different, the "difference" between the coin and its weight, because it qualifies a substance, viz. the coin, itself becomes attributive and must therefore be different from it. That is, we have to assume a second difference to explain the first, and a third to explain the second and so on—a process which leads to infinite regress. To escape from it, the advocate of the view in question has to postulate that the "difference" between substance and attribute does not itself require to be distinguished from its ground or support. In other words, he should admit that there is, at least, one exception to the rule that substance and attribute are distinct. It is this very explanation, viz. that there is no need to distinguish them, although they sometimes appear as two, which the dvaitin extends, on the basis of *viśeṣa*, to *all* cases where there is no difference but a distinction is made. In his view, *bheda* or "difference" is one of such cases, for, though identical with the essence of things, it is, as already stated, sometimes distinguished from them. This category of *viṣeṣa*, it should be carefully noted, is not the same as "difference" (*bheda*) but is what accounts for speaking of identical things as different.[13] The reader will here see, as in the case of an object and its provisional quality instanced above, a new attempt to solve an old problem we have come across already more than once in the course of this book, viz. the problem of things which appear neither wholly identical nor wholly different (pp. 65, 93) but we cannot say that the solution is more satisfactory.

By *viśesa* accordingly we should understand a speciality that characterizes a thing; and in each thing, as many *viśesas* are recognized as are necessary to account for linguistic usages (which imply corresponding modes of thought) of the kind alluded to above. It is postulated not only in the case of substances but in that of all categories—even non-existence, for all alike have characteristics which in common parlance sometimes are, and sometimes are not, distinguished from them.

Here we find a divergence from the conception of *viśesa* in the Nyāya-Vaiśeṣika which restricts it to substances and, among them, only to such as are eternal (p. 87). Another important difference between the two conceptions is that, while in the Nyāya-Vaiśeṣika *viśeṣa* accounts for the difference which is assumed to exist between two things, here it accounts for making a difference where there is assumed to be none.

The process of knowing is explained as in the Nyāya-Vaiśeṣika (p. 91), but the conception of knowledge itself is very different. It is regarded there as a quality which arises in the self when certain conditions, such as the contact of a sense organ with an appropriate object, are fulfilled. Here it is explained as a transformation or mode of the internal organ (*manas*), and therefore as characterizing it and not the self. This explanation should not be taken to stand in the way of the knowledge being felt as its own by the self, for, according to the doctrine, the latter is the agent which initiates the knowing process and is not therefore unconnected with the knowledge that arises. As in the Viśiṣṭādvaita, all knowledge is here regarded as pointing to a complex or qualified object, and there is consequently no justification for admitting any attributeless entity.

We have already described the doctrine as realistic. It is realism in the absolute sense, for Madhva denies that there can be any knowledge without reference to an object other than it, not excluding error as we shall soon see. Existence in space and time is the general criterion of reality. Anything that comes into relation with time and space is necessarily real, no matter for how long or to what extent. The Dvaita recognizes no distinction between the real and the empirical or between the empirical and the unreal as the Advaita does (p. 167). There is only one valid distinction ontologically, viz. that between the real and the unreal. If the Advaita explains the prevailingly absolutistic standpoint of Upanishadic teaching by postulating only one reality and explaining the rest of the universe as its appearance (p. 161), the Dvaita does the same by postulating God as the only supreme entity and explaining the rest as altogether dependent upon him.

In accordance with the realism of the doctrine, truth (*pramā*) is defined as correspondence with outside reality. In it, the object is apprehended just as it is (*yathārtha*). Dreams and recollection also are taken to be true. But the former are valid only so far as the particular objects, in themselves, are concerned. Their externality, experienced at the time, is admitted to be illusory. For example, an elephant seen in a dream is, as such, real; but its being then seen in the streets of a town (say) is false. The reason why dream objects are regarded as real is that they are not contradicted later. The dreamer, after he wakes, does not feel that it was not an elephant which he saw but only that it was not there outside. Recollection also is right knowledge when the object remembered is taken in the spatial and temporal context in which it appears, but not in relation to the time when or the place where it may be remembered. That is, it becomes false only if we think a past thing to be present or a remote thing to be near.

The Dvaita theory of error resembles that of the Nyāya-Vaiśeṣika with one important difference; and it is, for this reason, sometimes described as a new or improved version of it (*abhinavānyathā-khyāti*). The latter doctrine holds that the serpent, seen when only a rope is presented, is existent, though not in the place where it appears (p. 98). The Dvaita agrees that the serpent is not where it appears; but it dismisses the fact of its existence or being real elsewhere as irrelevant. Thus the error consists here in taking the absolutely non-existent for the existent.[14] This is the misapprehension (*anyathā-khyāti*) involved in error. That the serpent is non-existent altogether is to be deduced from the later correcting knowledge, which shows that what was taken to *be*, actually *was not*. Objects of error consequently are neither in the place where they seem to be, nor elsewhere. But still erroneous knowledge is explained as having its own "object," viz. the absolutely non-existent. The dvaitin, unlike many other thinkers, believes that the non-existent is knowable as shown, for instance, by the fact that we speak of a unicorn or a square-circle. To speak of *asat*, he says, is to grant that we know it. Though the *object* of error is thus unreal, the erroneous *knowledge* itself is looked upon as quite real. The dvaitin accordingly does not grant what some like the advaitins believe, viz. that the falsity of the object necessarily involves the falsity of its knowledge.

Like Rāmānuja, Madhva also accepts only three means to

valid knowledge (*pramāṇas*): perception, inference and verbal testimony. But over and above these, he regards valid knowledge itself as being a *pramāṇa* in the sense that it points directly to a *fact* and not in the sense that it is a means to valid *knowledge*. Thus perception as a *pramāṇa* points to a jar (say) mediately through perceptual knowledge, while the latter does so immediately. Similarly inference as a *pramāṇa* indicates the presence of fire mediately through inferential knowledge, while the latter does so directly. He thus makes a distinction, which appears to be too obvious to need affirmation, between what may be described as primary (*kevala-pramāṇa*) and secondary (*anupramāṇa*) means to the knowing of objects. It is the latter that are divided in a triple way as perception, inference and verbal testimony. Of these, we shall say a few words only about the first, viz. perception. In his view of scriptural testimony Madhva, like Rāmānuja, shows a greater leaning towards Āgamas and Purāṇas than Śaṁkara does.

The senses, which are instrumental in knowing, are reckoned as seven, including not only *manas* but also what is called the *sākṣin*. The conception of *sākṣin* as an organ of sense (*indriya*) is another distinctive feature of Dvaita. We have seen that God and the selves are of the nature of sentience. It is this sentience itself that is taken here, somewhat as in Advaita (p. 165), to be the *sākṣin*. That is, it not only finally knows things presented through one or other of the sense as commonly understood; it can also know directly, being of the nature of sentience—a view which resembles in part the Jaina view of knowing (p. 61). The knowledge gained through this means is regarded as invariably correct. Some things like one's own self, pain, pleasure, time and space are thus directly known; all else, through one or other of the remaining senses. In the case of the self then, according to Madhva, it knows itself by itself[15]—a view which Śaṁkara, as we have seen (p. 166), dismisses as a contradiction in terms. A consequence of ascribing the knowledge of pain, pleasure etc. to the self directly is to reduce the internal organ (*manas*) to merely a general aid in knowing; and it ceases to have its own specific objects to make known to the self as in several other doctrines, for instance, Nyāya-Vaiśeṣika (p. 91). It is an aid by itself only in respect of recollection.

## II

As in Advaita (p. 165), the prime source of *saṁsāra* is beginningless ignorance (*avidyā*), which is regarded as specific to each individual. But here it is conceived as real. It is, in fact, one of the twenty "substances" accepted in the system. There are two principal aspects of it. It obscures from man not only the true nature of God but also that of himself; and release consists in overcoming both. Of these, one attains a correct knowledge of one's self by the study of the scriptures; but it will be mediate. This mediate knowledge becomes immediate when final liberation is achieved through God's grace, to which we shall presently refer. A knowledge of God, as the author of the universe and the lord of all, is thus more essential than self-knowledge for release. It also is to be gained through the scriptures; but it is to be transformed into direct experience, chiefly through steadfast meditation. The ideal is the attainment by the selves of bliss, appropriate in each case to its intrinsic worth, so that the distinction of one self from another, though both become free, persists even in *mokṣa*. The bliss of the self in this state and, we may add, its knowledge also are finite as compared with the bliss and knowledge of God which are infinite; but even such bliss and knowledge are not completely realized in mundane life, as after liberation. A vessel may be big or small and even a small one, it is said in illustration of this view, may or may not be full of water. Similar is the difference between the states of transmigration and release in the case of selves.

We have pointed out that a knowledge of God is essential to release. But the final means to reaching it is unbroken love of God or devotion (*bhakti*), which springs from a realization of his greatness and goodness. This love leads to God's grace (*prasāda*) towards the self; and it is that grace, says Madhva, which is the crowning cause of salvation.[16] The rest are but aids to it. Herein is seen best the theistic character of the doctrine, and the true source of its popular appeal. This love should be infinitely more intense than that which one may possess for oneself, or for things belonging to oneself; and its promptings should be such as will not allow themselves to be thwarted by obstacles, be they ever so many. The realization of God's greatness and goodness, which is the penultimate means to salvation, arises through the cultivation of absolute detachment by performing one's duties in the spirit of the Gītā teaching (*karma-yoga*), the study (*śravana*) of the scriptures thereafter under a proper *guru*, reflection (*manana*) upon what is taught in them as well as constant meditation (*dhyāna*) upon it—a course of discipline which is identical with the one prescribed in the Upanishads, and to which we have referred more than once heretofore. Like Rāmānuja, Madhva also rejects the ideal of *jīvanmukti*, and insists upon the need for carrying out, till the very end, the duties of one's station in life, including the scriptural rites that are obligatory.

# NOTES AND REFERENCES

ABBREVIATIONS

| | |
|---|---|
| Bṛ. Up. | Bṛhadāraṇyaka Upanishad. |
| Ch. Up. | Chāndogya Upanishad. |
| NM. | Nyāya-mañjarī of Jayanta Bhaṭṭa (Vizianagaram Sans. Series). |
| RV. | Rigveda. |
| SB. | Śrī-bhāṣya of Rāmānuja with Śruta-prakāśikā, Sūtraś 1–4, (Nirn. Sag. Pr.). |
| SK. | Sāṅkhya Kārikā of Īśvara Kṛṣṇa. |
| SV. | Śloka-vārttika of Kumārila Bhaṭṭa (Chowkhamba Series). |
| TAS. | Tattvārthādhigama-sūtra of Umāsvāti (Bibliotheca Indica). |
| VS. | Vedānta Sūtra of Bādarāyaṇa. |
| YS. | Yoga Sūtra of Patañjali with the com. of Vyāsa and Vācaspati's gloss on it (Anandasrama Series). |

## CHAPTER ONE

[1] The Mantras are verse; the Brāhmaṇas are in prose, but they often contain quotations in verse. The whole of this material is grouped under four heads, each being designated a "Veda" (i.e. knowledge)—Rigveda, Yajur-veda, Sāma Veda and Atharva Veda. Each Veda thus includes both Mantras and Brāhmaṇas.

[2] *Six Systems of Indian Philosophy* (Collected Edition), p. 41.

[3] "Though the name of Uṣas is radically cognate to Aurora, the cult of Dawn as a goddess is a specially Indian development." Macdonnell, *Vedic Mythology*, p. 8.

[4] *Ethics of India*, by E. W. Hopkins, p. 8. The author adds: "The *bhakti* or loving devotion, which some scholars imagine to be only a late development of Hindu religion, is already evident in the Rigveda."

[5] Cf. Aitareya Up., iii, 3, where Brahmā is named at the head of living beings.

[6] RV., X, 129.

[7] RV., X, 90: *Sa bhūmim viśvato vṛtvā atyatiṣṭhat daśāṅgulam.*

[8] See e.g. *Mīmāṁsā-nyāya-prakāśa*, by Āpa Deva, p. 47 (Nirn. Sag. Pr.). It is this stage in the development of Indian religion that may be described as "Brahmanism." Its characteristic mark is the acknowledgment of the Veda as divine revelation. "Hinduism" is the name applied to a later phase of it. It also appeals to Vedic authority; but "it is much wider in scope and includes the worship of deities of post-Vedic origin and growth."

[9] Bṛ. Up., I, iv, 10.

[10] Cf. *id.* IV, iv, 22.

[11] Ch. Up., VII, 25, 2; Muṇḍaka Up., II, ii, 11.

[12] Aitareya Up., iii, 3.

[13] Ch. Up., VI, ii, 1–2.

[14] Bṛ. Up., I, iv, 2: *Dvitīyāt vai bhayam bhavati.*

[15] Cf. Praśna Up., v, 2.

[16] See *Indian Antiquary* for 1924, pp. 77–86.

[17] Bṛ. Up., V, ii. Hence it is not right to hold, as some do, that the Upanishads do not care much for social morality and concern themselves solely with pointing out the way to individual perfection. Cf. Hopkins, *op. cit.* p. 64.

[18] Kaṭha Up., II, ii, 7: *Yathā-karma yathā-śrutam.*

[19] Praśna Up., iii, 7: *Puṇyena puṇyam lokam nayati, pāpena pāpam.*

[20] Cf. Īśa Up., st. 1 and Br. Up., III, vii. One may think that the conception of Brahman (n.) is the same as that of Brahmā (m.), which sometimes occurs in the Upanishads. But it is not so, for the latter goes back, as pointed out in the text (p. 15), not to the Upanishadic Absolute but to Prajāpati. *See* Note 2 to Chapter Two.

CHAPTER TWO

[1] See, e.g., Jacobi's contribution to *Indian Studies in Honour of Lanman* (Harvard Oriental Series), where the Mīmāṁsā Sūtra is placed about 300–200 B.C.; the Vaiśeṣika Sūtra, about 100 B.C., and the Nyāya Sūtra, a little later.

[2] It has to be noted that even these Gods appear later (e.g. in the minor Upanishads) as the personifications of ātman or Brahman, in accordance with the general spirit of Upanishadic teaching.

[3] The Mahābhārata, for instance, says that Śiva sprang from Śri Krishna's forehead (Kumbhakonam Edn., III, xii, 37 ff.) thus repudiating the supremacy assigned to him in Śaivism.

[4] See Śaṁkara's com. on VS. II, ii, 45.

[5] Kaṭha Up., I, iii, 9: *Tat Viṣṇoḥ paramam padam.*

[6] *Yacca kim-cit jagatyasmin dṛśyate śrūyatepi vā*
*Antarbahiśca tat sarvam vyāpya Nārāyaṇaḥ sthitaḥ.*

[7] Gītā iv, 7–8.

[8] *Id.* ix, 23.

[9] *Id.* xii, 8, xiv, 2.

[10] *Ācāra-hīnam na punanti vedāḥ.* Vāśiṣṭha Dharma Sūtra, vi, 3.

[11] Cf. Mahābhārata, XII, 109, 14: *Dhāraṇāt dharmam ityāhuḥ.*

[12] There are also two other kinds of *karma*, viz., *kāmya* and *pratiṣiddha*. The former are optional, like sacrifices for attaining heaven, and are to be performed by those that seek their fruit; the latter are such as are prohibited, e.g. infliction of injury. See Chapter Six, pp. 147–8.

[13] Cf. Yājñavalkya Smṛti (I, iv, 122):
*Ahiṁsā satyamasteyam śaucam indriya-nigrahaḥ*
*Dānam damo dayā śāntiḥ sarveṣām dharma-sādhanam.*

[14] Bṛ. Up., II, iv.

[15] Cf. Gautama Dharma Sūtra, iii, 36.

[16] Cf. Āpastamba Dharma Sūtra, I, xxii, 2 *ff.*, and Gautama Dharma Sūtra, viii, 22–23.

[17] *Aprāpte śāstram arthavat.* Cf. Mīmāṁsā Sūtra, I, i, 5. This portion dealing with types of Indian thought, and the next one, dealing with the Karma doctrine, are based for the most part on two articles contributed by the author to the *Aryan Path* of September 1934 and January 1935 respectively.

[18] See e.g., Sāyaṇa's Introduction to his com. on RV.

[19] *Smṛti* is a general word for tradition or "what is remembered." But, as accepted by the orthodox, it is only such tradition as has a basis in *śruti* or "revelation" directly or indirectly.

[20] SV., p. 90.

[21] Similarly, the fact that man does not always reap in this life the fruit of the good and evil he does in it points to the need for postulating future births.

[22] Yājñavalkya Smṛti, i, 349. See also Manu Smṛti, vii, 205.

[23] *Philosophy of the Upanishads* (English Translation), p. 313 *n.*

[24] Cf. NM., pp. 513–515. See also Āpastamba Dharma Sūtra, xxiii–xxiv.

[25] *Nirupadrava-bhūtārtha-svabhāvasya viparyayaiḥ*
*Na bādhoyatna-vatvepi buddheh tat-pakṣa-pātataḥ.*

[26] Cf. ii, 47.

[27] Cf. ii, 31; iii, 35; xviii, 47–48.

[28] Cf. v, 11; vi, 12.

[29] Com. on Gītā, iii, 1: *Vihitasya karaṇākaraṇayoḥ duḥkha-rupatvāt.*

[30] xii, 10; Cf. xi, 54.

## CHAPTER THREE

[1] *Agnirusṇo jalam śitam sama-sparśaḥ tathānilaḥ*
*Kenedam citritam tasmāt svabhāvāt tadvyavasthitiḥ.*

[2] NM., p. 467.

[3] The other two are *dharma* and *adharma*. They do not, however, stand here for moral or religious merit and demerit as in Hinduism generally, but represent the principles of motion and of rest. The whole of space is divided, according to Jainism, into two parts, in one of which alone, where *dharma* is present, motion is possible. It is thus a condition of motion. The other principle of *adharma*, found in the remaining part of space, is similarly regarded as a condition of rest.

[4] These souls animating matter are not to be confounded with the animalculae that may live, say, in a drop of water.

[5] *Sarva-dravya-paryāyeṣu kevalasya* (TAS., i, 30).

[6] Some hold that sensory perception also in indirect on the ground that it needs the assistance of sense organs. See TAS., i, 11.

[7] *Sāmānya-viśeṣātmā tadartho viṣayaḥ.*

[8] *Utpāda-vyaya-dhrauvya-yuktam sat* (TAS., v, 29).

[9] *Guṇa-paryāyavat dravyam* (TAS., v, 37). See Jacobi, *Sacred Books of the East*, Vol. XLV, pp. xxxiv and 153 n. There is, however, a view that *guṇas* are essential or permanent attributes like touch or taste of matter, while *paryāyas* are its passing phases. See Pūjyapāda's com. on TAS., v, 41.

[10] The alternative of "is" and "is not" is only a combination of the first two, and is not therefore reckoned as a separate *koṭi*. Cf. *Syādvāda-mañjarī*, p. 195 (Bombay Sans. Series): *Amīṣāmeva trayāṇām mukhyatvāt śeṣa-bhaṅgānām ca saṁyoga-jatvena amīṣveva antarbhāvah.* The first of these three views would be that of the *Sāṅkhya*; the second, of nihilistic Buddhism; and the third, of one aspect of Upanishadic teaching. (Cf. Taittirīya Up., ii, 4: *Yato vāco nivartante aprāpya manasā saha.*)

[11] Altogether four standpoints are recognized in regard to every thing: its material (*dravya*), the place which it occupies (*kṣetra*), the time in which it exists (*kāla*) and the state in which it is (*bhāva*). We have illustrated the point, in the text, by taking the first of them.

[12] Pūjyapāda's com. on TAS. (x, 1) describes it as *apratarkya-vibhūti-viśeṣam*, i.e. "of inconceivable splendour."

[13] Cf. Śaṁkara on VS., II, ii, 33.

[14] See Jacobi, *Sacred Books of the East*, Vol. XXII, pp. xxii *ff*.

[15] *Dhyānam mokṣa-hetuḥ* (com. on TAS., vii, 57).

[16] The account in this section is based chiefly on the later writings of Mrs. C. A. F. Rhys Davids, such as *Outlines of Buddhism* and *What was the Original Gospel of Buddhism?* (1938).

[17] Cf.

*Ātmani sati para-saṁjñā sva-para-vibhāgāt parigraha-dveṣau*
*Anayoḥ sampratibaddhāḥ sarve bhāvāḥ prajāyante.*

[18] This is the doctrine of *pratītya-samutpāda* or "dependent origination."

[19] These five are—right resolve, right speech, right livelihood, right effort and right mindfulness.

[20] It is usual to consider two schools under Hīnayāna Buddhism also, viz. the Vaibhāṣika and the Sautrāntika; but we have not thought it necessary to dwell upon this distinction. These are termed *Sarvāsti-vāda* and dealt with together, for example, in VS. (II, ii, 18 *ff.*).

[21] *Mādhyamika-kārikā*, xvi, 8.

[22] *Na sat nāsat na sadasat na cāpyanubhayātmakam*
*Catuṣkoṭi-vinirmuktam tattvam Mādhyamikā viduḥ.*

[23] See e.g., NM. pp. 536–537.

[24] "We see here the influence of the doctrine of *bhakti* known to us from the Bhagavadgītā, and it is most probable that it was the Bhagavadgītā itself which influenced the development of the Mahāyāna." Winternitz, *History of Indian Literature*, Vol. ii, p. 229 *n*.

## CHAPTER FOUR

[1] The atoms, it is believed, can be perceived by *yogins*.

[2] Two or more different "elements" cannot combine in this manner. If they are found together, as in the human body, they are to be explained as only in mechanical combination with a product derived from some *one* of them.

[3] The Indian belief is that man alone is self-conscious and thus may strive for self-perfection or spiritual freedom. The other living beings are born merely to reap the fruit of past karma. It may appear that, in the absence of all scope for moral improvement, there is no justification for the punishment of such animals in accordance with their past karma. The explanation lies in the ethical view of the universe that underlies the doctrine. It is retributive justice.

[4] There is no contradiction in describing selves as all-pervading and yet as mutually exclusive, for they are not *physical* entities.

[5] It is said "generally" because the doctrine assumes, in accounting for the lack of experience in deep sleep, that there is a temporary disconnection between the self and *manas*.

[6] There is a ninth specific quality of the self also recognized, viz. *bhāvanā* or "residual impression." It is one of the three varieties of *saṁskāra* included in the list of qualities.

[7] See NM. p. 201.

[8] In order that two things may be in conjunction, it is necessary that one of them at least should be finite.

[9] These correspond to the "abstract universals" (*tiryak-sāmānya*) of Jainism. There is no recognition here of "concrete universals" (*ūrdhvatā-sāmānya*), for the idea of evolution or change is foreign to the system. We have now all the *three* views of *sāmānya* known to Indian philosophy: some, like the Buddhists, take it as purely conceptual; others, like the Jains, as configurations characterizing the particulars; and still others, like the followers of the present doctrine, as objective realities.

[10] *Samavāya* thus relates five sets of things: (1) whole and parts, (2) substance and quality, (3) substance and action, (4) particular and universal, and (5) ultimate substance and *viśeṣa*.

[11] See *Sapta-padārthī*, p. 25 (Vizianagaram Sans. Series): *Sarvam jñānam dharmiṇi abhrāntam, prakāre tu viparyayaḥ*.

[12] There is another set of circumstances where the Buddhist recognizes the legitimacy of inference, viz. genus and species. The fact of an object being a cow (say) is invariably connected with the fact of its being an animal, for the one is a species of the other (*tādātmya*).

[13] These are strictly to be called *liṅga* or "the sign" and the *liṅgin* or "the signified;" but they continue to be called *hetu* or "cause" and *sādhya* or "effect."

[14] Cf. *Nyāya-vārttika*, p. 23.

[15] *Nyāya Sūtra*, IV, i, 64.

## CHAPTER FIVE

[1] Considerable portions of this chapter are reproduced, with permission, from the author's article on the Sāṅkhya contributed to the *Heritage of Indian Culture*, published by the Ramakrishna Mission.

[2] There is an alternative view, ascribing the five organs of action (*karamendriya*) to this source. In that view, each *guṇa* would be responsible for the production of some entities. See *Sāṅkhya-pravacana-bhāṣya* (ii), 18.

[3] Cf. *Dharmi-svarūpo hi dharmaḥ* (com. on YS., iii, 13).

[4] See SK., st. 17. Strictly the statement here refers to the attempts made by the best minds in this direction.

[5] SK., st. 21.

[6] SK., st. 11.

[7] YS., i, 47–49. See also i, 51.

[8] SK., st. 64.

[9] See YS., ii, 19 (p. 85).

[10] *Puruṣārtha eva hetuḥ* (SK., st. 31).

[11] SK., st. 6.

[12] *Jñānasya eva parā kāṣṭhā vairāgyam* (YS., i, 16, com.).

[13] The view here set forth is of some like Bhoja. See his com. on YS, i, 23. Others do not seem to accept the alternative character of this discipline. Cf. Vācaspati on YS., ii, 45.

[14] It may, no doubt, be said that there is the past karma, or *puṇya* and *pāpa*, to govern the process; but that also is a phase of Prakṛti here.

[15] i, 3. See also iv, 10.

### CHAPTER SIX

[1] See Jaimini Sūtra, I, i, 3.

[2] *Indian Logic in the Early Schools*, p. 48 *n*.

[3] *Pratīti-siddham abādhitam na śakyam anyathā-kartum*; SV., pp. 560–561, 564 (com.).

[4] SV., p. 651, st. 49.

[5] *Na kadācit anīdṛśam jagat*. Cf. SV., pp. 650 ff.

[6] Ritualism, as represented in this stage, not only reasserted its old antagonistic attitude towards the Upanishads; it also developed naturalistic tendencies and had, by Kumārila's time, come to be looked upon "almost as the Lokāyata doctrine." See com. on SV., st.10 (p. 4).

[7] *Svarūpa-para-rūpābhyām sarvam sadasadātmatkam*, SV., p. 476.

[8] This question is really two-fold—whether knowledge is self-valid in respect of its origin (*utpattau*), and whether it is so in respect of its ascertainment (*jñaptau*). For the sake of simplicity, the problem is here considered without reference to this distinction.

[9] There is a fourth view also, viz. that both validity and invalidity are intrinsic to knowledge, held in the Sāṅkhya-Yoga, according to which doctrine whatever manifests itself at any time has already been there in an implicit form.

[10] The two varieties of *artha-vāda*, alluded to in the text, are known respectively as *anuvāda* and *guṇa-vāda*. There is also a third variety of it, called *bhūtārtha-vāda* as, for example, when the Veda says "Indra raised the thunderbolt against Vṛtra"—a statement which neither contradicts nor reiterates common experience.

[11] *Śāstra-dīpikā*, p. 122 and 131. It should be added that the Veda directly teaches the immortality of the self, though in its later portions. Cf. *Avināśī vā areyamātmā anucchittidharmā* (Bṛ. Up., IV, v, 14).

[12] The splinters into which the article may be reduced, it describes as "posterior non-existence;" and the bare ground (on which it was expected to be found) as its "absolute non-existence."

[13] The Prābhākara school restricts verbal testimony to the Veda, and explains the secular form of it as based upon perception, etc.

[14] *Yāgadireva dharmaḥ*: see *Artha-saṁgraha* (Nirn. Sag. Ed.), p. 6.

[15] *Prayojanam anuddiśya na mandopi pravartate*, SV., p. 653, st. 55.

[16] *Niyoga-nibandhanam anuṣṭhānam na phala-nibandhanam* (*Bhāvanā-viveka*, p. 111).

[17] Ananta Deva's *Bhāṭṭālaṁkāra*, p. 488.

[18] *Śāstra-dīpikā*, pp. 126–127.

### CHAPTER SEVEN

[1] Cf. Praśna Up., v, 2.

[2] *Na khalu ananytvamiti abhedam brūmaḥ: kim tu bhedam vyāsedhāmaḥ* (*Bhāmatī*, II, i, 14).

[3] The latter is described as *sopādhika-bhrama* or an illusion involving

the presence of an *upādhi*, which is the name given to intervening factors like the sheet of glass. In the former, there is no such factor, and it is therefore described as *nirupādhika-bhrama*.

4 Cf. com. on VS., II, i, 14–15.

5 See, e.g., under VS., I, i, 2.

6 There are differences in matters of detail, e.g. the senses are derived from *ahaṁ-kāra* in the Sāṅkhya-Yoga; but here they are traced to the elements, viz. *pṛthivī*, *ap*, etc.

7 Cf. NM. pp. 526 ff.

8 VS., II, iii, 7. *Ya eva hi nirākartā tadeva tasya svarūpam.* Śaṁkara's doctrine cannot, for the same reason, be identified with the *śūnya* of the Mādhyamika school of Buddhism (granting that it is not absolute nothing), for it is an *objective* something, transcendental though it be.

9 *Tyaktavyo mama-kāraḥ tyaktum yadi śakyate nāsau*
*Kartavyo mama-kāraḥ kim tu sa sarvatra kartavyaḥ.*

10 See *Kalpa-taru* (I, i, 20):
*Nirviśesaṁ param brahma sākṣātkartumanīśvarāḥ*
*Ye mandāstenukampyante saviśeṣa-nirūpaṇaiḥ.*

11 Cf. *Avagatireva gatiḥ*. Śaṁkara on Kaṭha Up., I, iii, 12.

12 See *Vedānta-paribhāṣā* on *uparati*, ch. viii.

13 The relation of reason to revelation, as set forth here, is acceptable to all schools of Vedānta.

14 See *Naiṣkarmya-siddhi*, iii, st. 5 and 53.

15 Cf. Bṛ. Up., IV, iii, 22. This passage, no doubt, refers to deep sleep; but *mokṣa* is, in this respect, only a replica of deep sleep. See Śaṁkara on VS. IV, i, 3.

16 *Anubhavāvasānatvāt brahma-jñānasya:* Śaṁkara on VS. I, i, 2.

## CHAPTER EIGHT

1 We should add that, so far as the higher classes of society were concerned, this revival also meant the revival of Vedic ritualism.

2 See SB. p. 53 (com.). No doubt, we may say, "the rose *has* redness;" but the point is that such optional usage is not permitted in the case of all distinct entities. It may be added, in this connection, that Rāmānuja criticizes the *bhedābheda* view as strongly as Śaṁkara does.

3 *Viśiṣṭāntarbhāva eva aikyam.* See SB. p. 132 (com.).

4 Bṛ. Up., III, v.

5 The relation between material cause and effect, in this sense, is one of identity (*Ananyatva*) see SB., II, i, 14 and 17.

6 But we should not forget that it is not physical, and is therefore different from the rays of a lamp flame (say) which also can show but cannot know. The distinction will become clear when we say that even these rays require the aid of *dharma-bhūta-jñāna* for being perceived. To use technical terms, it is *parāk* and not *pratyak* like the latter.

7 This is described as *sadvāraka-pariṇāma*, because it is mediated through *dharma-bhūta-jñāna*.

[8] See SB., p. 224 (com.). Strictly according to old texts, this relation does not differ from *apṛthak-siddhi*. See, e.g. SB., p. 205, where the latter term is defined so as to include the former. It is, however, clear that there is a distinction as indicated by the condition that one of the relata must be a *cetana* here.

[9] *Bhinnāśca bhinna-dharmāśca padārthā nikhilā amī.*

[10] *Svarūpa-pramiti-pravṛtti—lakṣaṇa-sattā-traividhye*
*parānapekṣam svatantram; tadapekṣam paratantram* (*Tīkā* on *Tattva-saṁkhyānam*).

[11] *Prakṛtyādi-sattā-pradatvam ca aṅgi-karyam Īśvarasya* (com. on VS. II, ii, 5).

[12] *Dravyam karma ca kālaśca svabhāvo jīva eva ca*
*Yadanugrahataḥ santi na santi yadupekṣayā.*

[13] Madhva admits (1) absolute identity as in the case of A is A (2) *saviśeṣābheda* as in the case of a coin and its weight (3) identity *and* difference as in the case of a flower and its provisional colour and (4) absolute difference as in the case of a man and his staff. Generally speaking, he explains what, according to thinkers like Kumārula, are instances of *Chedābheda*, on the basis of *either* (2) *or* (3).

[14] Or, alternatively, it consists in taking the existent for the absolutely non-existent.

[15] Here knowledge and the known become identical; and it may appear to contradict what has been stated in describing the Dvaita as realistic (p. 195). But it is pointed out that, even here, there is a distinction, viz. that between the *sākṣin* as manifesting (*vyañjaka*) and the same as manifested (*vyaṅgya*).

[16] *Mokṣaśca Viṣṇu-prasādena vinā na labhyate* (*Viṣṇu-tattvanirṇaya*).

## SANSKRIT GLOSSARY

N.B. (1) Figures refer to the pages on which the words are explained, or are used for the first time

(2) The glossary is confined to the words occurring in the body of the work, and does not include those that appear only within brackets.

| | |
|---|---|
| *Ajīva* | non-soul or the inanimate, 61. |
| *Adharma* | the opposite of *dharma* (*q.v.*), 91. |
| *Anumāna* | inference, 101. |
| *Apṛthak-siddhi* | inseparable relation, 177. |
| *Artha* | wealth, 50. |
| *Arhan* | "the worthy one" or a perfected saint, 63. |
| *Avatāra* | an incarnation of God, especially Viṣṇu, 35. |
| *Avidyā* | nescience, 163. |
| *Asat* | non-being, 196. |
| *Asat-kārya-vāda* | "doctrine of not-pre-existent effect," 88. |
| *Aham-kāra* | egoism or sense of "I," 110. |
| *Ākāśa* | (1) space, 24; *or* (2) ether or substratum of sound, 86. |
| *Ātman* | self or soul, 20. |
| *Ānanda* | bliss, 22. |
| *Upaniṣad* | "secret teaching," 18. |
| *Upāsana* | meditation, 26. |
| *Ṛta* | (1) cosmic order, 12; (2) principle of righteousness, 12; *or* (3) sacrificial correctness, 17. |
| *Karma* | deed—good or bad, religious or secular, 29. |
| *Karma-yoga* | devotion to disinterested action, 55. |
| *Kāma* | sensual pleasure, 50 |
| *Kevala-jñāna* | all-comprehensive or perfect knowledge, 61. |
| *Guṇa* | a (1) constituent, 108; (2) quality, 180; *or* (3) product, 191, of *Prakṛti*, viz. *sattva*, *rajas* and *tamas*. |
| *Guru* | an exemplary preceptor, 125. |
| *Gauḥ* | cow, 101. |
| *Cit* | sentence, 22 |
| *Jina* | "spiritual conqueror"—a title applied to Vardhamāna, the famous Jaina teacher, 60. |
| *Jīva* | individual soul, 60. |
| *Jīvanmukti* | liberation while still alive, 28. |
| *Jñāna* | knowledge, 56. |
| *Jñāna-yoga* | devotion to knowledge of (1) ultimate reality, 56, *or* (2) the soul, 185. |
| *Tanmātra* | a simple or subtle element. 110. |
| *Tamas* | see *Guṇa*. |

*Tādātmya* relation of identity-in-difference which subsists between substance and quality, the particular and the universal, whole and parts, etc., 131.
*Tri-mūrti* the Hindu Trinity: Brahma, Viṣṇu and Śiva, 176.

*Deva* "luminous," deity, 14.

*Dharma* "what holds together," the basis of all order—religious or moral merit, 37.
*Dharma-bhūta-jñāna* attributive intelligence, 180.
*Dhyāna* meditation, 26.

*Puruṣa* individual soul, 113.
*Prakāra* an inseparable accessory to substance, 181.
*Prakṛti* primal matter, 108.
*Prapatti* complete surrender of one's will to God, 184.
*Pramāṇa* (1) proximate means to valid knowledge, 42; *or* (2) test of its validity, 42.
*Pramā* true knowledge or truth, 42.

*Brahman* (1) prayer, 14; *or* (2) primary principle which is the source of the universe, 20.
*Brāhmana* liturgical treatise, 14.
*Bhakti* loving devotion to God, 33.
*Bhakti-yoga* (1) the way of devotion, 56; *or* (2) loving and enlightened meditation upon God, 185.
*Bhagavān* "the worshipful," 35.
*Bhavya* "what is to come" or auspicious, 51.
*Bheda* difference, 189.

*Manana* reflection, 26.
*Manas* (1) the internal organ, 90; *or* (2) one of its phases, 112.
*Mantra* hymn or religious song, 9.
*Mahat* intellect, 110.
*Mīmāṁsā* systematic investigation, 129.
*Mokṣa* final freedom or salvation, 25.

*Yoga* meditation as a means of (1) union with ultimate Reality, 26; *or* (2) separation of spirit from matter, 122.
*Yogin* an adept in meditation— 99.

*Rajas* see *Guṇa*.

*Lokāyata* "restricted to the world of common experience"—a name applied to the materialist, 57.

*Vivarta-vāda* doctrine of apparent change, 159.
*Viśeṣa* (1) particularity, conceived as a property of eternal entities, which distinguishes things otherwise the same, 87; *or* (2) speciality, associated with everything, which explains the distinction made between things that are really the same, 193.

| | |
|---|---|
| *Vedānta* | "end of the Veda" or final conclusion of Vedic teaching, 151. |
| *Śabda* | (1) sound or word, 43; *or* (2) verbal testimony, 43. |
| *Śiva* | "auspicious"—a designation of the supreme God, 33. |
| *Śravaṇa* | learning the ultimate truth through a formal study of scripture, 26. |
| *Śruti* | Hindu scriptures or revelation, 44. |
| *Saṁsāra* | mundane existence or the recurrent round of birth and death, 28. |
| *Saguṇa Brahman* | qualified Brahman (*q.v.*), 163. |
| *Saccidānanda* | Brahman, the ultimate Reality, conceived as Being, Sentience and Bliss, 22. |
| *Sat* | (1) being, 22; *or* (2) good, 51. |
| *Sat-kārya-vāda* | (1) "doctrine of pre-existent effect," 109; *or* (2) the doctrine that regards the already existing as an effect because of a transformation in its modes, 180. |
| *Sattva* | see *Guṇa*. |
| *Saṁnyāsa* | formal renunciation, 27. |
| *Sapta-bhaṅgī* | sevenfold way of expressing the real, 67. |
| *Samavāya* | a unique relation that subsists between substance and quality, particular and universal, whole and parts, etc., 89. |
| *Samādhi* | trance, representing the ultimate or penultimate stage in *yoga* discipline, 124. |
| *Sākṣin* | (1) the witness self, 165; *or* (2) the same conceived as an organ of sense, 197. |
| *Sāttvika* | derived from *sattva* (*q.v.*), 112. |
| *Sāmānya-lakṣaṇa* | general feature of things, 79. |
| *Sūtra* | aphorism, 42. |
| *Soma* | a creeper, from which an intoxicating drink was extracted in ancient times, 11. |
| *Smṛti* | tradition, 44. |
| *Sva-lakṣaṇa* | a bare particular or a thing-in-itself, 79. |

# INDEX


Absolute, the, 22, 23, 30, 31, 33, 83, 163; *see* Absolutism
Absolutism, 19, 21–4, 68–9, 83, 114, 127, 152–4; *see* Advaita
Activism, 28, 39, 51–2, 129–30, 186–7, 199
Advaita: origin, 151–2; its world-view in general, 152, 155–8; causation, 158–9; Māyā, 160–1; *nirguna* Brahman, 161–3; *saguṇa* Brahman and God, 163–4; the self, 164–5; conception of knowledge, 165–6; truth and error, 166–9; view of revelation, 169; goal of life, 169–70, 173–4; means to its attainment, 170–2; reason and revelation, 173; *see* Monism
Āgamas, 34, 35, 184
Asceticism, 27–8, 51–2, 53, 54, 69, 74, 105, 187
Atheism, 48, 83, 124–5, 134–5
Atomic theory, 61–2, 86–9, 132
Attributes, *see* Quality

Bhāgavata religion, 35, 53, 56
Bodhisattva, 83
Bondage, 70, 76, 102–3; *see* Goal of life
Brahman (*masc.*), 15, 32;—as supreme God, 32
Buddhism, 41, 46
  primitive: general character, 72; relation to Brahmanism, 72–3; conception of self, 73; goal of life, 73–4; means to its realisation, 74
  canonical: general character, 74–5; the Four Noble Truths: evil, its cause, its removal and the means thereto, 75–7
  systematized: its divisions, 77–8; doctrine of momentariness, 78; (1) Hīnayāna: conception of self and of external reality, 78–9; goal of life, 83; (2) Mahāyāna: as subjectivism, 80–1; as nihilism, 81–2; as absolutism, 83; goal of life, 83; ideal of Bodhisattva, 83

Causation, 76, 81–2, 88–90, 107, 109, 114, 132, 158–9, 173, 193
Comparison (*upamāna*), 141
Conjunction (*saṁyoga*), 88, 93, 179, 182
Creation, 24, 89–90, 110, 153

Devotion (*bhakti*), 13, 33, 36, 56, 125–6, 198
Difference (*bheda*), 187, 188–90, 196–7
Dissolution, 24, 110
Dreams, 196
Dualism, 84; *see* Dvaita
Duty, 37–9, 53–6, 147–8, 170–1
Dvaita: origin and history, 151–2, 187–8; principal features, 188–90; categories, 190–1; substance: God, 191–2; the self, 192; Prakṛti, 192–3; *viśeṣa* ("*speciality*"), 193–5; relation between substance and attribute, 191; view of knowledge, 195; conception of reality, 195; truth and error, 195–6; *pramānas*, 197; goal of life, 198; means to its attainment, 198–9

Eightfold path, the, 77
Elements, the, 24, 58, 86, 87, 110–11, 131
Empiricism, 44
Error, *see* Knowledge
Ether (*ākāśa*), 86–7
Evolution, 16, 109–10, 153; primary and secondary, 112

Fatalism, 47, 49–50
Freedom, 47–50

Goal of life, 13, 25–6, 28–9, 37, 39, 50–2, 58–9, 69, 73–4, 75, 76–7, 83, 102–3, 116, 122, 148–50, 153, 169–70, 173–4, 184–5, 197–8; means to its attainment, 13, 25–8, 69–70, 74, 103–5, 116–17, 122–4, 126, 149, 153, 170–2, 184–7, 198–9; *see* Value

God, the supreme, 29–30, 32–3, 59, 61, 89–90, 94, 127, 134–5, 146, 163–4, 176, 181–2, 191–2; *see under* Brahma (*m.*), Śiva *and* Viṣṇu
Gods, Vedic conception of, 11, 12–13
Grace, divine (*prasāda*), 13, 33, 36, 56, 186, 198

"I am Brahman" (*Aham Brahma asmi*), 21
Idealism, 19, 80, 85
Identity-in-difference (*tādātmya*), 65, 109, 131, 132, 134, 136–7, 152, 158
Ignorance, 25, 51, 75, 127, 160–2
Indra, chief god of Vedic hymns, 11; later, ruler of heaven, 12
Inference, 43, 57–8, 63, 64, 96–7, 99–101, 121, 132, 137, 141, 142–3, 183, 197
Internal organ, 112, 157, 165

THE END